Artificial Intelligence for Intrusion Detection Systems

This book is associated with the cybersecurity issues and provides a wide view of the novel cyber attacks and the defense mechanisms, especially AI-based Intrusion Detection Systems (IDS).

Features:

- A systematic overview of the state-of-the-art IDS
- Proper explanation of novel cyber attacks which are much different from classical cyber attacks
- Proper and in-depth discussion of AI in the field of cybersecurity
- Introduction to design and architecture of novel AI-based IDS with a transparent view of real-time implementations
- Covers a wide variety of AI-based cyber defense mechanisms, especially in the field of network-based attacks, IoT-based attacks, multimedia attacks, and blockchain attacks.

This book serves as a reference book for scientific investigators who need to analyze IDS, as well as researchers developing methodologies in this field. It may also be used as a textbook for a graduate-level course on information security.

Artificial Intelligence for Intrusion Detection Systems

Edited by
Mayank Swarnkar
Shyam Singh Rajput

CRC Press
Taylor & Francis Group
Boca Raton London New York

CRC Press is an imprint of the
Taylor & Francis Group, an **informa** business

A CHAPMAN & HALL BOOK

Front cover image: LeoWolfert/Shutterstock

First edition published 2024
by CRC Press
2385 NW Executive Center Dr, Suite 320, Boca Raton, FL 33431

and by CRC Press
4 Park Square, Milton Park, Abingdon, Oxon, OX14 4RN

CRC Press is an imprint of Taylor & Francis Group, LLC

Library of Congress Cataloging-in-Publication Data
Names: Swarnkar, Mayank, editor. | Rajput, Shyam Singh, editor.
Title: Artificial intelligence for intrusion detection systems / editor,
Mayank Swarnkar, Shyam Singh Rajput.
Description: Boca Raton, FL : CRC Press, 2024. | Includes bibliographical
references and index.
Identifiers: LCCN 2023018206 (print) | LCCN 2023018207 (ebook) |
ISBN 9781032386652 (hardback) | ISBN 9781032386966 (paperback) |
ISBN 9781003346340 (ebook)
Subjects: LCSH: Intrusion detection systems (Computer security) |
Artificial intelligence.
Classification: LCC TK5105.59 .A785 2024 (print) | LCC TK5105.59 (ebook)
| DDC 005.8/3--dc23/eng/20230729
LC record available at https://lccn.loc.gov/2023018206
LC ebook record available at https://lccn.loc.gov/2023018207

ISBN: 978-1-032-38665-2 (hbk)
ISBN: 978-1-032-38696-6 (pbk)
ISBN: 978-1-003-34634-0 (ebk)

DOI: 10.1201/9781003346340

Typeset in Times
by SPi Technologies India Pvt Ltd (Straive)

Contents

Author Biographies

Dr. Mayank Swarnkar is currently working as an Assistant Professor in the Department of Computer Science and Engineering at the Indian Institute of Technology (Banaras Hindu University) Varanasi. He completed his Ph.D. from the Indian Institute of Technology Indore in 2019. He completed his M.Tech in Wireless Communication and Computing from the Indian Institute of Information Technology Allahabad in 2013 and B.E. in IT from Government Engineering College Jabalpur in 2011. He also worked as Software Engineer at NEC Technologies India for 1 year from 2013 to 2014 and as Assistant Professor at Bennett University for 1 year from 2019 to 2020. His primary areas of interest are Network and System Security. He works mainly in the field of Network Traffic Classification, Zero Day Attacks, Intrusion Detection Systems, and VoIP Spam Detection. He has given many invited talks and he is a reviewer of many reputed conferences and journals.

Dr. Shyam Singh Rajput received a B.E. degree in Computer Science & Engineering (CSE) from R. G. P.V., Bhopal, Madhya Pradesh, India, in 2011. He earned his M.Tech degree and Ph.D. degree in CSE from ABV-Indian Institute of Information Technology & Management (ABVIIITM), Gwalior, India, in 2013 and 2019, respectively. He has more than seven years of experience teaching undergraduate and postgraduate classes. Presently, he is working as an assistant professor in the Department of CSE, National Institute of Technology Patna, India. His current research interests include image processing, computer vision, and wireless networks. He has published more than 40 journal articles, conference papers, and book chapters in the domain of image processing, biometrics, wireless ad hoc networks, and information security. He has published three Indian patents and edited books with Elsevier and CRC Press. He is a member of IEEE and ACM.

Contributors

Yutika Agarwal
The Northcap University
Gurugram, Haryana, India

Hrithik Bhat
NIT Karnataka
Mangaluru, India

Mahesh Chandra Govil
NIT Sikkim
Ravangla, India

Ramya Chinnasamy
Kongu Engineering College
Erode, India

Shuddhatm Choudhary
NIT Karnataka
Mangaluru, India

Avantika Gaur
Doon University
Dehradun, India

M Sukruth Gowda
Presidency University
Kolkata, India

Senthil Kumar Jagthessaperumal
Mepco Schlenk Engineering College
Sivakasi, India

Rajayan Christy Jeyavim Sherin
Vellore Institute of Technology
Chennai, India

Arun Cyril Jose
IIIT-Kottayam
Valavoor, India

Somesh Kartikeya
NIT Karnataka
Mangaluru, India

A Kathirvel
Sri Krishna College of Engineering and
    Technology
Coimbatore, India

Pankaj Kumar Keserwani
NIT Sikkim
Sikkim, India

Gaurav Kothari
Doon University
Dehradun, India

C P Maheswaran
Karunya Institute of Technology and
    Sciences
Coimbatore, India

Rashi Makwana
Christ University (Deemed to be
    University)
Bangalore, India

Preeti Mishra
Doon University
Dehradun, India

Mridul Mittal
Navi Bengaluru
Karnataka, India

R Pallavi
Presidency University
Kolkata, India

Krishnamoorthy Parkavi
Vellore Institute of Technology
Chennai, India

Galiveeti Poornima
Presidency University
Kolkata, India

Deepak S Sakkari
VTU
Belgaum, India

Arjun Singh
Doon University
Dehradun, India

Mahendra Pratap Singh
NIT Karnataka
Mangaluru, India

Malliga Subramanian
Kongu Engineering College
Erode, India

Y Sudha
Presidency University
Kolkata, India

Akshaya Suresh
IIIT-Kottayam
Valavoor, India

Tejaswi
Doon University
Dehradun, India

Preface

Technology is growing with the growth of the Internet. One decade ago, the Internet was usually connected to end devices like PCs, laptops, mobile phones, tablets, etc. Nowadays, the situation has changed over time and the Internet is connected to many more end devices like IoTs, drones, smart devices, smart grids, and vehicles, including the ones we were using previously. Moreover, many smart devices are either battery-operated or have low computation power or both. These issues in smart devices lure hackers toward them as they are more vulnerable to network-based attacks. Moreover, traditional Intrusion Detection Systems (IDS), Firewalls, Antiviruses, and other defense mechanisms are not suitable in such situations. The reason is that hackers launch network attacks specific for the devices with known vulnerabilities, and traditional IDS cannot detect such huge and novel variations in network-based attacks.

Toward this critical issue, many security researchers in academia and industry are working to develop Artificial Intelligence (AI) based IDS which can not only withstand the latest cyber attacks but also defend the network, system, and end devices against them. The proposal of the book is associated with the stated cybersecurity issues and provides a wide view of the novel cyber attacks and the defense mechanisms, especially AI-based IDS. Specifically, the book will make the following contributions:

A: Proper understanding of novel cyber attacks which are much different than the classical cyber attacks which are usually found in textbooks
B: Proper and in-depth understanding of AI in the field of cybersecurity
C: Introduction to design and architecture of novel AI-based IDS with a transparent view of real-time implementations
D: Covers a wide variety of AI-based cyber defense mechanisms, especially in the field of network-based attacks, IoT-based attacks, Multimedia attacks, and Blockchain attacks.

OUTLINE OF THE BOOK AND CHAPTER SYNOPSIS

Chapter 1 presents a review of several AI-based IDS and their advantages and drawbacks have been highlighted. The chapter will help clarify the numerous directions that IDS work has gone to. Future directions for this field of study are also provided in the chapter.

Chapter 2 provides an explanation of advanced malware detection techniques in detail. The techniques are mainly classified into three parts based on the recent advances in technology: (i) Adversarial machine learning (ML) based malware detection approach, (ii) optimization-based malware detection approach, and (iii) XAI-based malware detection approach. This chapter also discusses key research challenges of the field.

Chapter 3 elaborates on Smart Signature-based IDS (SIDS) with the details such as (i) definition of SIDS, (ii) flow diagram of SIDS, (iii) classification, (iv) signature structure, (v) various smart signature detection methods, and (vi) performance measures.

Chapter 4 mainly studies intrusion detection and its types. It then mainly studies anomaly-based IDS. It briefly describes four main techniques of machine learning, genetic algorithms, fuzzy logic, and neural networks. In several instances, AI methods have been shown to be more effective than conventional methods, which are frequently constrained by the complexity, lack of flexibility, and/or scalability of the deterministic or semi-analytical models on which they are dependent. Then finally, the IPS is used to prevent the attacks that are coming in the near future as also discussed.

Chapter 5 presents an intelligent malware detection framework based on static analysis of Windows API calls and PE header files. It uses an ensemble approach and the Chi-square-based feature selection method. The framework also uses locality-sensitive hashing (LSH) to store all previously seen malware and detect known variants to increase computational efficiency. Experimental results demonstrate the effectiveness of the proposed framework.

Chapter 6 offers a survey of IDSs advanced for IoT environments. Suggestions for designing a robust and lightweight IDS have been additionally worried. In this survey, several papers had been analyzed. These papers specifically examine the introduction and overall performance of IDSs for providers inside the IoT paradigm that can be worried in smart environments. The traits of all IDS strategies provided in these papers have been translated. Moreover, this chapter presents a few pointers that need to be evaluated while growing an IDS for the IoT, consisting of the requirement for a strong and light system with a proper placement method that does not adversely impact the integrity, confidentiality, and availability of the IoT area.

Chapter 7 proposes a network-based intrusion detection system (NIDS). The proposed NIDS utilizes a feature selection technique based on the random forest to produce a feature subset of relevant features. The relevant feature subset is inputted to various state-of-the-art ML algorithms (such as Random forest, K-NN, and SVM) and their output is applied to a voting classifier for better intrusion detection. For evaluation of the proposed NIDS model NSL-KDD dataset has been utilized to produce the values of performance matrices: Accuracy, Precision, Recall, and F-measure. The proposed model is achieving more than 99% for different attacks: DoS – 99.80%, Probe – 99.28%, R2L – 97.26%, and U2R – 99.75%.

Chapter 8 provides a two-tier process-oriented AI-based enhanced intrusion detection and response (EIDR) system. The chaotic ant optimization (CAO) algorithm performs optimal cluster formation as the first contribution of the proposed EIDR system. The second contribution uses the multi-objective differential evolution (MODE) technique to determine the trust value of each sensor node. The intrusion reaction action (IRA) system, which performs various functions and exhibits multiple features of response to lessen intrusion impacts, is designed using the computed trust value. According to the simulation results, the suggested EIDR system has a higher detection rate and lower false positive rate without compromising network performance.

Finally, Chapter 9 discusses the main concern in the convergence and speed of IDS. This chapter helps various advanced methodologies in AI for programming AI-based IDS.

Special Acknowledgments

The first editor gratefully acknowledges the authorities of the *Indian Institute of Technology (BHU) Varanasi*, India, for their kind support to come up with this book.

The second editor gratefully acknowledges the authorities of the *National Institute of Technology Patna*, India, for their kind support to come up with this book.

We are sincerely thankful to all authors, editors, and publishers whose works have been cited directly/indirectly in this book.

Dr. Mayank Swarnkar
Varanasi, India

Dr. Shyam Singh Rajput
Patna, India

1 Intrusion Detection System Using Artificial Intelligence

Galiveeti Poornima
Presidency University, Kolkata, India

Deepak S Sakkari
VTU, Belgaum, India

R Pallavi, Y Sudha and M Sukruth Gowda
Presidency University, Kolkata, India

CONTENTS

DOI: 10.1201/9781003346340-1

1

1.1 INTRODUCTION

Denial of Internet connectivity is now inconceivable in both personal and professional settings. Attackers have never had such a wide attack region, thanks to the unrestricted and expanding array of technological devices linked to the Internet. The question of how to effectively defend both against known and unknown threats is brought up by this. The issue is complicated, especially given that threats are occurring more frequently every year (Stampar & Fertalj, 2015).

Important network-accessible resources ought to be completely protected against any attempts to take, harm, expose, disable, or otherwise obtain unauthorized access to or utilize them. Systems must maintain their availability, confidentiality, and integrity. A system known as an intrusion detection system (IDS) is dedicated to identifying such malicious attempts.

Traditional IDSs' primary drawback is their inability to identify novel or variant attacks because they are mostly signature-based and only detect known threats (Lee et al., 2001). One area that immediately comes to mind as a potential remedy for this issue is machine learning (ML), a branch of artificial intelligence that gives computers the ability to learn without even being specifically trained for a specific task.

The Internet has ingrained itself into daily life and is widely used in a variety of contexts, including commerce, communication, entertainment, education, and daily activities of staff members, among others. The Internet, in particular, has been utilized as a crucial part of business operations to gain access to data. Access to information over the Internet offers a number of possibilities to attack computer systems. Businesses are more vulnerable to Internet-based intrusions and attacks. "Any series of actions which attempt to breach the security objectives" is the definition of an incursion or attack. Included among the crucial security goals are availability, Integrity, discretion, responsibility, and assurance (Halme & Bauer, 1995). There are four groups of intrusions that can be distinguished: probing, denial of service (DoS), user-to-root (U2R), and remote-to-local (R2L) attacks (Haines, Lippmann, Fried, Zissman, & Tran, 2001).

Several anti-intrusion technologies have been developed to stop numerous Internet attacks. IDS is one of the seven anti-intrusion systems, along with avoidance, preemption, deterrent, deflection, detection, and countermeasures, according to Halme and Bauer (1995). Accurate detection of an incursion is the most crucial of these elements.

Finding harmful or undesirable network's packets using a detecting technique is challenging. To check for any unexpected activity on the network, real-time traffic surveillance is used during this operation. Big data and sophisticated computer abilities, in addition to the expansion of the size of the network, raise the demand for the necessary operations that must be done concurrently in real-time. As a result, unlike outdated techniques, NIDS should conduct monitoring with caution, accuracy, and precision. On the other hand, the rate at which the precision of machine learning algorithms has increased is just astounding. Its inception is motivated by the expanding demand for improved performance across diverse network architectures (Alzahrani & Alenazi, 2021). The software defined network (SDN) implementation has given the network-based system for intrusion detection (NIDS) a new frontier for deployment, however, in light of the diversifying and expanding array of security threats that current networks must contend with. The increasing number of connected devices and packet headers provide security risks. The advent of technologies including the Internet of Things (IoT), artificial intelligence (AI), and quantum computing has raised the threat level (Shone, Ngoc, Phai, & Shi, 2018), making network security difficult and necessitating a new paradigm in its implementation. In many cases, attackers have outpaced older defenses (divided into signature-based and unusual case IDSs) (Gómez et al., 2013; Dey & Rahman, 2019), requiring the development of more effective, adaptable, and reliable security (Alzahrani & Alenazi, 2021). Because of this, the known network design framework turns into SDN implementation (Ngo, Pham-Quoc, & Thinh, 2020). The study and monitoring of data must be ongoing if future occurrences like risks, attacks, and diseases are to be predicted. More information will be generated, learned, and recorded through the evaluation of very large amounts of data. More resources are preserved and the workplace environment stays the same. The supply chain's use of big data analytics (BDA) research is the key to controlling and preventing risks (Bag, Gupta, & Wood, 2020). In circumstances like disasters, when it can enhance the response and decrease human suffering and deaths, BDA for supply chain can assist the contributors in their decision-making. BDA and data monitoring using machine learning may help in identifying and grasping the connections between the reasons, difficulties, barriers, and obstacles that drive businesses in making the most appropriate and accurate decisions in risk management processes. This could have a very positive impact on the procedure and have an impact on whole nations and businesses.

Network monitoring-based machine learning techniques have been used in numerous industries. A social media site monitoring system is presented for evaluating and identifying traffic accidents using bi-directional long-short-term memory neural networks (Ali et al., 2021). The suggested solution uses query-based crawling to gather sentences relating to any congested road occurrences and social media, such as information on traffic bottlenecks, and road closures (Facebook and Twitter). Utilizing a variety of pre-processing techniques, such as classification, text categorization, steaming, and POS tagging, the acquired data are subsequently converted into an orderly state. In order to automatically classify the data as "traffic" or "non-traffic," the latent Dirichlet allocation (LDA) method is then utilized. Positive, negative, and neutral traffic-labeled data categories are examined. The statement created at this phase involves the polarities of the traffic phrase and is classified as either travel or non-traffic (positive, negative, or neutral). Then, using the bag-of-words (BoW) technique, each sentence is supplied to the bidirectional long short-term memory (LSTM) neural network as a one-hot encoding form (Bi-LSTM). The neural nets use the softmax layer to execute multi-class classification after the learning experience in order to classify the sentence based on its location, the type of any ensuing communication, and its polarity. The suggested technique contrasts several conventional deep learning and tries to cut deep learning methods based on traits like efficiency, F-score, and others.

A system that is capable of recognizing or detecting invasive activity is referred to as an IDS. This encompasses all methods used to spot improper computer or network activity in a broader sense. This is accomplished using software designed specifically to find odd or abnormal behavior. IDS can be categorized into four groups, according to several research and references in the literature (Lazarevic, Kumar, & Srivastava, 2005) (HIDS, NIDS, WIDS, NBA).

As technology advances, cybercriminals also develop more effective attack strategies, tools, and ways to take advantage of businesses. Public online services, in particular, are common services that everyone can use, and so many companies offer such services through publicly accessible websites. A web service's failure or compromise could harm a company's reputation or income. Web services in the Internet Demilitarized Zone (DMZ) can indeed be restricted by firewalls since they are constantly accessible to the public. Security managers normally reject all black-list policies for idle services registered in the firewall to prevent intrusions from outside attackers. As a result, it's crucial for cybersecurity to distinguish between legitimate access and malicious attacks. In actuality, many security incidents – such as data breaches, service outages, and malware infections – began as web attacks.

For distributed, cooperative, and hypertext information systems, an application-level protocol is the hypertext transfer protocol (HTTP) (Fielding et al., 1999). Today's HTTP is changing the way data is transported from web sites and is also utilized for system commands to be sent to different devices including command-line interfaces, update scripts, and mobile apps. Web attacks frequently target application flaws in open online services rather than trying to penetrate hosts' systems. The attacker attempts to initiate an attack by providing exploitational code via a web-server flaw in a certain subdomain or path file. The attacker may then compromise the webserver or other device that was injected with the code (Atienza, Herrero, & Corchado, 2015).

High security and service quality in massive networks are persistent research topics. For the exchange of crucial information, the connection of network and associated applications grows daily into increasingly sophisticated networks. About 3 trillion IoT device connections were anticipated globally till the end of 2020, with an estimated economic effect rate of $3.9–11.1 trillion annually. Numerous applications, including those for home automation, cities, healthcare, and other areas, improve the quality of life and the widespread connection of connections with other networks and communication devices. IoT network design based on layers is depicted in Figure 1.1. Some gadgets employ sensors to automatically collect actual information that is transferred across networks for analysis (Khan et al., 2019; He et al., 2021).

1.2   ARTIFICIAL INTELLIGENCE

Conceptually, artificial intelligence is a field of mental processes using computing models (Charniak, 1985). The primary fields of AI research are robotics, general intelligence, computer vision, natural language processing computerized planning and scheduling, reasoning, information retrieval, and computer vision (strong AI). The main focus of this work is ML, as it seems to be the most practical AI sub-field for the problem of intrusion detection. However, additional methods that do not use ML will also be described.

Key to machine learning is the research and creation of algorithms that can truly adjust (i.e., learn) using small amounts of data (ML). These algorithms work by

Application layer

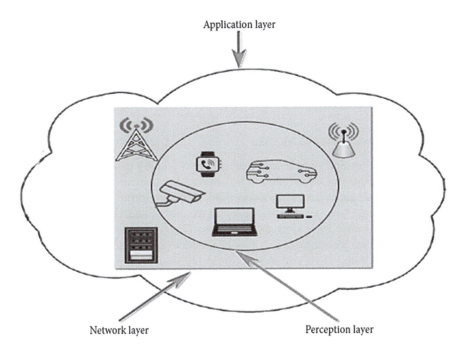

Network layer   Perception layer

FIGURE 1.1   Different devices communicate across network tiers in IoT network design.

building models based on data and applying those predictions to produce predictions or judgments, as opposed to just following explicitly written instructions. They are the best choices for intrusion detection tasks since they possess these qualities.

Classification, regression, and clustering are the three common challenges that machine learning attempts to address. In classification, group membership is determined, in regression, a response is estimated or predicted, and through research and advancement in a cluster, a set of data is divided into groups with similar characteristics. Depending on the output, we can talk about classification, regression, or clustering. Classification is the topic if the output accepts classifiers. Regression is used when the output variable allows continuous numeric values. Regression, as opposed to categorization and clustering, is thus suited to problems of the type that can be predicted.

ML can be further divided into three primary groups based on learning methods: supervised, unsupervised, and reinforcement learning. When trying to teach a computer our own categorization scheme, supervised learning is frequently employed to solve classification difficulties. Unsupervised learning appears to be more difficult. The objective is to teach the computer how to perform a task that we do not expressly instruct it to perform. It is an effective method for spotting structure in unsupervised learning, representing the statistical characteristics of the total set of input formats. Instead of being formally taught, reinforcement learning involves the learning agent interacting with the environment and learning by doing by seeing the outcomes of its activities.

There isn't a single AI system that achieves the highest accuracy in every circumstance. Therefore, using numerous algorithms in combination to produce better quality reasoning than any one algorithm is one strategy to improve results. Ensemble and hybrid techniques are the two most common types. When utilizing ensemble classifiers, various merging techniques (such as majority voting) are commonly used to integrate several yet homogeneous weak models at the level of their individual output (Cordón, Kazienko, & Trawiński, 2011). In turn, hybrid algorithms incorporate many, heterogeneous AI techniques (e.g., through cascading).

1.2.1 MACHINE LEARNING MODELS

Supervised and unsupervised learning are the two primary categories of machine learning. The important information in tagged data is essential to supervised learning. The most frequent activity in supervised learning (and in IDS) is classification; nevertheless, labeling data manually is expensive and time-consuming. As a result, the primary obstacle to supervised learning is a lack of enough labeled data. Unsupervised learning, on the other hand, draws out useful features extracted from unlabeled data, which makes it considerably simpler to gather training data. Unsupervised learning approaches typically do less well at detection than supervised learning methods, though. Figure 1.2 demonstrates the common machine learning techniques used in IDSs.

1.2.1.1 Shallow Models

Typical classic machine learning architectures (shallow models) for IDS include artificial neural systems (ANN), support vector algorithms (SVM), k-nearest neighbor (KNN), naïve Bayes, regression models (LR), decisions trees, clustering, in addition to mixed and hybrid techniques. In fact, some of these methods have been examined for a long time and have proven approaches. They provide equal attention to practical issues like detection effectiveness and data management in addition to the detection effect. Table 1.1 lists the benefits and drawbacks of several shallow models.

Artificial Neural Network (ANN): An ANN is intended to function similarly to how human brains function. There are numerous hidden layers, an output layer, and an input layer in an ANN. Units in neighboring strata are completely interconnected. An ANN has a powerful ability to fit functions, especially nonlinear ones because it has a very large number of components and can potentially approximate any function. Training ANNs is a time-consuming operation due to the complex model structure. The use of the backpropagation technique, which cannot be used to create deep networks, to train ANN models is extraordinary. An ANN is so distinct from deep learning models and belongs to the category of shallow models.

Support Vector Machines (SVM): Finding a max-margin separating hyperplane in the n-dimensional feature space is the SVM strategy. Because only a few support vectors control the separation hyperplane, SVMs can produce satisfying results even with limited training data. However, noise near the hyperplane represents a threat to SVMs. SVMs work well to resolve linear problems. Typically, kernel functions are employed for nonlinear data. To separate the original nonlinear data, a kernel function converts the original

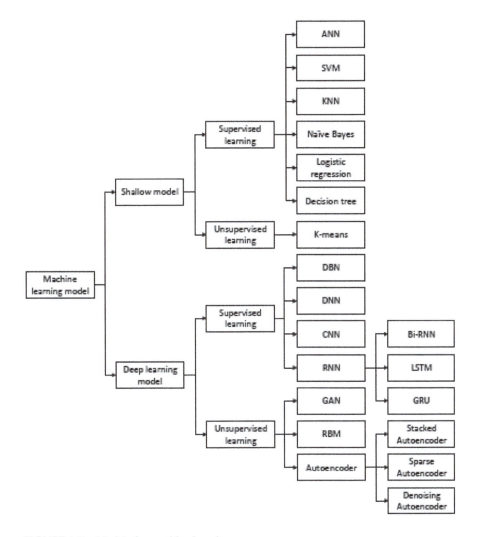

FIGURE 1.2   Models for machine learning.

area into a new space. Both SVMs as well as other machine learning methods commonly use kernel techniques.

k-Nearest Neighbors (kNN): The manifold hypothesis serves as the foundation for KNN. A sample does have a high likelihood of belonging to a class
if the majority of its neighbors do as well. The top k nearest neighbors are
the only ones who are relevant to the categorization outcome. KNN model
performance is heavily influenced by the parameter k. The danger of overfitting increases as k gets smaller, making the model more complex. On the
other hand, as k increases, the model becomes simpler and its ability to fit
data becomes weaker.

Naïve Bayes: The conditional distribution and the assumption of attribute independence are the foundations of the naïve Bayes algorithm. The naïve Bayes

TABLE 1.1

Benefits and Drawbacks of Various Shallow Models

Algorithms	Benefits	Drawbacks	Improvement Measures
Artificial Neural Network	capable of dealing with nonlinear data; outstanding fitting abilities	being overly fitted; being susceptible to being caught in a locally optimal; model training that takes a lot of time	enhanced optimizer, activation, and loss functions
SVM	Gain knowledge from a simple train set; powerful generation ability	do poorly on tasks involving huge data or different classifications; kernel function parameters are sensitive	Particle swarm optimization-assisted parameter optimization (PSO)
k-Nearest Neighbor	apply to large amounts of data; suitable for nonlinear data exercise swiftly; resilient to noise	Long test times; low accuracy for the minority class; sensitivity to the parameter K	Trigonometric inequality reduced comparison times; Particle swarm optimization (PSO)-optimized parameters; Synthetic minority over-sampling technique (SMOTE)-balanced Datasets
Näive Bayes	robust to noise; capable of incremental learning	Poor attribute-related performance	Latent variables have been included to weaken the independent assumption.
Linear Regression	Quickly trainable and simple; automatically scales features	perform poorly with non-linear data; Suitable to oversizing	Regularization of imported data to prevent overfitting
Decision Tree	Automatic feature selection; powerful interpretation	Classification outcome tends toward the majority class; Disregard the data's correlation	SMOTE-balanced datasets; latent variables added
K-means	Strong scalability; simple, quick training; able to fit large data	perform poorly with non-convex data; capable of startup; aware of the K parameter	enhanced initialization technique

Notes: KC – KDD Cup; NK – NSL-KDD; UN – UNSW-NB15; C7 – CICIDS2017; C8 – CSE-CIC-IDS2018; OT – Others Curve; ACC – Accuracy; PRE – Precision; REC -Recall; F-M – F-Measure; FAR – False Alarm Rate; ROC – Receiver Operating Characteristic; TPR – True Positive Rate; OTH – Others.

classifier determines the likelihood function for several classifications for each sample. The sample is put into the class with the highest probability. The calculation for the conditional formula is provided in Formula (1.1).

$$P(A = a \mid B = x_i) = \prod_{j=1}^{n} P(A^{(j)} = a^{(j)} \mid B = x_i) \qquad (1.1)$$

The naïve Bayes method yields the best result when the criterion for characteristic independence is satisfied. Unfortunately, evaluation of the naïve Bayes algorithm poorly on attribute-related data since it is difficult to verify that hypothesis in practice.

Logistic Regression (LR): A specific kind of logarithm generalized linear is the LR. The LR algorithm uses a parametric logistic distribution to calculate the probabilities of various classes, as illustrated in Formula (1.2)

$$P(Y = i \mid a) = \frac{e^{w_i * a}}{1 + \sum_{i}^{K-1} e^{w_i * a}} \tag{1.2}$$

where $i = 1, 2, ..., K - 1$. The sample x is classified into the maximum probability class. The construction of a linear regression is simple, and the learning algorithm is effective. However, LR's use is constrained because it struggles with nonlinear data.

Decision Tree: Data are categorized using a set of criteria using the decision tree algorithm. Since the model looks like a tree, it can be understood. The decision tree algorithm has the ability to automatically omit repetitive and irrelevant features. Feature selection, tree generation, and tree pruning are all parts of the learning process. The approach chooses the most appropriate features for each child node from the root node when building a decision tree model. Decision trees are the most basic type of classifier. Some advanced algorithms, such as randomized forests and severe gradient boosting, use a variety of decision trees.

Clustering: Similarity theory is the foundation for clustering, which involves putting remarkably Less comparable data in one cluster and more similar data in another. Different from classification, clustering is a form of unsupervised learning. Because clustering algorithms don't require previous knowledge or labeled data, their dataset needs are quite minimal. However, external data must be referred to when utilizing clustering techniques to detect assaults.

A common clustering approach is K-means, K indicates how many clusters there are, and means indicates how many attributes there are on average. Distance is used as a semantic similarity criterion in the K-means algorithm. The likelihood of two data objects being placed within the same cluster increases with decreasing distance between them. Although the K-means algorithm performs well on linear data, it produces less-than-ideal results on nonconvex data. Additionally, both the initialization conditions and the parameter K have an impact on the K-means algorithm. In order to determine the correct parameter value, numerous repeated tests must be performed.

Ensembles and Hybrids: Each classifier is unique and also has advantages and disadvantages. Combining numerous weak classifiers to create a powerful classifier is a logical strategy. Multiple classifiers are trained using ensemble methods, and the final outcomes are decided by the classifiers themselves. Hybrid approaches are composed of several steps, each of which employs a classification model. More researchers are starting to examine ensemble and hybrid classifiers because they typically outperform solo classifiers in classification tasks. The important decisions involve choosing which classifiers to combine and how to combine them.

1.2.1.2 Deep Learning Models

Different deep networks make up deep learning models. Among them, autoencoders, restricted Boltzmann machines (RBMs), and generative adversarial networks (GANs) are unsupervised learning models. Deep brief networks (DBNs), deep neural networks (DNNs), convolutional neural networks (CNNs), and recurrent neural networks (RNNs) are supervised learning models. Since 2015, there have been a lot more research on IDSs based on deep learning. Without the need for manual feature engineering, deep learning models immediately learn visual features from the original information, such as images and texts. Deep learning techniques can therefore be used end to end. Deep learning techniques significantly outperform shallow models for huge datasets. Network design, hyperparameter choice, and optimization approach are the three primary focuses of deep learning research. Table 1.2 compares various deep learning models on exhibit.

Autoencoder: As seen in Figure 1.3, an autoencoder consists of two symmetrical parts – an encoder and a decoder. From the raw data, the encoder extracts features, and the decoder uses those characteristics to reassemble the data. The gap between the encoder's input and the decoder's output gradually decreases during training. When the decoder is able to recreate the data using the features extracted, it indicates that the characteristics the encoder

---

TABLE 1.2
Comparison of Various Deep Learning Models

Algorithms	Suitable Data Types	Supervised or Unsupervised	Functions
Autoencoder	Raw data; Feature vectors	Unsupervised	Feature extraction; feature reduction; denoising
RBM	Feature vectors	Unsupervised	Feature extraction; feature reduction; denoising
DBN	Feature vectors	Supervised	Feature extraction; classification
DNN	Feature vectors	Supervised	Feature extraction; classification
CNN	Raw data	Feature vectors	Matrices supervised feature extraction
RNN	Raw data	Feature vectors	Sequence data supervised feature extraction; classification
GAN	Raw data	Feature vectors	Unsupervised data augmentation; adversarial training

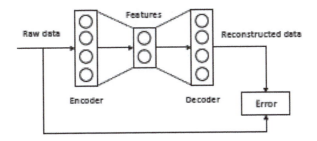

FIGURE 1.3   Structure of auto-encoder.

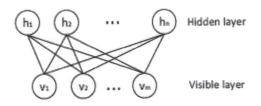

FIGURE 1.4   Structure of RBM.

extracted accurately capture the core of the data. It's crucial to remember that no supervised information is needed for any part of this process. There are numerous well-known autoencoder variations, including sparse autoencoders (Deng, Zhang, Marchi, & Schuller, 2013) and denoising autoencoders (Vincent, Larochelle, Bengio, & Manzagol, 2008; Vincent et al., 2010).

Restricted Boltzmann Machine (RBM): A randomized perceptron with units that follow the Boltzmann distribution is known as an RBM. A visible layer plus a concealed layer make up an RBM. As illustrated in Figure 1.4, the unit in different levels are fully connected but the units within the same level are not. where layer hi is a hidden layer and layer vi is the visible layer. RBMs do not differentiate between forward and backward motion; as a result, the weights are identical in both directions. RBMs are unsupervised learning models that have been trained using the contrastive divergence algorithm (Hinton, 2012) and are frequently used for feature extraction or denoising.

Deep Brief Network (DBN): As depicted in Figure 1.5, a DBN is made up of numerous RBM layers as well as a softmax classification layer. Unsupervised pretraining or supervised fine-tuning are the two stages of training a DBN (Sarikaya, Hinton, & Deoras, 2014). Prior to training each RBM, greedy layer-wise pretraining is used. The softmax layer's weight is then determined by labeled data. DBNs are utilized for the extraction and classification of features in attack detection (Zhao, Zhang, & Zheng, 2017).

Deep Neural Network (DNN): An approach called "tier pretraining and fine-tuning" can be used to construct DNNs with many layers, as shown in Figure 1.6. A DNN is trained by initially learning its parameters from

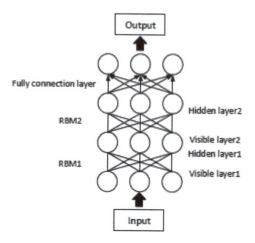

FIGURE 1.5   Structure of DBN.

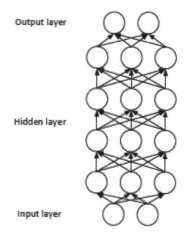

FIGURE 1.6   Structure of DNN.

unsupervised learning, which is known as an unsupervised learning stage. Labeled data are then used to make adjustments to the network, which is known as an unsupervised learning stage. The unsupervised learning stage is mostly responsible for the astounding successes of DNNs.

Convolution Neural Networks (CNN): CNNs have made tremendous advancements in the area of machine learning since they are designed to emulate the visual system of humans (HVS) (Lawrence, Giles, Tsoi, & Back, 1997). As seen in Figure 1.7, a CNN is stacked with alternative convolutional and pooling layers. The convolutions are used to improve the generalizability of the features while the convolution layer is employed to extract features. Matrix conversion of the input data is necessary for attack detection because CNNs operate on 2-dimensional (2D) data.

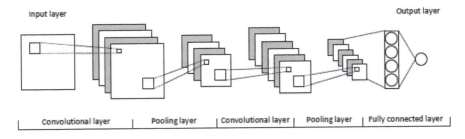

FIGURE 1.7 Structure of CNN.

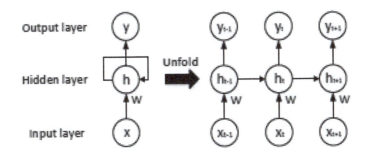

FIGURE 1.8 Structure of RNN.

Recurrent Neural Network (RNN): Natural language processing (NLP) makes extensive use of RNNs, which are networks created for sequential data (Graves, Mohamed, & Hinton, 2013). Sequential data have contextual properties, hence it makes little sense to analyze individual data points from the sequence. Every component in an RNN receives both the previous states and the present state in order to gather contextual information. Figure 1.8 illustrates an RNN's structural layout, where Figure 1.8's W elements are all identical. Due to this property, RNNs frequently experience disappearing or exploding gradients. In practice, typical RNNs only work with short sequences. Many RNN versions, including LSTM (Hochreiter & Schmidhuber, 1997), gated recurrent unit (GRU) (Chung, Gulcehre, Cho, & Bengio, 2014), and bi-RNN (Schuster & Paliwal, 1997), have been proposed to address the long-term reliance problem.

Hochreiter and Schmidhuber proposed the LSTM model in 1997 (Hochreiter & Schmidhuber, 1997). A gate, an input entrance, and an outer loop are all present in each LSTM unit. The input gate accepts fresh data, the forget gate purges out-of-date memory, as well as the output gate, mixes short-term and long-term memory to produce the present memory state. Chung et al. proposed the GRU in 2014 (Chung et al., 2014). The GRU model, which is less complex than the LSTM, incorporates a number into a single implemented number that combines a memory gate with a gate.

Generative Adversarial Network (GAN): Two subnetworks, a generator and a discriminator, are part of a GAN model. The generator's objective is to create fake data that looks like real data, but the discriminator's objective is to distinguish between the two. As a result, both the generator and the discriminator get better. Currently, GANs are a popular study area utilized to supplement data in attack detection, helping to partially resolve the issue of IDS dataset shortages. GANs, on the other hand, are an adversarial learning strategy that can improve model detection accuracy by including adversarial samples in the training set.

1.2.2 Deep Learning Models Compared to Shallow Models

In most application settings, deep models outperform traditional deep learning (or shallow model) techniques. Deep learning is a subset of machine learning. The following characteristics mostly illustrate how shallow models and deep models differ from one another.

Length of play: Training and testing time are both included in the running time. Deep models take substantially longer to train and test than shallow models do due to their high level of complexity. **The quantity of parameters**: Learnable variables and hyperparameters are the two different categories of parameters. The hyperparameters are manually set prior to training, while the learnable variables are determined during training. Deep models require more time to train and optimize since there are significantly more learnable parameters and hyperparameters in deep networks than in shallow models.

Representation of features: A feature vector is the input to conventional machine learning models, and feature engineering is a crucial stage. Deep learning models, on the other hand, are not affected by feature engineering and are capable of learning feature representations from unprocessed data. The ability to run end-to-end gives deep learning techniques a significant edge over more conventional machine learning techniques.

Capacity for learning: Deep learning models have intricate structures and a vast number of variables (generally millions or more). Since they can fit data more accurately than shallow models, deep learning methods are more effective. Deep learning algorithms, however, run the danger of overfitting and need significantly more training data. The impact of deep learning models is superior because of their better ability to interpret the data.

Interpretability: A crucial aspect of deep learning is that the algorithms are black boxes; the outcomes are essentially incomprehensible. The decision tree and naïve Bayes, two conventional deep learning algorithms, have strong interpretability.

1.3 INTRUSION DETECTION SYSTEM

Intrusion detection detects attempts to undermine resource confidentiality, integrity, or availability (Jaramillo, 2018). IDS is a hardware or software tool that gathers and examines data from various computer or network components to find security flaws, such as infiltration and misuse. Different IDS "flavors" detect suspicious behavior in various ways.

IDS can be either host-based (HIDS), which inspects the behavior of the system at individual devices, or network-based (NIDS), which inspects network events at a single collection point (s). To safeguard a system from network-based dangers, utilizing a network tap, bridge port, or hub requires the usage of NIDS to monitor and examine network traffic. On a particular device, HIDS tries to spot unauthorized, illegal, and aberrant behavior. HIDS typically entails the installation of an agent on each machine, which monitors and alerts on both OS and application activities from a distance.

IDS might be anomaly-based (misuse) or signature-based (based on an underpinning detection logic). A signature-based IDS (SIDS) keeps track of suspicious activity and compares its traits to a database of known harmful threat signatures or properties. The primary problem is the delay between the appearance of a new hazard and the application of the IDS signature to identify that danger. IDS is not able to find the danger during that latency time. An anomaly-based IDS (AIDS) monitors behavior and assesses its characteristics in comparison to a predetermined guideline. The guideline will define what is "normal" for that person and will raise an alarm when abnormal behavior is seen or when the baseline is noticeably different. The greater false positive rate is the main problem.

IDS can indeed be inactive or reactive depending on how it responds to a threat that is detected. Passive IDS just recognizes and warns, leaving it up to the administrator to decide if action should be taken to halt the activity or if another response is appropriate. Reactive IDS, sometimes referred to as an intrusion prevention system (IPS), would respond to the danger by taking predetermined preemptive measures. Usually, this entails preventing any more network communication from the user or source IP address.

An attempt to illegally or uninvitedly access computer system data or interfere with system performance is referred to as an intrusion for an IDS. A computer security technology called an IDS looks for several types of security breaches, such as insider abuse and system penetration attempts to outside intrusion attempts (Denning, 1987). Examining the activity of computer systems, keeping track of hosts and networks, issuing warnings, and responding to suspicious behavior are the primary duties of IDSs. IDSs are often placed close to the protected network nodes because they watch over linked hosts and networks (e.g., switches in significant network segments).

In order to monitor security and protection, IDS are the tools that automatically spot unsettling behavior on a host or network and investigate it. The invasion is simply found using intrusion detection. It sometimes specifies the rules for evidence in certain circumstances. An intrusion occurs when a network or computer deviates from normal operation and is used as a pretext for an attempt to steal or corrupt network data (Yang, Li, Liang, He, & Zhao, 2019; Kolias, Kambourakis, Stavrou, & Gritzalis, 2015; Abdulhammed, Musafer, Alessa, Faezipour, & Abuzneid, 2019). Today, people share and keep private information on the Internet as well as other networks. IDS is a cybersecurity tool utilized by firewall and antivirus software, according to Liao, Ali, Nazir, He, and Khan (2020).

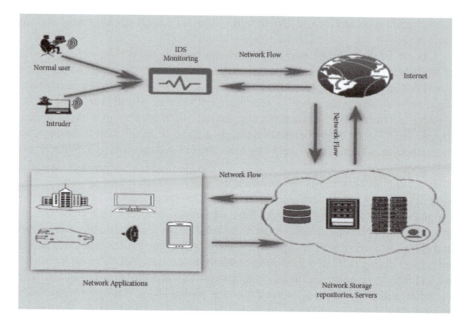

FIGURE 1.9 Network movement across the networks and IDS.

Additionally, the firewall only superficially examines the web traffic. Despite the fact that IDSs can govern, monitor, and keep all networks functioning, they nonetheless inform network administrators when there is unusual behavior or a threat of an attack. Figure 1.9 depicts the movement of network communication as well as intrusion prevention measures across networks (Tavallaee, Bagheri, Lu, & Ghorbani, 2009; Moustafa & Slay, 2015).

IDS classification techniques fall into two categories: methods based on data sources and methods based on detection. IDSs fall under two categories among detection-based techniques: abuse prevention and anomaly detection. Among the data source-based strategies, IDSs can be divided into host-based and network-based methods (Snapp et al., 1991). These two IDS categorization categories are combined in this study, with the detection technique acting as a supportive classification component and the data source acting as the main classification factor. In Figure 1.10, the suggested taxonomy is displayed. The survey focuses on machine learning techniques for detecting approaches.

1.3.1 IDENTIFICATION BASED ON DETECTION TECHNIQUES

The term "signature-based detection" also applies to misuse detection. the fundamental concept of representing attack methods as signatures. Using a signature database, the detection method compares the samples' signatures to the database. The creation of effective signatures is the key challenge in misuse detection system construction. The benefits of abuse detection include a low incidence of false alarms and

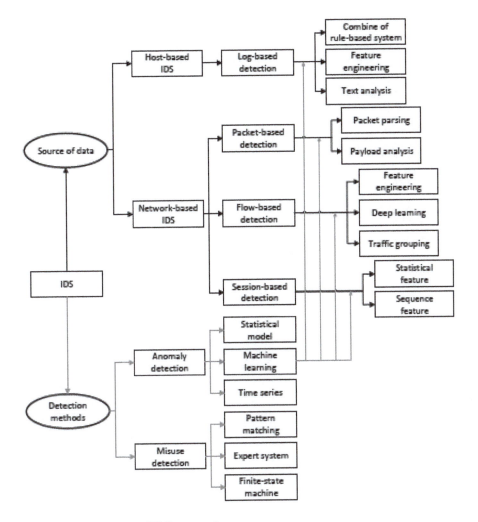

FIGURE 1.10   System of IDS taxonomies.

detailed reporting of attack types and potential causes; the drawbacks include a high percentage of missed alarms, the inability to identify unknown attacks, and the need to maintain a sizable signature database. The concept underlying detection methods is to characterize aberrant activities according to the degree to which they deviate from the usual profile. Therefore, defining a normal profile precisely is essential when creating an anomaly detection system. Strong generalization and the capacity to identify unidentified attacks are two advantages of anomaly detection; nevertheless, a high rate of false alarms and the inability to offer potential explanations for anomalies are two drawbacks. Table 1.3 lists the primary distinctions between abuse detection and anomaly detection.

Misuse detection comprises approaches based on pattern matching, expert systems, and finite state machines, as demonstrated in Figure 1.10 of the detection

TABLE 1.3

Differences between Abuse and Anomaly Detection

	Abuse Detection	Anomaly Detection
Detection Capability	Low false alarm rate; High missed alarm rate	Low missed alarm rate; High false alarm rate
Efficiency of detection	High, Falling with the size of the signature database	Depends on the intricacy of the model
Reliance on domain knowledge	Nearly all detections are subject to domain knowledge.	Low, only feature design is subject to subject matter expertise.
Interpretation	Excellent interpretive skills and domain knowledge-based design	Produces just detection results and has poor interpreting skills.
Detection of an unknown attack	Only detects known attacks	Detects known and unknown attacks

method-based taxonomy. Methods for identifying anomalies include those based on time series, machine learning, and statistical models.

1.3.2 CLASSIFICATION BASED ON DATA SOURCE

Because host-based IDSs (HIDSs) can watch the actions of important objects, they have the ability to precisely locate intrusions and launch replies (e.g., sensitive files, programs, and ports). HIDSs have the drawbacks of consuming host resources, depending on the host's dependability, and being unable to recognize network threats. Major servers or switches are typically used to deploy a network-based IDS (NIDS). The majority of p2p IDSs are OS-independent, allowing them to be used in a variety of OS scenarios. Furthermore, particular kinds of protocols and network attacks can be found using NIDSs. They only monitor traffic passing through a specific network slice, which is a drawback. Table 1.4 lists the main differences between network-based and host-based intrusion detection solutions.

TABLE 1.4

Differences between Host-Based and Network-Based IDSs

	Host-Based IDS	Network-Based IDS
Origin of the data	Operating system or application program logs	Network activity
Deployment	every host; dependent on operating systems; challenging to deploy	Important network nodes; deployable
Precision of detection	Low, many logs must be processed	High, real-time attack detection rate
Traceability of intrusions	Track the intrusion process using the system call pathways	Utilize IP addresses and times tamps to track the location and date of an intrusion
Limitation	unable to examine network behavior	only keep an eye on the traffic going through a certain network segment.

Audit records are used as a source of data by an HIDS, as seen in Figure 1.10. The majority of log identification techniques are hybrids based on log attributes, deep learning, and text analysis, as well as rule- and deep-learning-based hybrids. Network traffic, often in the form of packets, the fundamental building blocks of network communication, serves as the data source for an NIDS. A flow is a collection of packets that occur within a given time window and represent the state of the network. A session is a grouping of packets based on a 5-tuple of network information (IP addresses for clients, client ports, servers, and protocols). A session represents high-level significant traffic information. Packet detection comprises frame-by-frame and payload analysis-based techniques since packets contain network packets and payloads. The separation of flow identification into approaches based on feature engineering and deep learning is made possible by feature extraction. As an additional approach to flow detection, traffic clustering is unique. Statistics functionality and sequencing feature-based strategies for session detection can be distinguished from one another depending on whether sequence information is employed.

1.3.3 CATEGORIES OF IDSs

IDSs primarily consist of three segments. In order to assess and identify the cyber-attacks in the second segment, cyberattack evidence data must first be collected from input data and processed. The attacks are finally described in the third section. Recent advances in input data analysis have enabled the use of machine- and deep-learning-based approaches to forecast both typical and anomalous network activity as well as previously unknown network attacks. IDS techniques can be categorized into a number of categories, such as HIDS, network-based IDS (NIDS), AIDS, specification-based detection, hybrid-based detection, SIDS, and distributed IDS (DIDS) (Koroniotis, Moustafa, Sitnikova, & Turnbull, 2019).

1.3.3.1 Signature-Based Intrusion Detection Systems (SIDS)

Knowledge-based detection is SIDS. It compares network connectivity and activities to famous patterns or signatures to locate attack signatures in signature databases. It records network attack behavior and signature (Abou Khamis, Shafiq, & Matrawy, 2020). The saved signature database alerts when the attack profile matches. SIDS only detects attacks with database signatures. SIDS detects new attacks but cannot distinguish attack variations. False alarms are decreased through proactive and precise misbehavior recognition and classification to evaluate network administrators' defensive measures. However, acts that are not included in the database can be considered normal, aberrant, or attack versions. SIDS requires frequent revisions to its knowledge base to account for new assault variants. SIDS methods just compare packets to database patterns. It ignores fresh attacks. AIDS (anomaly-based intrusion detection system) can solve this problem by profiling attack behavior (Sewak, Sahay, & Rathore, 2020).

The SIDS restriction is addressed using the AIS (Artificial Immune System) technique. This method makes use of the immune cells model, which analyzes attack patterns or signatures and categorizes them as normal or aberrant. Additionally, it finds new signatures by continuously monitoring the system. In addition, Linux-based Suricata signature IDS is utilized to address the resource issue.

1.3.3.2 Anomaly-Based Intrusion Detection System (AIDS)

Due to its effectiveness against new attacks, AIDS, also known as prole-based or dynamic behavior abnormality detection, is the model that is utilized the most frequently in comparison to SIDS. The limits of SIDS are frequently bypassed with AIDS. Unidentified attack detection at various phases triggers alarms to identify vulnerabilities and prevent them using potential countermeasures. AIDS continuously monitors the system to gather information for the identification of normal and abnormal behavior. Because pattern databases are concerned with emerging unusual behavior, the primary goal of AIDS is to recognize zero-day attacks (Arqub & Abo-Hammour, 2014). Within the networks, it might pick up on strange behavior. For instance, the alarm is set off in the event of any unauthorized activity or account theft. A large false-positive rate is caused by abnormal behavior being new, routine behaviors rather than unnoticed incursions (Abo-Hammour, Arqub, Alsmadi, Momani, & Alsaedi, 2014).

There are a number of modern techniques for identifying and categorizing abnormal behaviors that have been created and discussed in the literature. The problems have been researched for the past 20 years, yet they remain unsolved (Mundher, Muhamad, Rehman, Saba, & Kausar, 2014).

1.3.3.3 Customized Intrusion Detection Methods

This technique manually develops requirements and rules to depict ordinary network behavior, though customized and AIDS work similarly. The system is watched over in accordance with the suggested set of guidelines and norms. Due to complexity and other constraints regarding construction, time consumption, and cost, the customized IDS has downsides (A. R. Khan, 2022), but it has a low false positive rate because it is resistant to new attack variations.

1.3.3.4 Hybrid Intrusion Detection Methods

These techniques, often referred to as compound detection, were created by combining anomalous, misuse, and requirement detection techniques in order to address their shortcomings and improve the detection of both current and emerging attack behavior. For 6LoWPAN systems in the IoT connected by IP, For instance, the hybrid approach was used to construct the SVELTE IDS technology (SIDS and AIDS). To achieve the consistency of these techniques' storage, processing, cost, and complexity, a hybrid technique was devised.

For new and unidentified attacks on communication networks, DSNSF (digital signature of network segment using flow analysis) was developed. It provided misbehavior signs that were classified as port scan, flash crowd, DoS, or DDoS attacks (Sicato, Singh, Rathore, & Park, 2020).

1.3.3.5 Host-Based IDS (HIDS)

By looking through firewalls, servers, or database logs, the HIDS software, which is placed investigates, examines, accumulates, and examines the data operations continuously taking place inside the host and network network on the channel's host computer. HIDS can only identify aberrant assaults on a single host while missing attacks across the network (Fernandes, Rodrigues, Carvalho, Al-Muhtadi, & Proença, 2019).

1.3.3.6 Network-Based IDS (NIDS)

NIDS keeps track of system activity by collecting packet captures and other data from NetFlow. Its primary goal is to protect networks. when a malicious attack occurs, a warning or alarm is generated from the exterior attacks. Through the use of hardware or software, this IDS monitors and analyzes network traffic for use with numerous hosts on many networks and outside firewalls. Servers have observing software installed, and sensors are connected to the servers for analysis. the communications of the network. Consequently, NIDS is extremely reliable and secure in identifying malicious attacks.

The large amount of network data that NIDS cannot handle and analyze because of the high capacity and velocity of traffic flow. Network packets that are encrypted cannot be processed by NIDS (A. R. Khan, 2022).

1.3.3.7 Distributed IDS (DIDS)

In order to assess communications monitoring administration, malicious attack data, and events, DIDS combines several distinct IDS on a large network. In order to oversee intrusion detection and prevention, information is combined using a number of sensors (based on NIDS and HIDS) and a central analyzer (Sagar, Jhaveri, & Borrego, 2020).

Thus, this discussion can be summarized as shown in Table 1.5.

TABLE 1.5
Summary of Various IDS

Name of the System	Processing Criteria	Source of Audit Data	Type of Response
NSM	Hybrid	N/w	Passive
Bro	Signature	N/w	Passive
MIDAS	Hybrid	Host	Passive
Haystack	Hybrid	Host	Passive
IDES	Anomaly	Host	Passive
W&S	Anomaly	Host	Passive
Comp Watch	Anomaly	Host	Passive
ASAX	Signature	Host	Passive
USTAT	Signature	Host	Passive
IDIOT	Signature	Host	Passive
GrIDS	Hybrid	Hybrid	Passive
NIDES	Hybrid	Host	Passive
EMERLARD	Hybrid	Hybrid	Active
Janus	Signature	Host	Active
Tripwire	Signature	Host	Passive
OSSEC HIDS	Hybrid	Host	Active
Snort	Hybrid	N/w	Active
AAFID	Anomaly	Host	Active
NAIDR	Anomaly	N/w	Passive
OSSEC HIDS	Hybrid	Host	Active
RealSecure	Signature	Hybrid	Active

1.4   RELATED WORK

In the literature, numerous algorithms and techniques for deep learning and machine learning techniques for intrusion detection have been documented. As a result, this section examines a variety of deep-learning-based methodologies and solutions.

In order to improve the system's accuracy, the study in Maithem and Al-sultany (2021) proposed a hybrid machine learning system (decision trees with SVM techniques). The classification of the recognized attack types uses the Decision Tree algorithm. The standard data are categorized using the SVM technique. NSL-KDD Dataset was utilized in this model. This system was 96.4% accurate. In Aslahi-Shahri et al. (2016), the researchers employed a SVM and a genetic algorithm (GA) to detect intrusion packets that are used with specific attributes. Researchers utilize SVM to solve classification and regression difficulties. The efficiency of detection in this paper was 97.3% and the dataset used was KDD Cup 1999. Yin, Zhu, Fei, and He (2017) developed a network detection method utilizing the NSL-KDD dataset and the RNN algorithm. The output of this study is broken down into binary classification, with an accuracy rate of 83.28%, and multiclass classification, with an accuracy rate of 81.29%. To identify network intrusion, the suggested system in Liu et al. (2017) uses a CNN. The KDD Cup 1999 dataset was used to build the datasets, and test data for the CNN-IDS model underwent two-depersonalization. This model's detection rate was 97.7%. The KDD Cup 1999 dataset was utilized by Singh and Ahlawat (2016) to test an artificial neural network in network intrusion detection. Principal Component Analysis (PCA) was utilized in the preprocessing of this system to reduce the amount of features and the min/max method to standardize the data. This study uses the Feed Forward Neural Network (FFNN), Levenberg–Marquardt (LM) Backpropagation, and mean square error as a loss function in artificial neural network architecture. This model's accuracy was 97.97%. In Potluri and Diedrich (2016), a DNN using NSL-KDD datasets was the suggested system. They suggested using a label-encoder, min-max normalization, and an auto-encoder network for preprocessing and learning the deep learning layers. This model is constructed using five categories. The dos attack category had the highest accuracy detection rate (97.7%), followed by the probe (89.8%), etc. The KDD Cup 99 dataset was used to examine and test the researchers' proposed artificial intelligence (AI) IDS, which used a DNN. They constructed their neural network using four hidden layers, the Adam optimizer for back-propagation training, and the ReLU function as the activation function in the forwarding. The accuracy of the binary categorization type, which may be either normal or an attack, was 99.08%. DNN and the DARPA 1999 dataset were used in the system that was suggested. ReLU is employed as that of the non-linear activation function in the hidden layer, and there are just two neurons in the output layer (Attack and Benign) (Vigneswaran, Vinayakumar, Soman, & Poornachandran, 2018). It was 93% accurate.

The approach of feature selection has been found to be improved in current research trends in order to improve the performance of the classifier of the created model. Iman and Ahmad (2020) observed that the model's classification performance improves as a result of feature selection and data reduction. The performance of the classification model improved when the amount of the data was minimal, according to a test the authors conducted on three separate sets of features to support their hypothesis of improving the performance of the model based on different characteristics. The three different feature section techniques used are Multimodal, IG + Correlation, and GA + LR and fusion. Performance was assessed without data reduction, and accuracy and precision were computed for two different circumstances. It was discovered that the performance of the three selected features increased by 0.02% in the second situation and by 0.03% in the first.

Drewek-Ossowicka, Pietrołaj, and Rumiński (2021) conducted a survey regarding the application of neural networks for IDS. The analysis of many datasets used frequently for resigning IDS, such as the KDD Cup 1999, NSL-KDD, UNSW-NB-15, and Kyoto2006+, is included in the survey. Hybrid models are frequently used in conjunction with neural network technology to improve performance. The various datasets under investigation demonstrate certain disadvantages of being redundant and older.

IDS encounters difficulties when newly developed cyberattacks arise. Based on the assault pattern, the model can quickly identify the current cyberattacks.

In order to analyze the IDS using naïve Bayes and the enhanced BAT method by examining certain features, Pokuri et al. (2021) presented a hybrid technique. The feature section methodology's ability to enhance the performance of an anomaly detection model is supported by the author. The IG algorithm is used to rank the features according to their weight values. The characteristics marked with the same ranks or falling under the same weight categories are then combined together to form sets, which are subsequently applied using the BA method.

When subsets are processed, features are optimized. The improved features are then put to the random forest method using various size-selected features, such as 15, 20, and 35, and it is discovered that the random forest algorithm performs better when used for classification. Talita, Nataza, and Rustam (2021) created an IDS for advanced metering systems (AMI) in grid systems, which are the target due to their two-way inter-network communication capability. LSTM networks, based on the CNN algorithm, are combined with cross-layer features over AMI IDS to solve the issue of taking into account the global and temporal properties of harmful information. The authors suggested a cross-layer IDS that uses LSTM-CNN feature fusion to track both legitimate and erroneous data behavior. The suggested algorithm was used to test and train the model using the KDD Cup 99 and NSL-KDD datasets. The proposed model demonstrated a 99.79% overall accuracy. In order to obtain a low false alarm rate and a high sensing rate, an IDS model based on data integrity targeted the DI-EIDS (Benisha & Ratna, 2020). The suggested approach is categorized as sampling and feature selection based on IDS-tracked attack patterns. The model was trained using the black forest classifier (BFC), and the ratio was optimized using the grey wolf optimization (GWO), deviation forest (d-forest), and the elimination of obstacles for the sampling selection. The training process takes longer than usual and is solely employed again for the detection of threats based on data integrity, which creates a research gap. The DI-EIDS algorithm's overall accuracy is 94.7%; its overall precision, recall, and F-measure are, respectively, 62.7%, 67.1%, and 62.5%. The algorithm exhibits a reduced false alarm rate when compared to the NB, ELM, and SVM algorithms for the prediction measures. Singh, Krishnamoorthy, Nayyar, Luhach, and Kaur (2019) provide a brand-new hybridization strategy to protect the environment of cloud computing against phishing, fake identity, and data absconding detection. The suggested algorithm automatically improves the fitness value by altering clusters with fuzzy-based ANN. Dataset and dimension reduction are accomplished using the spider monkey optimization method. The FCM-SMO cluster classifier reduces and optimizes the NSL-KDD dataset. It is discovered that the proposed approach performs better than other algorithms like ANN, FCM+SVM, and ANN+FCM. The hybridization algorithm's overall accuracy ranges from 80% to 85%, with precision, sensitivity, F-measure, specificity, and other metrics being 0.85%, 85%, 95%, 67%, 75%, 85%, and 88%, respectively.

Halim et al. (2021) discovered that because larger dimensionality has a negative effect on the efficiency of the machine learning algorithm, the application of machine learning techniques depends on the validity and availability of data. The authors created a genetic algorithm that retains the information using penetration testing for information security. It is based on a novel fitness value and features selection process. GbFS, a newly created methodology, increases accuracy by 99.80%. In Li, Ghoreishi, and Issakhov (2021), the authors used a metaheuristic consensus technique over an overlapping layout to improve DNA assembly fragments. The methodology's results over 25 datasets demonstrate the average performance when compared to other approaches. Tu et al. (2021) used a reinforcement learning attack technique to guarantee the detection of spoofing attacks during device-to-device communication. The number of false, detection rate, and error rate are used to describe how well the algorithm performed. The authors investigated how it is established that a reduced level of stress is the primary factor in accident mitigation since different levels of driver stress have an impact on vehicle control and the danger associated with road accidents involving high levels of stress. To investigate the connections between brain waves and physiology, the scientists employed a machine learning methodology. With an accuracy of 97.95%, the study finds that SVM outperforms other classification algorithms. According to Di Mauro, Galatro, Fortino, and Liotta (2021), the IDS is essential to attaining information security. A sophisticated assault is detected using the signature-based anomaly detection approach, which often modifies its patterns and is tracked based on these changes. The authors offer an experimental evaluation of a deep learning and neural network-based network intrusion management technology. The empirical analysis is carried out taking into account accuracy and time complexity. According to Lee, Pak, and Lee (2020), network IDS is used to gauge the frequency of both regular and abnormal network traffic in order to spot anomalous activity. The authors suggested a classification method based on deep learning for feature extraction. When compared to other algorithms across the most recent dataset, a reliability of 99% was attained. Injadat, Moubayed, Nassif, and Shami (2020) suggested a network intrusion detection-oriented multi-stage optimization strategy. The influence of interpolation on modeling various training samples using a variety of feature selection strategies forms the basis of the work. They discovered showed the CCIDS and UNSW-15 dataset performances of the model were improved with 99% accuracy. In the network IDS described in Di Mauro, Galatro, and Liotta (2020), authors analyzed the KDD 99 dataset using a considerable supervised feature selection approach. They then employed a variety of experimental analysis techniques to gauge the dataset's complexity, correlation, and performance. Belgrana, Benamrane, Hamaida, Chaabani, and Taleb-Ahmed (2021), discovered, by lowering the false negative rate, the various artificial intelligence-based algorithms that are used to detect anomalies improve the quality of detection. For the classification and regression of samples on the NSL-KDD dataset, the condensed closest neighbor's method is applied. The experimental research demonstrates how the detection rate increases with a shorter processing time. A red-black tree full-nodes-based integrity technique over multi-copy dynamic data was suggested by Liu, Liu, Yang, and Li (2021). Referring to Yu, Lee, Park, and Hong (2021), it was discovered that authentication based on a special ID is necessary to address the problem of harmful actions through cloud storage systems. According to Latif et al. (2021) and Huma et al. (2021), the industrial sector uses traditional IoT technology. Information security is being hampered by the widespread adoption of IoT in the industrial sector. The authors suggested a unique HDRaNN technique for detecting network intrusions and discovered that the algorithm exhibits high accuracy of 98% and 99% for two different datasets, such as UNSW-NB15 and DS2OS.

Table 1.6 lists related works that use models, features, datasets, and performance metrics to focus on intrusion detection using DL methods.

According to Liu et al. (2017), the intrusion prevention model based on a CNN have had the highest detection accuracy and precision when compared to other IDS classifiers. It has been demonstrated that using a CNN in extremely intrusive detection is feasible. The authors contend that CNN-based algorithms perform more effectively than other machine learning categorization methods. In order to train and check for traffic characteristics, Wang et al. (2017)'s design of an IDS with a CNN significantly lowers the rate of false alarms (FAR). This study demonstrates how detailed network traffic characteristics may be extracted from and learned using deep learning algorithms. An RNN-IDS was proposed by Yin et al. (2017) and evaluated against ANN, random forest (RF), SVM, and other machine learning techniques. An RNN-IDS is suitable for developing a classification model with high accuracy, and it performs better in binary and multiclass classification than typical machine learning approaches.

For unsupervised feature learning, Shone et al. (2018) demonstrated a non-symmetric deep auto-encoder (NDAE). This work compares an auto-encoder with an NDAE in order to increase the classification performance of KDD99 and NSLKDD99 (NDAE). For the purpose of attack detection, Wu et al. (2018) developed CNN and RNN; however, their model is different from the model utilized in this study since it carried out independent experiments on the CNN and RNN models. The usefulness of deep learning techniques for AIDSs was examined by Naseer et al. (2018). The effectiveness of models using multi-class classification was compared to the effectiveness of conventional machine learning techniques by Ding and Zhai (2018).

In addition to developing DL for an IDS available on WSNs, Otoum et al. (2019) also contrasted the adaptively supervised and clustered hybrid IDS and the Boltzmann machine-based clustered IDS (RBC-IDS) (ASCH-IDS). For the purpose of detecting network intrusions, Chouhan et al. (2019) suggested a Channel Boosted and Residual learning-based deep Convolutional Neural Network (CBR-CNN) architecture. Stacked Auto-encoders (SAE) and unsupervised training were used in this study, and an NSL-KDD dataset was used to assess how well the suggested CBR-CNN technique performed. In order to identify and categorize unexpected and unpredictable cyberattacks by DNN, Vinayakumar et al. (2019) created an IDS. The NSL-KDD, UNSW-NB15, Kyoto, WSN-DS, and CICIDS2017 datasets were used to test the

TABLE 1.6
Related Works on IDS

Year	Authors	Focus Area	Deep Model	Features	Dataset	Performance
2017	Liu et al. (2017)	Attack classification	CNN	41 features	KDD Cup 1999	DR = 97.66%
2017	Wang et al. (2017)	Feature learning for intrusion detection	CNN	16 Features based on net-flow	DARPA 1998, ISCX2012	DR = 99.89%, FAR = 0.02%
2017	Yin et al. (2017)	Binary and multi-class intrusion detection	RNN	41 features mapped into 122	NSL-KDD	ACC = 83.28%
2018	Shone et al. (2018)	Attack classification using unsupervised feature learning	Non-Symmetric Deep Auto-Encoders	41 features	KDD Cup 1999, NSL-KDD	ACC = 97.85%
2018	Wu, Chen, and Li (2018)	Attack classification	CNN, RNN	41 features	NSL-KDD	ACC = 79.48%
2018	Naseer et al. (2018)	DL approaches for anomaly-based IDS	DNN, CNN, RNN	41 features	NSL-KDD	DR = 85–89%
2018	Ding and Zhai (2018)	multi-class intrusion detection	CNN	41 features	NSL-KDD	ACC = 80.13%
2019	Otoum, Kantarci, and Mouftah (2019)	Intrusion detection on wireless sensor networks (WSNs)	Restricted Boltzmann Machine (RBM)	41 features	KDD Cup 1999	DR = 99.91%
2019	Chouhan et al. (2019)	Intrusion detection based on unsupervised training	CNN	41 features	NSL-KDD	ACC = 89.41%
2019	Vinayakumar et al. (2019)	Intrusion detection on ML/DL approaches	DNN	41/41/49/23 features	KDD Cup 1999 NSL-KDD, UNSW-NB15, WSN-DS	KDD Cup 1999, NSL-KDD: ACC = 95–99%, UNSW-NB15, WSN-DS: ACC = 65–75%

Year	Authors	Purpose	Method	Features	Datasets	Results
2019	Chiba et al. (2019)	Intrusion detection on cloud environment	DNN	80/41/14 features	CICIDS2017, NSL-KDD version 2015, CIDDS-001	ACC = 99–99.9%
2019	Zhang et al. (2019)	Identify SQL injection attacks in network traffic	Deep Belief Network (DBN)	6 features	Private datasets	ACC = 92–96%
2019	Faker and Dogdu (2019)	Attack classification on ML/DL approaches	DNN, Random Forest (RF), Gradient Boosting Tree (GBT)	80/49 features	CICIS 2017, UNSW NB15	ACC = 91–98%
2019	Aloqaily, Otoum, Al Ridhawi, and Jararweh (2019)	Intrusion detection for connected vehicles	Deep Belief Network (DBN), Decision Tree (DT)	41 features mapped into 122	NSL-KDD, NS-3 Featured Traffic	ACC = 99.43% DR = 99.92%
2020	Kim et al. (2020)	Intrusion detection for real-time web-service	CNN-LSTM	256 features (all extended ASCII characters)	Real-time web traffic data, CSIC-2010, CICIS 2017	ACC = 98.07% DR = 99.22%

21

performance using the DNN model. Utilizing recent datasets such as CICIDS2017, NSL-KDD version 2015, and CIDDS-001, Chiba et al. (2019) developed a DNN model in a cloud-environment-based anomalous network IDS using a hybrid optimization framework (IGASAA) based on the Improved Genetic Algorithm (IGA) and Simulated Annealing Algorithm (SAA). A deep belief network (DBN) model was utilized by Zhang et al. (2019) to detect SQL injection attacks in network traffic. Using a DNN and two ensemble approaches, RF and gradient boosting tree, Faker and Dogdu (2019) tested with enhancing the performance of IDSs on the CICIS2017 and UNSW NB15 datasets (GBT). A novel approach or strategy for enhancing deep learning algorithms has been proposed by prior research. In order to provide an IDS against security assaults, Aloqaily et al. (2019) designed an automated secure continuous cloud service availability framework for smart connected automobiles.

1.5 DATASETS USED AS BENCHMARKS FOR IDS

Machine learning's job is to extract useful information from data, so how well it performs is dependent on the caliber of the input data. The foundation of machine learning methodology is data understanding. The adopted data for IDSs should be simple to obtain and reflect host or network behavior. Packets, flows, sessions, and logs are the typical source data formats for IDSs. A dataset requires a lot of work and effort to build. A benchmark dataset can be created and then utilized regularly by numerous researchers. Using benchmark datasets has two additional advantages in addition to convenience. (1) The benchmark datasets are reliable and increase the credibility of experimental findings. (2) A lot of published studies have made use of standard benchmark datasets, making it possible to compare the findings of current studies to those of earlier ones. Table 1.7 provides a thorough review of the dataset and the attack types contained inside each.

1.5.1 DARPA1998

The MIT Lincoln laboratory created the DARPA1998 dataset (Zissman et al., 1999), which is a benchmark dataset frequently used in IDS studies. The first seven weeks

TABLE 1.7

List of Benchmark Datasets

Dataset	Year	Attack Types	Attacks
KDD Cup'99 (Cup, 2007)	1998	4	DoS, Probe, R2L, U2R
NSL-KDD (Liu & Lang, 2019)	2009	4	DoS, Probe, R2L, U2R
UNSW-NB15 (Moustafa & Slay, 2015)	2015	9	Backdoors, DoS, Exploits, Fuzzers, Generic, Port scans, Reconnaissance, Shellcode, worms
CIC-IDS2017 (Sharafaldin et al., 2018)	2017	7	Brute Force, HeartBleed, Botnet, DoS, DDoS, Web, Infiltration
CSE-CIC-IDS2018 (Sharafaldin et al., 2018)	2018	7	HeartBleed, DoS, Botnet, DDoS, Brute Force, Infiltration, Web

served as the training dataset, and the final two weeks served as the test set, while the researchers gathered Internet traffic over a nine-week period to create it. Labels and raw packets are also included in the collection. Normal, DoS), Probe, U2R, and Remote to Local (R2L) are the five different sorts of labeling. Machine learning models can indeed be directly applied to raw packets, hence the KDD99 dataset was created to address this issue.

1.5.2   KDD99

The KDD99 data (Cup, 2007) is currently the most used IDS benchmark dataset. Data from DARPA1998 was used by its compilers to extract 41-dimensional characteristics. The tags in KDD 1999 and DARPA 1998 are identical. Basic features, content features, host-based statistical features, and moment statistical features are the four different categories of features in KDD99. Unfortunately, there are numerous flaws in the KDD99 dataset. The classification findings are skewed toward the classes that make up the majority due to the data's significant unbalance. Additionally, there are a lot of redundant records and duplicate records. Before using the dataset, many researchers must properly filter it. As a result, it is not always possible to compare the experimental outcomes of various investigations. Additionally, KDD data are just too old to accurately reflect the state of the network.

1.5.3   NSL-KDD

The NSL-KDD (Liu & Lang, 2019) was presented as a solution to the problems with the KDD99 dataset. Based on the KDD99, the entries in the NSL-KDD have been carefully selected. The NSL-KDD prevents classification bias by balancing records from several classes. Only a small number of records remain after the NSL-KDD deleted any duplicates and redundant data. As a result, the entire dataset may be used for the tests, as well as the results from other studies are similar and consistent. The issues of data biases and data redundancy are somewhat mitigated by the NSL-KDD. The NSL-KDD, however, does not contain fresh data; as a result, minority class data are still absent and its data are still dated.

1.5.4   UNSW-NB15

The University of South Wales created the UNSW-NB15 (Moustafa & Slay, 2015) dataset, and researchers there set up three virtual servers to record network traffic and extract 49-dimensional features using a tool called Bro. In comparison to the KDD99 dataset, the dataset has more features and more attack types. Normality tests and nine different sorts of attacks are among the data categories. Among the features are labeled features, flow characteristics, basic features, features, time features, and other features. Recent investigations have made use of the UNSW-NB15, a sample of new IDS datasets. Even while UNSW-NB15 currently has less of an impact than KDD99, new datasets must be created in order to create new, machine learning-based IDS.

1.5.5   CIC-IDS2017

The Canadian Institute of Cyber Security (CIC) produced this dataset in 2017 (Sharafaldin, Lashkari, & Ghorbani, 2018). Both updated real-world attacks and the typical flows are included. CICFlowMeter uses data from timestamps, destination address Email accounts, protocols, and assaults to assess the network traffic (Lashkari et al., 2017). Also included in CICIDS2017 are typical attack scenarios including Brute Force Attacks, HeartBleed Attacks, Botnet, Distributed DoS (DDoS), DoS, Web Attacks, and Infiltration Attacks (Abdulhammed, Musafer, Alessa, Faezipour, & Abuzneid, 2019).

1.5.6   CSE-CIC-IDS2018

In 2018, the Communications Security Establishment (CSE) and the CIC collaborated to generate this dataset (Karatas, Demir, & Sahingoz, 2020). The creation of user profiles that include an abstract depiction of the many events. All of these profiles are integrated with a special set of features to create the dataset. Brute-force, Heartbleed, Botnet, DoS, DDoS, Web attacks, and network infiltration from within are just some of the seven various attack scenarios that are covered (Sharafaldin et al., 2018).

1.6   EVALUATION METRICS

The performance of ML and DL methods for IDS is evaluated using the most popular evaluation metrics, which are described in this section. The Confusion Matrix is a two-dimensional matrix that contains data on the Actual and Predicted class (Deng et al., 2013) and includes the foundation for all evaluation metrics. It contains information about the various qualities utilized in class and includes the following:

i. True Positives (TP): Data instances that the classifier properly identified as Attacks.
ii. False Negative (FN) examples are data instances that were incorrectly classified as Normal instances.
iii. False Positives (FP): Those instances of data that were incorrectly categorized as an attack.
iv. True Negatives (TN): These situations were categorized as Normal situations appropriately.

The right predictions of a particular classifier are indicated by the diagonal of the confusion matrix, while non-diagonal entries are the incorrect predictions. These confusion matrix attributes are shown in Table 1.8. Additionally, the many evaluation metrics included in the most recent studies are:

Precision: This is the proportion of attacks properly predicted to all attacks predicted in all samples.

$$Precision = \frac{TP}{TP + FP}$$

TABLE 1.8
Confusion Matrix

		Predicted Values	
		Attack	**Normal**
Actual Class	**Attack**	True Positive	False Negative
	Normal	False Positive	True Negative

Recall: Remember that it is a ratio between all samples that were accurately identified as attacks and all samples that truly are attacks. Another name for it is Detection Rate.

$$\text{Recall} = \text{Decision Rate} = \frac{TP}{TP + FP}$$

False Alarm Rate: The ratio of incorrectly predicted Attack samples to all samples that are Normal is known as the false alarm rate, also known as the false positive rate.

$$\text{False Alarm Rate} = \frac{FP}{FP + TN}$$

True Negative Rate: The ratio of correctly identified Normal samples to all of the samples that are Normal is known as the true negative rate.

$$\text{True Negative Rate} = \frac{TN}{FP + TN}$$

Accuracy: This is the proportion of cases that are correctly categorized into all instances. It also goes by the name "Detection Accuracy," and a balanced dataset is a requirement for its usefulness as a performance indicator.

$$\text{Accuracy} = \frac{TP + TN}{TP + FP + TN + FN}$$

F-Measure: The harmonic mean of Precision and Recall is what is meant by the term "F-Measure." In other words, it is a statistical technique for evaluating a system's correctness while taking into account both its precision and recall.

$$\text{F-Measure} = 2 \times \left(\frac{\text{Precision} \times \text{Recall}}{\text{Precision} + \text{Recall}} \right)$$

Several studies that use the datasets stated in Section 1.5 and the evaluation criteria (explained in Section 1.6) to assess the effectiveness of their suggested methods are summarized and given an overview in Table 1.9.

TABLE 1.9
Datasets and Performance Evaluation Metrics

Study	Dataset						Evaluation Metrics							
	KC	NK	UN	C7	C8	OT	ACC	PRE	REC	F-M	FAR	ROC	TPR	OTH
Yin et al. (2017)	Y	Y					Y	Y	Y	Y	Y		Y	
Shone et al. (2018)	Y	Y					Y	Y	Y	Y	Y			
Ali et al. (2021)	Y						Y							
Wang et al. (2017)		Y				Y	Y	Y	Y	Y	Y	Y		
Naseer et al. (2018)		Y					Y	Y	Y			Y		Y
Vinayakumar et al. (2019)	Y	Y	Y	Y		Y	Y	Y		Y	Y	Y	Y	
Gao et al. (2020)		Y	Y				Y	Y	Y	Y				
Zhang et al. (2019)			Y	Y			Y	Y	Y		Y			
Karatas et al. (2020)			Y		Y		Y	Y	Y	Y				
Yang et al. (2019)		Y	Y				Y	Y	Y	Y	Y			
Yu et al. (2021)		Y		Y			Y	Y	Y	Y	Y			

REFERENCES

Abdulhammed, R., Musafer, H., Alessa, A., Faezipour, M., & Abuzneid, A. (2019). Features dimensionality reduction approaches for machine learning based network intrusion detection. *Electronics*, *8* (3), 322.

Abo-Hammour, Z., Arqub, O. A., Alsmadi, O., Momani, S., & Alsaedi, A. (2014). An optimization algorithm for solving systems of singular boundary value problems. *Applied Mathematics & Information Sciences*, *8* (6), 2809.

Abou Khamis, R., Shafiq, M. O., & Matrawy, A. (2020). Investigating resistance of deep learning-based IDS against adversaries using min-max optimization. In *ICC 2020-2020 IEEE international conference on communications (ICC)* (pp. 1–7).

Ali, F., Ali, A., Imran, M., Naqvi, R. A., Siddiqi, M. H., & Kwak, K.-S. (2021). Traffic accident detection and condition analysis based on social networking data. *Accident Analysis & Prevention*, *151*, 105973.

Aloqaily, M., Otoum, S., Al Ridhawi, I., & Jararweh, Y. (2019). An intrusion detection system for connected vehicles in smart cities. *Ad Hoc Networks*, *90*, 101842.

Alzahrani, A. O., & Alenazi, M. J. (2021). Designing a network intrusion detection system based on machine learning for software defined networks. *Future Internet*, *13* (5), 111.

Arqub, O. A., & Abo-Hammour, Z. (2014). Numerical solution of systems of second-order boundary value problems using continuous genetic algorithm. *Information Sciences*, *279*, 396–415.

Aslahi-Shahri, B., Rahmani, R., Chizari, M., Maralani, A., Eslami, M., Golkar, M. J., & Ebrahimi, A. (2016). A hybrid method consisting of GA and SVM for intrusion detection system. *Neural Computing and Applications*, *27* (6), 1669–1676.

Atienza, D., Herrero, Á., & Corchado, E. (2015). Neural analysis of http traffic for web attack detection. In *Computational intelligence in security for information systems conference* (pp. 201–212).

Bag, S., Gupta, S., & Wood, L. (2020). Big data analytics in sustainable humanitarian supply chain: Barriers and their interactions. *Annals of Operations Research*, *319*, 1–40.

Belgrana, F. Z., Benamrane, N., Hamaida, M. A., Chaabani, A. M., & Taleb-Ahmed, A. (2021). Network intrusion detection system using neural network and condensed nearest neighbors with selection of NSL-KDD influencing features. In *2020 IEEE international conference on internet of things and intelligence system (IOTAIS)* (pp. 23–29).

Benisha, R., & Ratna, S. R. (2020). Detection of data integrity attacks by constructing an effective intrusion detection system. *Journal of Ambient Intelligence and Humanized Computing*, *11* (11), 5233–5244.

Charniak, E. (1985). *Introduction to artificial intelligence*. Pearson Education India.

Chiba, Z., Abghour, N., Moussaid, K., Rida, M., et al. (2019). Intelligent approach to build a deep neural network based IDS for cloud environment using combination of machine learning algorithms. *Computers & Security*, *86*, 291–317.

Chouhan, N., Khan, A., et al. (2019). Network anomaly detection using channel boosted and residual learning based deep convolutional neural network. *Applied Soft Computing*, *83*, 105612.

Chung, J., Gulcehre, C., Cho, K., & Bengio, Y. (2014). Empirical evaluation of gated recurrent neural networks on sequence modeling. *arXiv preprint arXiv:1412.3555*.

Cordón, O., Kazienko, P., & Trawiński, B. (2011). Special issue on hybrid and ensemble methods in machine learning. *New Generation Computing*, *29* (3), 241–244.

Cup, K. (2007). http://kdd.ics.uci.edu/databases/kddcup99/kddcup99.html. October.

Deng, J., Zhang, Z., Marchi, E., & Schuller, B. (2013). Sparse autoencoder-based feature transfer learning for speech emotion recognition. In *2013 Humaine association conference on affective computing and intelligent interaction* (pp. 511–516).

Denning, D. E. (1987). An intrusion-detection model. *IEEE Transactions on Software Engineering* (2), 222–232.

Dey, S. K., & Rahman, M. M. (2019). Effects of machine learning approach in flow-based anomaly detection on software-defined networking. *Symmetry, 12* (1), 7.

Di Mauro, M., Galatro, G., Fortino, G., & Liotta, A. (2021). Supervised feature selection techniques in network intrusion detection: A critical review. *Engineering Applications of Artificial Intelligence, 101*, 104216.

Di Mauro, M., Galatro, G., & Liotta, A. (2020). Experimental review of neural-based approaches for network intrusion management. *IEEE Transactions on Network and Service Management, 17* (4), 2480–2495.

Ding, Y., & Zhai, Y. (2018). Intrusion detection system for NSL-KDD dataset using convolutional neural networks. In *Proceedings of the 2018 2nd international conference on computer science and artificial intelligence* (pp. 81–85).

Drewek-Ossowicka, A., Pietrołaj, M., & Rumiński, J. (2021). A survey of neural networks usage for intrusion detection systems. *Journal of Ambient Intelligence and Humanized Computing, 12* (1), 497–514.

Faker, O., & Dogdu, E. (2019). Intrusion detection using big data and deep learning techniques. In *Proceedings of the 2019 ACM southeast conference* (pp. 86–93).

Fernandes, G., Rodrigues, J. J., Carvalho, L. F., Al-Muhtadi, J. F., & Proença, M. L. (2019). A comprehensive survey on network anomaly detection. *Telecommunication Systems, 70* (3), 447–489.

Fielding, R., Gettys, J., Mogul, J., Frystyk, H., Masinter, L., Leach, P., & Berners-Lee, T. (1999). *Rfc2616: Hypertext transfer protocol–http/1.1*. RFC Editor.

Gao, M., Ma, L., Liu, H., Zhang, Z., Ning, Z., & Xu, J. (2020). Malicious network traffic detection based on deep neural networks and association analysis. *Sensors, 20* (5), 1452.

Gómez, J., Gil, C., Baños, R., Márquez, A. L., Montoya, F. G., & Montoya, M. (2013). A pareto-based multi-objective evolutionary algorithm for automatic rule generation in network intrusion detection systems. *Soft Computing, 17* (2), 255–263.

Graves, A., Mohamed, A.-R., & Hinton, G. (2013). Speech recognition with deep recurrent neural networks IEEE international conference on acoustics. In *IEEE International Conference on Acoustics, Speech and Signal Processing (ICASSP)* (pp. 6645–6649).

Haines, J. W., Lippmann, R. P., Fried, D. J., Zissman, M., & Tran, E. (2001). *1999 DARPA intrusion detection evaluation: Design and procedures* (Techical Report). Lincoln Lab, Massachusetts Institute of Techology, Lexington.

Halim, Z., Yousaf, M. N., Waqas, M., Sulaiman, M., Abbas, G., Hussain, M., … Hanif, M. (2021). An effective genetic algorithm-based feature selection method for intrusion detection systems. *Computers & Security, 110*, 102448.

Halme, L. R., & Bauer, R. K. (1995). Ain't misbehaving – A taxomony of anti-intrusion techniques. In *18th National Information Systems Security Conference* (p. 163).

He, Y., Khan, H. U., Zhang, K., Wang, W., Choi, B. J., Aly, A. A., … Baz, M. (2021). D2D-V2X-SDN: Taxonomy and architecture towards 5G mobile communication system. *IEEE Access, 9*, 155507–155525. doi: 10.1109/ACCESS.2021.3127041

Hinton, G. E. (2012). A practical guide to training restricted Boltzmann machines. In Montavon, G., Orr, G.B., Müller, K.R. (eds.) *Neural networks: Tricks of the trade. Lecture notes in computer science* (pp. 599–619). Springer. doi: 10.1007/978-3-642-35289-8_32

Hochreiter, S., & Schmidhuber, J. (1997). Long short-term memory. *Neural Computation, 9* (8), 1735–1780.

Huma, Z. E., Latif, S., Ahmad, J., Idrees, Z., Ibrar, A., Zou, Z., … Baothman, F. (2021). A hybrid deep random neural network for cyberattack detection in the industrial internet of things. *IEEE Access, 9*, 55595–55605.

Iman, A. N., & Ahmad, T. (2020). Data reduction for optimizing feature selection in modeling intrusion detection system. *International Journal of Intelligent Engineering and Systems, 13* (6), 199–207.

Injadat, M., Moubayed, A., Nassif, A. B., & Shami, A. (2020). Multi-stage optimized machine learning framework for network intrusion detection. *IEEE Transactions on Network and Service Management, 18* (2), 1803–1816.

Jaramillo, L. E. S. (2018). Malware detection and mitigation techniques: Lessons learned from Mirai DDOS attack. *Journal of Information Systems Engineering & Management, 3* (3), 19.

Karatas, G., Demir, O., & Sahingoz, O. K. (2020). Increasing the performance of machine learning-based IDSS on an imbalanced and up-to-date dataset. *IEEE Access, 8,* 32150–32162.

Khan, A. R. (2022). Facial emotion recognition using conventional machine learning and deep learning methods: Current achievements, analysis and remaining challenges. *Information, 13* (6), 268.

Khan, A. Y., Latif, R., Latif, S., Tahir, S., Batool, G., & Saba, T. (2019). Malicious insider attack detection in IoTs using data analytics. *IEEE Access, 8,* 11743–11753.

Kim, A., Park, M., and Lee, D.H. (2020). AI-IDS: Application of deep learning to real-time web intrusion detection. *IEEE Access, 8,* 70245–70261. doi: 10.1109/ACCESS.2020. 2986882

Kolias, C., Kambourakis, G., Stavrou, A., & Gritzalis, S. (2015). Intrusion detection in 802.11 networks: Empirical evaluation of threats and a public dataset. *IEEE Communications Surveys & Tutorials, 18* (1), 184–208.

Koroniotis, N., Moustafa, N., Sitnikova, E., & Turnbull, B. (2019). Towards the development of realistic botnet dataset in the internet of things for network forensic analytics: Bot-IoT dataset. *Future Generation Computer Systems, 100,* 779–796.

Lashkari, A. H., Draper-Gil, G., Mamun, M. S. I., Ghorbani, A. A., et al. (2017). Characterization of tor traffic using time based features. In *ICISSp* (pp. 253–262).

Latif, S., Huma, Z., Jamal, S. S., Ahmed, F., Ahmad, J., Zahid, A., ... Abbasi, Q. H. (2021). Intrusion detection framework for the internet of things using a dense random neural network. *IEEE Transactions on Industrial Informatics, 18* (9), 6435–6444. doi: 10.1109/ TII.2021.3130248

Lawrence, S., Giles, C. L., Tsoi, A. C., & Back, A. D. (1997). Face recognition: A convolutional neural-network approach. *IEEE Transactions on Neural Networks, 8* (1), 98–113.

Lazarevic, A., Kumar, V., & Srivastava, J. (2005). Intrusion detection: A survey. In Kumar, V., Srivastava, J., Lazarevic, A. (eds.) *Managing cyber threats. Massive computing* (pp. 19–78). Springer. doi: 10.1007/0-387-24230-9_2

Lee, J., Pak, J., & Lee, M. (2020). Network intrusion detection system using feature extraction based on deep sparse autoencoder. In *2020 international conference on information and communication technology convergence (ICTC)* (pp. 1282–1287).

Lee, W., Stolfo, S. J., Chan, P. K., Eskin, E., Fan, W., Miller, M., ... Zhang, J. (2001). Real time data mining-based intrusion detection. In *Proceedings DARPA information survivability conference and exposition II. DISCEX'01* (Vol. 1, pp. 89–100).

Li, Y., Ghoreishi, S.-M., & Issakhov, A. (2021). Improving the accuracy of network intrusion detection system in medical IoT systems through butterfly optimization algorithm. *Wireless Personal Communications, 126,* 1999–2017. doi: 10.1007/s11277-021-08756-x

Liao, B., Ali, Y., Nazir, S., He, L., & Khan, H. U. (2020). Security analysis of IoT devices by using mobile computing: A systematic literature review. *IEEE Access, 8,* 120331–120350.

Liu, H., & Lang, B. (2019). Machine learning and deep learning methods for intrusion detection systems: A survey. *Applied Sciences, 9* (20), 4396.

Liu, Y., Liu, S., Zhao, X., et al. (2017). Intrusion detection algorithm based on convolutional neural network. *Beijing Ligong Daxue Xuebao/Transactions of Beijing Institute of Technology, 37* (12), 1271–1275.

Liu, Z., Liu, Y., Yang, X., & Li, X. (2021). Integrity auditing for multi-copy in cloud storage based on red-black tree. *IEEE Access, 9,* 75117–75131.

Maithem, M., & Al-Sultany, G. A. (2021). Network intrusion detection system using deep neural networks. In *Journal of physics: Conference series* (Vol. 1804, p. 012138).

Moustafa, N., & Slay, J. (2015). UNSW-NB15: A comprehensive data set for network intrusion detection systems (UNSW-NB15 network data set). In *2015 military communications and information systems conference (MILCIS)* (pp. 1–6).

Mundher, M., Muhamad, D., Rehman, A., Saba, T., & Kausar, F. (2014). Digital watermarking for images security using discrete slantlet transform. *Applied Mathematics & Information Sciences, 8* (6), 2823.

Naseer, S., Saleem, Y., Khalid, S., Bashir, M. K., Han, J., Iqbal, M. M., & Han, K. (2018). Enhanced network anomaly detection based on deep neural networks. *IEEE Access, 6,* 48231–48246.

Ngo, D.-M., Pham-Quoc, C., & Thinh, T. N. (2020). Heterogeneous hardware-based network intrusion detection system with multiple approaches for SDN. *Mobile Networks and Applications, 25* (3), 1178–1192.

Otoum, S., Kantarci, B., & Mouftah, H. T. (2019). On the feasibility of deep learning in sensor network intrusion detection. *IEEE Networking Letters, 1* (2), 68–71.

Pokuri, S. R., et al. (2021). A hybrid approach for feature selection analysis on the intrusion detection system using Navi Bayes and improved Bat algorithm. *Turkish Journal of Computer and Mathematics Education (TURCOMAT), 12* (11), 5078–5087.

Potluri, S., & Diedrich, C. (2016). Accelerated deep neural networks for enhanced intrusion detection system. In *2016 IEEE 21st international conference on emerging technologies and factory automation (ETFA)* (pp. 1–8).

Sagar, R., Jhaveri, R., & Borrego, C. (2020). Applications in security and evasions in machine learning: A survey. *Electronics, 9* (1), 97.

Sarikaya, R., Hinton, G. E., & Deoras, A. (2014). Application of deep belief networks for natural language understanding. *IEEE/ACM Transactions on Audio, Speech, and Language Processing, 22* (4), 778–784.

Schuster, M., & Paliwal, K. K. (1997). Bidirectional recurrent neural networks. *IEEE Transactions on Signal Processing, 45* (11), 2673–2681.

Sewak, M., Sahay, S. K., & Rathore, H. (2020). DeepIntent: ImplicitIntent based android ids with E2E deep learning architecture. In *2020 IEEE 31st annual international symposium on personal, indoor and mobile radio communications* (pp. 1–6).

Sharafaldin, I., Lashkari, A. H., & Ghorbani, A. A. (2018). Toward generating a new intrusion detection dataset and intrusion traffic characterization. *ICISSp, 1,* 108–116.

Shone, N., Ngoc, T. N., Phai, V. D., & Shi, Q. (2018). A deep learning approach to network intrusion detection. *IEEE Transactions on Emerging Topics in Computational Intelligence, 2* (1), 41–50.

Sicato, J. C. S., Singh, S. K., Rathore, S., & Park, J. H. (2020). A comprehensive analyses of intrusion detection system for IoT environment. *Journal of Information Processing Systems, 16* (4), 975–990.

Singh, B., & Ahlawat, A. K. (2016). Innovative empirical approach for intrusion detection using ann. *International Journal of Innovative Research in Computer Science & Technology (IJIRCST), 4.*

Singh, P., Krishnamoorthy, S., Nayyar, A., Luhach, A. K., & Kaur, A. (2019). Soft-computing-based false alarm reduction for hierarchical data of intrusion detection system. *International Journal of Distributed Sensor Networks, 15* (10), 1550147719883132.

Snapp, S. R., Brentano, J., Dias, G. V., Goan, T. L., Heberlein, T., Ho, C., … Mansur, D. (1991). DIDS-(distributed intrusion detection system)-motivation, architecture, and an early prototype. In *Proceedings of the 14th national computer security conference,* Washington, DC (pp. 167–176).

Stampar, M., & Fertalj, K. (2015). Artificial intelligence in network intrusion detection. In *2015 38th international convention on information and communication technology, electronics and microelectronics (MIPRO)* (pp. 1318–1323).

Talita, A., Nataza, O., & Rustam, Z. (2021). Naïve bayes classifier and particle swarm optimization feature selection method for classifying intrusion detection system dataset. In *Journal of physics: Conference series* (Vol. 1752, p. 012021).

Tavallaee, M., Bagheri, E., Lu, W., & Ghorbani, A. A. (2009). A detailed analysis of the KDD cup 99 data set. In *2009 IEEE symposium on computational intelligence for security and defense applications* (pp. 1–6).

Tu, S., Waqas, M., Rehman, S. U., Mir, T., Abbas, G., Abbas, Z. H., ... Ahmad, I. (2021). Reinforcement learning assisted impersonation attack detection in device-to-device communications. *IEEE Transactions on Vehicular Technology*, *70* (2), 1474–1479.

Vigneswaran, R. K., Vinayakumar, R., Soman, K., & Poornachandran, P. (2018). Evaluating shallow and deep neural networks for network intrusion detection systems in cyber security. In *2018 9th international conference on computing, communication and networking technologies (ICCCNT)* (pp. 1–6).

Vinayakumar, R., Alazab, M., Soman, K., Poornachandran, P., Al-Nemrat, A., & Venkatraman, S. (2019). Deep learning approach for intelligent intrusion detection system. *IEEE Access*, *7*, 41525–41550.

Vincent, P., Larochelle, H., Bengio, Y., & Manzagol, P.-A. (2008). Extracting and composing robust features with denoising autoencoders. In *Proceedings of the 25th international conference on machine learning* (pp. 1096–1103).

Vincent, P., Larochelle, H., Lajoie, I., Bengio, Y., Manzagol, P.-A., & Bottou, L. (2010). Stacked denoising autoencoders: Learning useful representations in a deep network with a local denoising criterion. *Journal of Machine Learning Research*, *11* (12), 3371–3408.

Wang, W., Sheng, Y., Wang, J., Zeng, X., Ye, X., Huang, Y., & Zhu, M. (2017). Hast-ids: Learning hierarchical spatial-temporal features using deep neural networks to improve intrusion detection. *IEEE Access*, *6*, 1792–1806.

Wu, K., Chen, Z., & Li, W. (2018). A novel intrusion detection model for a massive network using convolutional neural networks. *IEEE Access*, *6*, 50850–50859.

Yang, J., Li, T., Liang, G., He, W., & Zhao, Y. (2019). A simple recurrent unit model based intrusion detection system with dcgan. *IEEE Access*, *7*, 83286–83296.

Yin, C., Zhu, Y., Fei, J., & He, X. (2017). A deep learning approach for intrusion detection using recurrent neural networks. *IEEE Access*, *5*, 21954–21961.

Yu, D., Lee, H., Park, S.-H., & Hong, S.-E. (2021). Deep learning methods for joint optimization of beamforming and fronthaul quantization in cloud radio access networks. *IEEE Wireless Communications Letters*, *10* (10), 2180–2184.

Zhang, H., Zhao, B., Yuan, H., Zhao, J., Yan, X., & Li, F. (2019). SQL injection detection based on deep belief network. In *Proceedings of the 3rd international conference on computer science and application engineering* (pp. 1–6).

Zhao, G., Zhang, C., & Zheng, L. (2017). Intrusion detection using deep belief network and probabilistic neural network. In *2017 IEEE international conference on computational science and engineering (CSE) and IEEE international conference on embedded and ubiquitous computing (EUC)* (Vol. 1, pp. 639–642).

Zissman, M., et al. (1999). *DARPA intrusion detection evaluation*. MIT Lincoln Laboratory. http://www.ll.mit.edu/IST/ideval/index.html

2 Robust, Efficient, and Interpretable Adversarial AI Models for Intrusion Detection in Virtualization Environment

Arjun Singh, Avantika Gaur and Gaurav Kothari
Doon University, Dehradun, India

Yutika Agarwal
The Northcap University, Gurugram, India

Tejaswi and Preeti Mishra
Doon University, Dehradun, India

Senthil Kumar Jagthessaperumal
Mepco Schlenk Engineering College, Sivakasi, India

CONTENTS

DOI: 10.1201/9781003346340-2

2.1 INTRODUCTION

During and post-COVID, virtualization technology has seen an impactful surge in the market. With the introduction of work from home, many IT companies have shifted to virtualization, saving a substantial amount of money and time. Security has become a significant concern for organizations as technology is still growing. For instance, since the start of the Ukraine–Russia war, 25 significant cyber attacks against Ukraine's government and military sector have been recorded till July 2022, as per the report published by European Parliament [1]. Similarly, the European Union Agency for Cybersecurity (ENSIA) reported in June 2022 that Machine Learning (ML) models have become the target of most cyber attacks. According to the S & P Global Market Intelligence research,[1] a 4% increment has been seen from Indian participants facing cloud-based attacks from the last year, i.e., 2021. Recently, AIIMS Delhi and Safdargunj Hospital faced severe cyber attacks jeopardizing the confidential data of millions of people.[2] With such attack incidents in the era of emerging technologies, security has become a significant concern for organizations.

Virtualization allows the user to separate the operating system (OS) from the primary hardware, allowing multiple OS, such as Windows and Linux, to run on a single physical machine. Various physical hardware components of the system, such as processors, memory, and storage, are segmented into numerous virtual domains called virtual machines (VM). There is a particular software layer that is placed on top of the hardware/OS, called a virtual machine monitor (VMM) or Hypervisor [2]. VMM is responsible for creating, managing, and monitoring the VMs [3]. Furthermore, the VMs are installed on the respective VMM, where the guest OS and user applications are hosted/deployed. Distinct VMs running on the same physical server can run simultaneously. Hence, a crucial concern arises that the co-located VMs must be isolated to restrict malicious activities within a VM. A securely designed VMM layer should guarantee the isolation of VMs. Hence, VMM is considered to be secure. However, malware injection is still possible at VM-level applications. Therefore, defensive solutions to deal with various recent malware attacks are a need of time.

Intrusion Detection System (IDS) [4] is a defensive solution to counter-measure these attacks. IDS is a system or a security tool that captures and monitors the network traffic as well as system logs and scans the system or network for suspicious activities. Based on the deployment location, IDS can be classified as host-based IDS, network-based IDS, and hypervisor-based IDS. A host-based intrusion detection system (HIDS) [5] monitors independent hosts (physical/virtual) or devices on the network and sends alerts to the administrator about suspicious activities. A network-based intrusion detection system (NIDS) is positioned at the network points, such as gateway or routers, to examine the traffic for irregularities. Hypervisor-based IDS is set at the hypervisor/VMM or privileged VM. It collects the logs passing through the physical/virtual network and event channels. Various techniques exist that fall under misuse and anomaly detection approaches and are used to detect intrusion in the virtualization environment. Misuse detection techniques maintain rules for known signature attacks either by using the knowledge-based systems with the databases of known signature attacks or by the supervised ML algorithm. Anomaly detection systems are based on the expected behavior of the system. If there is a sign of any other behavior (beyond the typical behavior), it is considered anomalous behavior [6].

It should be noted that ML models, which are being used in the IDS, can also be attacked [7]. The attack in ML models, where the attacker tries to degrade the performance of the classifier, is called Adversarial Machine Learning (AML). Hence, there is a dire need to work towards developing advanced security approaches to make IDS robust and efficient. Furthermore, the mechanism of IDS should be interpretable for a better understanding of the results. In this chapter, we have provided a detailed study on the use of AML, optimization techniques, and explainable AI (XAI) for intrusion detection while focusing on three key design parameters, i.e., robustness, efficiency, and interpretability. Optimization techniques such as the ant colony algorithm [8] and genetic algorithm [9] are being used in the identification of unique features of malware which are helpful while designing an efficient IDS [10]. Various XAI libraries, such as SHAP [11] and LIME [12], can be used to demonstrate the working of IDS [13]. The significant contributions of this chapter can be summarized as follows:

1. A comprehensive description and a comparative study are provided on various XAI-based malware detection models.
2. A detailed comparative study is provided on various optimization-based malware detection models.
3. A classification of various adversarial ML approaches is provided to generate attacks and a comparative study.
4. A case study is provided on using XAI libraries and ML models for intrusion detection.
5. The key research challenges are discussed.

The chapter is organized as follows: Section 2.2 contains the related work done in the different aspects of Artificial Intelligence in malware detection; Section 2.3.1 discusses various approaches through which malware detection can be attacked; Section 2.3.2 describes optimization techniques used in malware detection. Section 2.3.3 provides different approaches included in XAI-based malware detections. A case study is provided in Section 2.4, in which malware classification is performed, and results are explained using XAI libraries. Section 2.5 includes various research challenges in each domain of our interest. Finally, we conclude the chapter in Section 2.6.

2.2 RELATED WORK

With the broad consideration of virtualization in cloud computing environments, the issues of hacking and leakage of confidential information are the biggest concerns. Let us now discuss some of the related surveys in this area. Martines et al. [3] discussed a detailed study on adversarial ML for intrusion detection. They have discussed the gradients attacks such as attacks based on the box limited-memory Broyden–Fletcher–Goldfarb–Shanno (L-BFGS) optimization, Fast Gradient Sign Method, DeepFool, Carlini & Wagner attack, and many more. The defensive approaches are provided in detail in their survey. The authors have explored the applications of both attack and defensive strategies in malware and intrusion detection. The survey paper [3] is limited to only intrusion and malware datasets, and limited defensive approaches are discussed.

Sadeghi et al. [14] proposed a systematic taxonomy for adversarial system models. Different taxonomies are provided on the datasets ML architectures, adversarial sample generation, and defensive techniques for attacks. Moreover, the AML cycle is introduced to model the arms race between attackers and defenders. Attack techniques are divided based on the differentiability of the loss function. Hence, techniques like FGSM and Universal Adversarial Perturbation are categorized as differentiable attacks, whereas ZOO, hill climbing, etc., are grouped under non-differentiable attacks. Similarly, defense approaches are divided into two groups based on whether the classifier is modified or a specialized detector is introduced to counter-measure the attack.

Recently, in [15], a summary of using XAI approaches for cybersecurity applications was presented. It narrates the usage of ML, DL, and other conventional signature-based and rule-based approaches to address the cybersecurity issues related to malware detection, intrusion detection, and spam filtering. Further, the focus was also on the necessary conditions to incorporate the XAI frameworks emphasized to impart effective cyber defense mechanisms.

In the survey presented by the authors in [16], the impact of explainable ML models such as KNN and Decision Trees to build interpretable ML models was discussed. For their work, it is emphasized that the development of model-specific inferences and explanations may deliver multiple dimensions of predictions, which lead to ambiguity issues. Considering such issues, the work summarizes standard approaches to build XAI models to address the challenges mentioned above. With the availability of numerous challenges in many areas of cybersecurity, the XAI model delivers promising outcomes that accurately elaborate the reasons for the decisions made and misclassifications. Mainly, deeper diagnosis and analysis of cyber systems could be provided by the XAI modes, which helps to improve our understanding of the decisions made by such systems.

The author of the review paper in [17] presents the structured and explained view of genetic algorithms (GA) and analyzes recent advances in genetic algorithms. For analysis, the research community has chosen a few genetic algorithms of particular interest. This paper [17] provides a broader vision of genetic algorithms. It is beneficial for research and gratitude teaching. The author gives a general framework of GA and hybrid GA with a mathematical formulation. Then the author mentions various GA operators with their pros and cons. At last, the author gives some details about the applicability of GA in the multimedia field. The challenges and issues mentioned in this paper [17] will help researchers conduct their research.

The work by the authors in a survey of optimization algorithms used in the field of intrusion detection over the last ten years, including Artificial Bee Colony (ABC), Genetic Algorithm (GA), Cuttlefish Algorithms (CFA), and Particle Swarm

Optimization (PSO). According to the author, the PSO algorithm always improves solutions to improve the problem. It can be used in conjunction with other algorithms to improve method performance. However, this algorithm does not guarantee an optimal solution. The ABC algorithm is simple to implement but requires many evaluation functions, which could reduce its accuracy. Nevertheless, CFA was successfully used for feature selection in a different study. But CFA is a highly complicated mathematical algorithm. The GA can handle large datasets and effectively optimize parameters, but it has some limitations. Researchers can use this review to get a basic understanding of the various intrusion detection methods.

2.3 ADVANCED MALWARE DETECTION TECHNIQUES IN VIRTUALIZATION

In this section, advanced malware detection techniques are explained in detail. The techniques are mainly classified into three parts based on the recent advances in technology: (i) Adversarial ML-based malware detection approach, (ii) optimization-based malware detection approach, and (iii) XAI-based malware detection approach.

The attacks in the ML model have resulted in severe consequences. Attacks are generated during either training time or testing time (Figure 2.1). The study of these attacks comes under AML. Attackers modify clean malware samples to generate perturbed samples to fool classifiers. The XAI approaches can provide interpretable features that provide valuable insights for the network administrators to identify the attacks. Further, the XAI models also guide the administrators and developers to enforce robust security policies.

2.3.1 ADVERSARIAL MACHINE LEARNING APPROACHES FOR INTRUSION DETECTION

With the advancement of technology, ML is now being used in malware detection. As a result, malware detection techniques have become more profound, accurate, and precise. The drawback of using ML is that an attacker can attack the classifier itself. These attacks are studied under AML, where the basic idea of crafting an adversarial sample is to fool the classifier. Various attack techniques are introduced

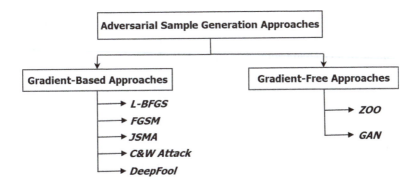

FIGURE 2.1 Classification of different adversarial sample generation approaches.

TABLE 2.1

A Brief Description of Various Adversarial Samples Generation Approaches

Strategy	Description	Limitations
L-BFGS	The approach finds a similar sample to the input having different classes using L2 distance. It then changes the magnitude of the noise with respect to the input.	L-BFGS is a computationally costly approach.
FGSM	This method considers the gradient of the loss function and modifies an input sample based on the sign of gradients. It can be used under L2 metrics.	FGSM adds perturbation to each feature and is less effective than other methods.
C&W	An Improvised version of L-BFGS. Instead of a cross-entropy loss function, it uses a hinge loss function.	It is an expensive strategy though it is efficient.
JSMA	The approach uses the saliency map based on features. The noises are added to features having higher saliency values.	JSMA is a slow process as saliency maps are generated.
Deepcool	The strategy involves the addition of a minimum value perturbation to an input so that the input shifts to the hyperplane of the desired sample.	Effective than FGSM and JSMA but more costly than both approaches.
ZOO	This strategy generates adversarial samples in a black box environment. It uses zeroth-order-based stochastic descent to estimate the gradient of the targeted model.	It requires raising a large number of queries, hence easy to detect.
GAN	The approach is based on the game theory where two players, Generator and Discriminator, try to fool each other. The generator generates samples, and the discriminator tries to classify them.	It is highly unstable, hence training of GAN becomes strenuous.

to implement the attack. The first AML attack was carried out by Dalvi et al. [18] in the Naive Bayes classifier. With the introduction of L-BFGS [19], the research pace in the field of AML grew very fastly. Various approaches involved in generating adversarial attacks are introduced to the date. The distinguishing difference among these approaches is some use gradient to create adversarial samples, and others use different methods, as shown in Table 2.1. Table 2.1 briefly highlights the characteristics of each approach.

1. **Fast Gradient Sign Method (FGSM):** The FGSM is introduced by Goodfellow et al. [20] as an approach to generate adversarial attacks. The FGSM minimizes the maximum amount of noise introduced in the input sample to misclassification. The mathematical equation for FGSM is

$$\eta = \epsilon \times sign\left(\nabla_x J\left(x, y\right)\right) \qquad (2.1)$$

η is the noise, ϵ is the hyperparameter that regulates the quantity of noise and J is the cost function where x is the input sample and y is the target label of x. The gradients are taken with respect to the input sample to generate the adversarial sample that maximizes the loss function. The FGSM approach is efficient for noise computation but less effective than other approaches.

2. **Limited-Memory Broyden–Fletcher–Goldfarb–Shanno (L-BFGS)**:
   L-BFGS was one of the first gradient methods, proposed by Szegedy et al.
   [19], to generate adversarial samples. Using this method, an adversary
   searches for similar input misclassified by a classifier under L_2 distance. The
   generation of an adversarial sample is considered an optimization problem
   and can be mathematically written as

$$\min \| z \|^2 \; s.t. : f\left(x+z\right) = y \tag{2.2}$$

   where z is the noise, x is the input sample, f is the model and y is the tar-
   geted/untargeted class label. The issue with the generation of the adversarial
   sample using L-BFGS is that it is computationally costly.

3. **Carlini & Wagner**: Carlini & Wagner is proposed by Carlini and Wagner,
   based on the L-BFGS method [21]. The authors considered adversarial sample generation as an optimization problem. The method involves the hinge
   loss function rather than the cross-entropy loss function (used in L-BFGS).
   The mathematical equation is

$$\text{minimize} : D\left(x, x+\eta\right) \tag{2.3a}$$

$$\text{such that} : C\left(x+\eta\right) = y \tag{2.3b}$$

$$x+\eta \in \left[0,1\right]^n \tag{2.3c}$$

   Here, x is the input sample, η is the noise, y is the target label, C is the classifier, D is the distance between the adversarial sample and original samples
   and n is the dimensions. $C(x + \eta) = y$ ensures that the input sample is misclassified while $x + \eta \in [0, 1]^n$ ensures that generated adversarial sample
   lies in the normalized version of the input sample (x). It is an expensive
   approach compared to FGSM and other approaches.

4. **Jacobian-Based Saliency Map Attack (JSMA)**: JSMA is introduced by
   Papernot et al. [22]. This method is focused on feature selection in order
   to minimize the number of modifications of features. The saliency map for
   an input sample is computed which has saliency values. Saliency values
   indicate the impact of modification of inputs in the classification. If the
   saliency value is minimum, the corresponding feature is selected and modified accordingly. The process is carried out till the modification of features
   causes misclassification. The major disadvantage of using JSMA is that
   though it requires only a few features to be modified, it has high computation cost.

5. **DeepFool**: DeepFool was given by Moosavi-Dezfooli et al. [23] to carry
   out an adversarial attack. The basic idea of this approach is to minimize
   the L2 distance, i.e., the euclidean distance between generated adversarial

samples and original input samples. For a binary classifier, for example, a malware detector, the noise must be projected from the input sample to the hyperplane of the classifier for the misclassification of an input sample. The mathematical equation to find out the value of noise in a binary classifier is given as follows:

$$r(x) = -\frac{f(x_0)}{\|w\|_2^2} w \qquad (2.4)$$

$r(x)$ is the noise with respect to the input x, f is the binary classifier which is divided by the L2 norm of the gradient of the loss function, i.e., w. The negative sign in the equation is introduced to increase the loss function.

6. **Zeroth Order Optimization Attack (ZOO)**: ZOO was presented by Chen et al. [24] to carry out black box attacks. ZOO considers a scenario where attackers don't have access to the classifier model. So, in order to carry out an attack, attackers estimate the gradient of the model using zeroth order stochastic descent. The noises are added to each feature of input samples, The optimal adversarial with respect to the first order is searched using different optimizers. The ZOO requires raising a large number of queries to the classifier in order to estimate the gradient and hence, a time-consuming approach.

7. **Generative Adversarial Network (GAN)**: GAN is the deep learning technique, introduced by Goodfellow et al. [25], which can be used to generate adversarial attacks. GAN consists of two networks which are Generator and Discriminator. The goal of the generator is to generate an adversarial sample that must be misclassified by the discriminator. While the discriminator tries to classify samples accordingly. The mathematical formula for the loss function is as follows:

$$E_x\left[\log(D(x))\right] + E_z\left[\log(1 - D(G(z)))\right] \qquad (2.5)$$

E_x is the expected value of the input sample, $D(x)$ is the function of the discriminator which estimates the probability of whether the input sample x is real, $D(G(z))$ is the function of the discriminator that tells whether the input sample is real or fake. The generator aims to minimize the loss function while the discriminator has the opposite goal, i.e., to maximize the loss function.

The major limitation of using GAN is that it is highly unstable and its training requires high computational power.

2.3.2 OPTIMIZATION APPROACHES BASED FOR INTRUSION DETECTION

The availability of suitable and validated data is a vital issue in multiple domains for implementing ML methods [26]. High data dimensionality has adverse effects on the learning algorithm's performance. Optimization preserves the most unique information-related data with a minimum number of features. Optimization aims to identify essential elements in building systems like IDS [4] such that they are computationally efficient and effective. Some optimization techniques (Table 2.2) which we are going to discuss are PSO, Ant Colony Optimization (ACO), Genetic Algorithm (GA), and some advanced optimization techniques.

TABLE 2.2

Comparative Analysis of Various Optimization Approaches Used in Intrusion Detection

References	Optimization Techniques	Classifier	Result (%)	Dataset	Limitation
Penmatsa et al. [33]	ACO and Rough Sets	Random Forest	95.2	claMP	Accuracy decreased for both raw datasets
Peng et al. [34]	ACO	SVM	98	KDDCUP99	Only suitable with SVM and KNN
Sreelaja [35]	ACO	ACOLBSR	100	Signature database	Do not compare part-by-part hash values of files
Bilaiya and Sharma [42]	Whale Optimization	GA		Network Traffic Collection	Slow convergence speed
Halim et al. [26]	Generic Algorithm	SVM, k-NN, XgBoost	96.48	CIRA-CIC-DOHBrw-2020,UNSW-NB15, and Bot-IoT	Approach is slow
Xu et al. [28]	PSO-FCAIW	SVM	96.13	Benign and malicious apps dataset	Overfitting problem with other classifiers.
Jurecek et al. [29]	PSO+Distance metric	KNN	96.72	Windows program PE	Not satisfactory results with differentiating between malware families
Ghosh et al. [30]	CUCKOO search +PSO	LR, Ada, RF	75.5	NSL-KDD dataset	Tested with old datasets and conventional ML algorithms
Javaheri et al. [37]	GA	DNN, J48DT	98.5	Adminus, Virus-Sign, and VirusShare	Instead of two, one sample malware was used
Ghatasheh et al. [38]	GA	SVM, RF	99	Tweet dataset	Not tested with multilingual spam
Jeyakarthic et al. [41]	EHO	WELM	96.94	CIC Evasive-PDFMal2022, Contagio dataset	Still need feature selection and reduction improvements

2.3.2.1 Particle Swarm Optimization (PSO)

ML models have been used for decades in network resource pooling, business process automation, predictions, etc. Cybersecurity and virtualization are two such domains that have recently piqued the interest of researchers. Following traditional models, there arises a problem of complex implementation, mathematical efficiency, and controlling parameters. To avoid these problems, PSO is among the top bio-inspired algorithms that offer solutions to all these stated issues by looking for the best solution in the search space. According to Zhang et al. [27], the extensive use of PSO has significantly increased model accuracy and aided in extracting features of extreme importance.

Let us now consider the following PSO-based optimization approaches.

Xu et al. [28] proposed a method based on PSO with a computing adaptive feature weight technique. The key goal of the approach is to increase swarm diversity in order to achieve the best Fitness. The authors considered a dataset containing both benign and malicious applications with a total of 104 permission features. As a result, due to the choice of Information Gain (IG) for feature selection, accuracy increased from 0.5% to 100% when fewer than 5% of features were selected. The top 20 features were tested with different inertia weight strategies while adjusting PSO. One of the strategies used was a dataset using Fitness-based and chaotic adaptive inertia weights (FCAIW) wrapped with SVM models. The conclusion was that FCAIW-PSO outperformed all other methods with 96.13% accuracy but has a limitation of overfitting with other models.

Jurecek and Lorencz [29] proposed a Particle Swarm Optimization (PSO) algorithm-based distance metric learning method for determining the appropriate weight for feature extraction, which catalyzes static malware detection. Static analysis has limitations as it does not describe behavior because the program is not running. They proposed a detection model with two phases: metric learning and classification using a KNN classifier (Figure 2.4). A Gain Ratio (GR) was used to determine a useful ratio for distinguishing between malware and benign files. Through an experiment with a database containing 150,145 window programs in PE File Format: 74,975 malware and 75,167 benign, the KNN classifier performed better with feature weight with an accuracy of 96.72%, yielding an error rate reduction of 12.77%. They suggested that a future goal would be to work with some more distance learning algorithms to distinguish between different malware families.

Ghosh et al. [30] introduced a cuckoo search (CS) Particle Swarm Optimizer (PSO) IDS for Cloud Environment. This model consists of two phases: feature selection and classification. The authors employed Logistic Regression (LR), Adaboost (AB), and Random Forest (RF) for classification purposes. The key aim was to reduce irrelevant features of the dataset without compromising its accuracy and yield an effective IDS. In their experiment, they used the NSL-KDD dataset having 41 features, 1,25,973 training, and 22,544 testing samples. It provides the best results with LR, i.e., 96.46% TPR, 3.54% FPR, and 75.5% accuracy. The approach works with optimal memory usage and minimal time complexity. The limitation is that it has been validated with a significantly older dataset, and a conventional ML algorithm has been used, which may not produce good results with a larger dataset having enriched set of feature vectors.

2.3.2.2 Ant Colony Optimization (ACO)

There are many optimization techniques used for feature selection in IDS that gives a good result, but there are many issues that cannot rectify by these optimization techniques. Some of the issues like cluster building and combinational optimization problems [31] finding optimum solutions are solved with nature-inspired algorithms like ACO [32]. It is a population-based metaheuristic, a probability algorithm that can be used to find approximate solutions to complex problems. The purpose of ACO is to identify essential features in building an IDS that is computationally efficient and effective. Let us now consider some ACO-based optimization approaches:

Penmatsa et al. [33] introduced a feature reduction mechanism for malware detection where features were extracted from the portable executable (PE) header of Windows. The authors employed the Rough Set (RS) method as a filter-based feature reduction method to reduce the features. The authors used the clamp[3] dataset, which has 55 features of 5184 benign and malware samples. Authors considered 10-fold cross-validation for the classification using two more datasets: raw malware dataset and integrated claMP dataset, which contain 60 and 72 features, respectively. Various classifiers have been used for classification. The random forest gives the best results at 98.3% and 99.25% on the raw and integrated claMP datasets, respectively. Ant Colony Optimization with Rough sets based Feature Selection (ACORFS) extracts 4 and 2 features, respectively, from both datasets. On the optimized feature set, the random forest gives 95.2% and 90.55% accuracy for the raw data set and integrated dataset, respectively. The ACORFS reduces the features significantly; however, It also decreased the accuracy of the classifier (ACC) by 3.04% and 8.76% for the raw dataset and integrated dataset respectively.

Peng et al. [34] proposed a new feature selection algorithm based on Fuzzy Ant Colony Optimization (FACO). The improved fitness function was designed for efficient feature selection & path transfer probability. The author considered the KDD CUP99 KDD CUP99[4] dataset having large amounts of network traffic data marked as normal or abnormal. A total of 41 features were tested on the MATLAB® 2014 platform. In the improved FACO fitness function, a two-stage pheromone updating rule was adopted. It optimized the heuristic path transaction probability and avoided falling into the local optimum, which helps find the optimal feature subset. This simulation experiment tested various classifiers: KNN, SVM, Bayes, and Decision Tree. The FACO algorithm improved the performance of each classifier most significantly, and it gave the best results with KNN and SVM classifiers. The ACC increases with the number of samples. The authors observed convergence after achieving 98% accuracy at the 12th iteration.

Sreelaja et al. [35] introduced an Ant Colony Optimization-Based Light weight Binary Search for Signature-Based Ransomware Detection (ACOLBSR) algorithm. In this defense method, the ant agent finds the search space in the signature database, and if the search space exists in the database, then the ant agent employs a binary search to match the incoming signature hash value with the signature in the search space. The author considered the dataset, which had 582 ransomware belonging to 11 families and merged with the 942 goodware applications. The computational complexity of ACOLBSR is log(c), where c is the total number of signature hash values in the search space. The author compares the ACOLBSR with different methods such as the CalmAV, Split Screen, fuzzy hashing, and binary search. The classification accuracy of this method is better than the existing classification method in terms of accuracy. The classification accuracy for ACOLBSR is 100%.

2.3.2.3   Genetic Algorithm (GA) Based Optimization

The GA [36] is a stochastic method for function optimization based on natural genetics and biological evolution. It is a search heuristic that is routinely used to generate useful solutions for optimization and search problems. It is inspired by natural evolution, such as inheritance, mutation, selection, and crossover. Let us now consider some GA-based optimization approaches:

Javaheri et al. [37] addressed the issue of the significant increase in advanced malware that is more intelligent and complex. This malware uses techniques such as packing, obfuscation, metamorphism, and scarcity of targeted malware. As a result, they proposed using the GA algorithm to evolve rare malware via gene crossover and mutation and generated a suitable model for training. They used the Adminus, Virus-Sign, and VirusShare datasets with Deep Neural Network (DNN) & J48 Decision Tree (DT) models for training. To optimize the dataset for DNN training, they converted all malware and benign binaries into grayscale. Following 10-fold cross-validation and model validation, they discovered that their model accuracy increased and improved the new generation's malware quality, with an accuracy of 98.5%, TPR of seven classes enhancing between 12% and 14% for DNN, and between 12% and 17% for J48 DT. Furthermore, the FPR decreased by 3–4% for both classifiers. The model is limited due to a lack of one more sample malware, as two were required. This model is also applicable to platforms other than Microsoft Windows, such as ELF on Linux and ART on Android.

Ghatasheh et al. [38] improved feature selection and hyperparameter optimization using a modified Genetic algorithm (GA). Spam modeling is a difficult task due to the high dimensionality of feature spaces and the classification algorithm's bias toward the majority class. As a result, they proposed a modified GA method that aims at directing the stochastic selection aspect towards a finite subset of features. They set up Google Colaboratory (Colab) for the experiment and used a tweet dataset with 5096 tweets, 17 of which were labeled as "Spam" and the rest as "Ham." This tweet spam modeling approach outperformed the chi-square and PCS approaches by selecting ten features and achieving an average total accuracy and geometrical mean of 92.67% and 82.32%, respectively. Furthermore, this model performed best with SVM and RF with 99% accuracy. At last, the author highlighted this model's limitations, such as the lack of parallel processing to reduce time complexity, the effect of natural language processing to improve accuracy, and the fact that the experiment with multi-language spam remains unexplored.

Halim et al. [26] proposed a novel Genetic Algorithm (GA) based approach for the feature selection (GbFS) to enhance the detection accuracy of the IDS. Their approach selects the most appropriate features from datasets. The authors considered three benchmark network traffic datasets namely, CIRA-CIC-DOHBrw-2020, UNSW-NB15 [39], and Bot-IoT [40] with 34, 29, and 49 features, respectively. A total of 8–9 features are selected by employing the GbFS method. The authors used three different classifiers, i.e., SVM, k-NN, and XgBoost, for above mentioned individual datasets. The average accuracy of all these classifiers is 90.98% with all features. The accuracy is further improved by 5.5% after considering the feature selection method. One of the limitations of their approach is that it is slower due to the multiple repetitive iterations and reproduction operations.

2.3.2.4 Other Advanced Algorithms

Chandran et al. [41] developed an Elephant Herd Optimization based on Weighted Extreme Learning Machine (EHO-WELM) for malware detection and classification in Portable Document Format (PDF). This model is divided into three sub-processes: data preprocessing for removing null values and categorical encoding, WELM classification for classifying PDF malware, and EHO-based parameter optimization to improve the classifier's efficacy. They used the CIC Evasive-PDFMal2022 dataset and the Contagio dataset, which includes 32,136 attributes, in their study. Superior classification outcomes were achieved using EHO-WELM, with an accuracy of 96.94% and a precision of 96.82%. In addition, the authors also suggested developing feature selection & reduction methods to improve model detection efficiency.

Bilaiya et al. [42] constructed a hybrid intrusion detection technique. It consists of two phases: whale search and genetic algorithm. The whale optimization algorithm is based on population, which improves the rule pool. This improved pool is supplied to the next part as an input, where GA is used to construct a rule base that has been used in the IDS. The author implemented this work on the MATLAB® programming tool. Algorithms regarding accuracy rate (AR) and detection rate (DR) have been compared. The author compared the DR and AR of both GA-Tabu and GA-Whale algorithms. The author ran both algorithms many times, and the GA-Whale algorithm outperforms the GA-Tabu algorithm for each of the varied population sizes. As the number of iterations increases, the accuracy of the proposed algorithm increases. The accuracy of the GA-whale technique becomes more than 95%.

2.3.3 XAI-Based Approaches

Initially, a decade back, the system developers largely depended on antivirus software for malware detection. As technology proliferates, the threats are also predominant in cloud platforms and smart gadgets. However, with the help of trending learning techniques through artificial intelligence and blockchain, even the most recent antiviruses started using trustworthy and powerful ML algorithms. The potential of XAI for predicting cybersecurity attacks was extensively reviewed in [43], where the authors summarized the transparency of the system on different types of attacks for various applications. Table 2.3 summarizes some popular means of addressing security attacks using XAI-based models.

In [48], the authors surveyed the use of various ML techniques for intrusion detection attacks. With the core focus on detecting low-frequency attacks, the authors employed various data mining tools on the network attack dataset. The accomplishments of this study impart enough inspiration to address the malware issues in virtualization environments. Imparting virtualization security through XAI approaches ensures collective, transparent, and trustworthy procedures and processes for protecting the virtualization environment. The most prominent threats in the

TABLE 2.3

Summary of Using XAI-Based Models for Addressing the Security Attacks

References	XAI Models	Applications	Dataset	Results	Inferences
Zhang et al. [15]	ML and DL	Cyber defense	Cybersecurity datasets	Effective and improved metrics.	Compares with conventional signature-based as well as rule-based approaches
Iadarola et al. [44]	ML techniques	Malware in Android Apps	Delivers a classification accuracy of 97%	Android Malware dataset	Estimates the malicious behavior of malware
Liu et al. [45]	ML techniques	Malware in Android Apps	165,000 Android applications	Explanation for 18.34% added and 84.45% for removed malware	Estimates the distinction between benign and malware as well as malicious behavior
Sauka et al. [46]	DNN	Adversarial attacks	NSL-KDD	12.79% reduction in the trained model's ROC-AUC	Addresses the vulnerabilities with better convergence
Tian et al. [47]	DL	Cloud virtualization	Processor Trace data	Encryption time overhead reduced by 1.57%	Intel Processor Trace strategy is used to trace the attacks

virtualization environments are service provider attacks, hypervisor attacks, VM jumping, and host traffic interception. The attacker, by gaining unauthorized access to the hypervisor, could attack a virtualized data center or the cloud, which controls all the active VMs in the data center. They usually attack the hypervisor through the host OS or the guest OS.

In a survey presented by the authors in [49], the role of XAI in providing cybersecurity solutions was analyzed. This work was compiled on the detection of malware, intrusions, botnets, phishing, and spam. It emphasizes the importance of transparency in decision-making by anticipating the most obvious threats well in advance.

The authors in [44] proposed an XAI-driven model for detecting a family of malware in Android applications. Such interpretable predictions on categorizing the malware could be typically equipped for the virtualization environments. A similar category of work was reported by Liu et al. in [45] for Android malware detection using XAI approaches (Figure 2.2). Here, the authors explored ML-based models for training, interpretation, and malware classifications under a diversified range of environmental settings. The results from the work highlight the crucial distinction between benign and malware in Android platforms based on malicious behaviors. Further, such findings could be reliably applied to the virtual machines to assist the

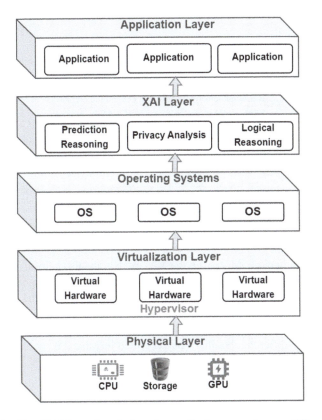

FIGURE 2.2 The XAI layer interfacing the applications running on different operating systems.

developers in identifying and addressing the malware-based obstacles in the virtualization environments.

A robust XAI-based network IDS using DNNs was developed in [46], where the authors focused on addressing the vulnerabilities that occurred due to adversarial attacks. From the experimentation, it was observed that the XAI-based model, which was adversarial-trained, provided better performance by assessing the area under the ROC curve. The malware detection strategy in [47] focuses on defending against attacks in cloud virtualization environments using hardware trace and deep learning models. Here, the authors focus on defending the attacks in the cloud virtualization environments using hardware trace and deep learning models. They have used the Intel Processor Trace strategy to accumulate the flow statistics of the target and convert them into images. Subsequently, those images were trained using CNN models to identify the malware. Further, the performance of such a detection mechanism was enhanced using Lamport's ring buffer algorithm.

The authors in [50] used API function calls to detect malware and emphasized a mechanism to trace the malware behavior in virtual machines. Further, they have confirmed the malware's existence and implemented a dynamic malware analysis

TABLE 2.4
Description of Different XAI Libraries [58]

Name of the Library	Description
SHAP	It is a mathematical method to explain the predictions of ML models
LIME	Explains the classifier for a specific single instance and is, therefore, suitable for local explanations.
Shapash	Provides several types of visualization which display explicit labels that everyone can understand
InterpretML	It supports training interpretable models (glass box), as well as explaining existing ML pipelines (BlackBox)
OmniXAI	OmniXAI aspires to provide a one-stop comprehensive library that makes explainable AI simple

with a volatile framework. Moreover, the XAI models are also helpful in assessing the exact metrics and properties of the explanations generated that supports the cyberse-curity community. In [51], a similar instance was reported where the attackers' goal was well identified and classified, and the model generated better explanation reports without any hindrance in the classification outcomes. Experimental results of mal-ware detection in different classifiers are presented in Table 2.6.

2.4 CASE STUDY

This section explains a case study for intrusion detection using XAI libraries (Table 2.4). The analysis is performed on a physical machine having UBUNTU 20.04 OS, Intel core i7 processor, 16 GB RAM, and 512 GB SSD. Two virtualization machines (VMs) have been created with Windows 7 OS installed on the top of the Xen hypervisor [52]. The malware dataset (executables) have been taken from San Jose State University[5] (SJSU) on request which consists of four malware families: Zbot, Vundo, Vobfus, and Zeroaccess [53]. The deep memory introspection has been performed using the Drakvuf [54] tool and logs of malware and benign files are gener-ated. We extracted 807 features through pre-processing of generated logs of malware and benign. Out of 807 features, 149 distinct features representing the frequency of system calls have been considered for the analysis. To reduce the noisy data, feature extraction has been performed and a feature importance table with F-score has been drawn using the SHAP XAI library. A feature with a high F-score indicates that the feature has high discriminating power between classes. Let us Consider two features f15 and f17 of the dataset, having F-scores of 586 and 537, respectively, as shown in Figure 2.3. It indicates that f15 has more discriminative power than f17. F-score help to select features that produce effective results in ML modeling. Finally, the top 28 features were chosen based on F-score. We have considered four ML classifiers: CatBoost,[6] XGBoost [55], Random Forest [56], and Support Vector Machine [57] for training/testing. The evaluation metrics used in the discussion of the results are shown in Table 2.5. Most of the classifiers provided an accuracy above 73%. Random Forest gives the best accuracy of 97.48%. The SHAP XAI library has been used to explain results and improve the interpretability of IDS.

Feature importance

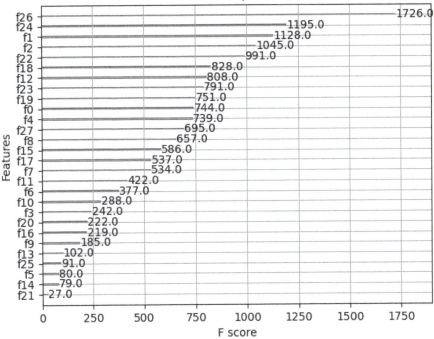

FIGURE 2.3 Feature scores by using XGBoost.

TABLE 2.5

Different Parameters to Evaluate the Performance of IDS

Parameter	Description
True Positive (TP)	IDS flags intrusion as malicious
False Positive (FP)	IDS flags normal system execution as malicious
True Negative (TN)	IDS flags normal system execution as normal
False Negative (FN)	IDS flags normal system execution as normal
TPR	Correctly flags intrusions & actual size of attack
FPR	Incorrectly flags intrusions & actual size of attack
FNR	Incorrectly flags normal program & actual size of attack
TNR	Correctly flags normal program to the actual size of normal class
Accuracy	Percentage of correct classifications across all test results

Result: The performance of all ML models is compared and it has been found that SVM has an accuracy of 73.58% with 90.83% TNR and 63.35% TPR, XGBoost has an accuracy of 92.02% with 96.35% TNR and 80.57% TPR, and CatBoost has an accuracy of 92.02% with 98.00% TNR and 91.99% TPR. Finally, Random Forest outperforms all other classifiers with an accuracy of 97.48% with 99.37% TNR and 91.99% TPR. Results are analyzed using the SHAP XAI library to ease interpretability.

TABLE 2.6

Experimental Results of Malware Detection on Different Classifiers

Classifier	TNR	TPR	FNR	FPR	Accuracy (%)
Random Forest	99.37	97.48	2.52	0.63	97.48
CatBoost	98.00	91.99	8.00	1.99	92.02
SVM	90.83	63.35	36.64	9.16	73.58
XGBoost	96.35	80.57	19.42	3.64	85.70

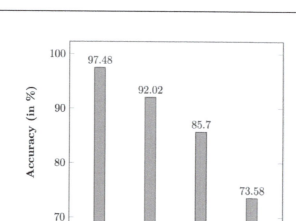

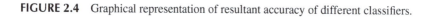

FIGURE 2.4 Graphical representation of resultant accuracy of different classifiers.

2.5 RESEARCH CHALLENGES

In this section, the existing technological challenges that serve to deploy trustworthy virtual machines were presented, with an attempt to determine the opportunities that they provide to support interpretable ML models. Some of the future works that need much attention are listed below:

Transparency: Traditional ML-based IDS are "black boxes" that fail to explain the logic behind models' decision-making, predictability, classification, and so on. Moreover, categorizing the model in a way that allows users to build a case in which they can state their assumptions at various points. Further, justification (or auditing) why the system, or how a specific component of the architecture, is producing certain results has become a mandatory choice for enabling transparency in the systems. Particularly, in the virtualization environment, this also allows the users to evaluate the robustness of the data models. However, to address these issues, there is a strong demand for XAI models to enhance the transparency behind the decisions made by the models.

Distance Metric Algorithms: Broadly, with a variety of ML algorithms available from supervised and unsupervised approaches, the use of distance metrics aims to determine the input intrusion data pattern in order to make any data-based detection decision. In this context, a good distance metric significantly improves the performance of the classification, clustering, and information retrieval processes. Despite these algorithms producing reasonable outcomes with feature extraction, however, they need more weight-based training and testing to enhance detection results. From this perspective, the quality of distance metrics in the interpretable ML approaches is seldom utilized so far in virtualization environments.

Nature-Inspired Optimization: In addition to the various bio-inspired algorithms developed, their performance in malware detection greatly improves the optimization of the resources in making trustworthy decisions. It is theoretically possible by most of the nature-inspired optimization techniques in offering adaptive computation procedures for complex optimization problems for a wide range of engineering applications. In other words, as nature-inspired algorithms are simple and versatile, many researchers around the globe have been drawn to the development of some advanced intelligent algorithms and their applicability in solving a wide range of complex intrusion detection problems efficiently. Therefore, vicious behaviors and evil intruders could be quickly identified and prevented with the support of intense research demands and experiments through newly developed interpretable ML algorithms.

Multi-Class Problems: In intrusion detection, there are various cases in which we have to deal with multi-class problems. Classification issues like the presence of multiple classes in an imbalanced dataset present a different challenge than a binary classification problem. Due to the skewed distribution nature, most of the traditional ML algorithms are less effective, particularly in predicting minority-class malware. We need to improve our systems so we can efficiently distinguish between various malware families. Particularly, interpretable ML models can be used to address multi-class problems and enhance the distinction among the malware present in virtualization environments.

Advanced Security Systems: Today, new kinds of malware, spyware, worms, viruses, etc., are developed by attackers on a daily basis. Every day, malware infects hundreds of thousands of files on computers and websites. According to the AV-Test Institute's latest statistics, more than 17 million new malware instances are registered each month. These contain newly developed features that may be missed by older models. So we need to create a more advanced system that can detect future malware and viruses. Apparently, a single feasible solution cannot reflect the malware attacks in the entire system. It is crucial to use robust interpretable ML approaches to impart advanced security solutions in an earlier stage; however, multiple ranges of attacks could be accumulated into a serious issue in the virtualization environment later on.

Redundancy: In intrusion detection, conventional ML techniques struggle with data that contains redundant and irrelevant features. Such presence of redundant and/or unnecessary features in datasets is one of the malware detection community's concerns, which could be easily exploited. Indeed, redundant/irrelevant behaviors that are irrelevant to a specific class can significantly increase operational costs and reduce most learners' accuracy. As a result, generating datasets, including feature extraction and selection phases, is still a challenging task that must be continually improved in order to improve the overall performance of the developed IDS models. The entire spectrum of virtualization environments may have different OS and applications. This makes overcoming redundancy a highly challenging task. By using interpretable ML models, we can carefully define metrics to include and extract the necessary features from the learning platform.

Lack of Interpretable IDS Architectures: In order to impart sophisticated features in the virtualization environment, it is often recommended to deploy and manage a distributed range of systems from a diversified range of devices in the network. Particularly from such a perspective, one of the most challenging issues falls in deploying transparent, attack-free virtual machines. Nowadays, in order to reduce the delay encountered in the accumulation of the decisions made from the distributed range of devices, multiple remote platforms, may require high computing GPUs. However, the challenging phase is imparting the transparency characteristics in their decision-making phases and integrating those decisions made from the distributed platforms. It is, therefore, an urgent demand to accumulate enough evidence on incorporating distributed XAI solutions for virtualization environments and in the adoption of other reliable alternate solutions for handling distributed ML models.

2.6   CONCLUSION

To detect advanced attacks in virtualization environments, there is a huge demand to establish robust, efficient, and interpretable IDS. In this chapter, we have provided a detailed study of various techniques for providing advanced interpretable IDS solutions in virtualization environments. These techniques include AML, optimization approaches, and XAI to achieve robustness, efficiency, and interpretability in the classification of the features of IDS. Among the different adversarial approaches, the role of FGSM, and JSMA have been discussed in association with the adversarial samples. Subsequently, the usage of a few popular optimization techniques such as ACO and GA were used to boost IDS performance. With the analysis of such bio-inspired optimization algorithms, advanced and search optimum solutions were included in the study. Further, by using XAI approaches, the inherent decision-making capabilities of the XAI-driven IDS can be interpretable even for people who were novices in ML. In addition, we have provided a case study on detecting malware and used the SHAP and LIME libraries to interpret the trustworthy observations of IDS detection. In the end, we studied the challenges that are currently restricting the usage of interpretable ML for its practical applicability in virtualization environments.

ACKNOWLEDGMENTS

The Science and Engineering Research Board, Department of Science and Technology (SERB-DST), provided funding for this study under Project File No. SPG/2021/002003. The authors would like to express their gratitude to SERB-DST for their intellectual generosity and research assistance.

NOTES

1 https://www.thalesgroup.com/en/india/pressrelease/cloud–data–breaches–and–cloud–complexity–rise–reveals–thales
2 https://www.thalesgroup.com/en/india/pressrelease/cloud–data–breaches–and–cloud–complexity–rise–reveals–thales
3 https://www.kaggle.com/datasets/saurabhshahane/classification-of-malwares
4 http://kdd.ics.uci.edu/databases/kddcup99/kddcup99.html
5 https://www.sjsu.edu/
6 https://catboost.ai/

REFERENCES

[1] Przetacznik Jakub. *Russia's war on Ukraine: Timeline of cyber-attacks.* Technical report, 2022.
[2] Preeti Mishra, Ishita Verma, Saurabh Gupta, Varun S. Rana, and Kavitha Kadarla. vProVal: Introspection based process validation for detecting malware in KVM-based cloud environment. In *2019 Fourth International Conference on Fog and Mobile Edge Computing (FMEC)*, pages 271–277, 2019.
[3] Preeti Mishra, Emmanuel S. Pilli, Vijay Varadharajan, and Udaya Tupakula. VAED: VMI-assisted evasion detection approach for infrastructure as a service cloud. *Concurrency and Computation: Practice and Experience*, 29(1–12):e4133, 2017.
[4] Preeti Mishra, Emmanuel S. Pilli, Vijay Varadharajan, and Udaya Tupakula. Intrusion detection techniques in cloud environment: A survey. *Journal of Network and Computer Applications*, 77:18–47, 2017.
[5] Amrit Pal Singh and Manik Deep Singh. Analysis of host-based and network-based intrusion detection system. *IJ Computer Net-work and Information Security*, 8:41–47.
[6] Preeti Mishra, Emmanuel S. Pilli, Vijay Varadharajan, and Udaya Tupakula. Intrusion detection techniques in cloud environment: A survey. *Journal of Network and Computer Applications*, 77:18–47, 2017.
[7] Maryam Shahpasand, Len Hamey, Dinusha Vatsalan, and Min-hui Xue. Adversarial attacks on mobile malware detection. In *2019 IEEE 1st International Workshop on Artificial Intelligence for Mobile (AI4Mobile)*, pages 17–20, 2019.
[8] Marco Dorigo and Mauro Birattari. *Ant Colony Optimization*, pages 36–39. Springer US, Boston, MA, 2010.
[9] Kumara Sastry, David Goldberg, and Graham Kendall. *Genetic Algorithms*, pages 97–125. Springer US, Boston, MA, 2005.
[10] Mohd Faizal Ab Razak, Nor Badrul Anuar, Fazidah Othman, Ahmad Firdaus, Firdaus Afifi, and Rosli Salleh. Bio-inspired for features optimization and malware detection. *Arabian Journal for Science and Engineering*, 43(12):6963–6979, 2018.
[11] Dylan Slack, Sophie Hilgard, Emily Jia, Sameer Singh, and Himabindu Lakkaraju. Fooling LIME and SHAP: Adversarial attacks on post hoc explanation methods. In *Proceedings of the AAAI/ACM Conference on AI, Ethics, and Society*, pages 180–186, 2020.

[12] Marco Tulio Ribeiro, Sameer Singh, and Carlos Guestrin. "Why should I trust you?" Explaining the predictions of any classifier. In *Proceedings of the 22nd ACM SIGKDD international conference on knowledge discovery and data mining*, pages 1135–1144, 2016.

[13] Martin Kinkead, Stuart Millar, Niall McLaughlin, and Philip O'Kane. Towards explainable CNNS for android malware detection. *Procedia Computer Science*, 184:959–965, 2021. In *The 12th International Conference on Ambient Systems, Networks and Technologies (ANT) / The 4th International Conference on Emerging Data and Industry 4.0 (EDI40) / Affiliated Workshops*.

[14] Koosha Sadeghi, Ayan Banerjee, and Sandeep K. S. Gupta. A system-driven taxonomy of attacks and defenses in adversarial machine learning. *IEEE Transactions on Emerging Topics in Computational Intelligence*, 4(4):450–467, 2020.

[15] Zhibo Zhang, Hussam Al Hamadi, Ernesto Damiani, Chan Yeob Yeun, and Fatma Taher. Explainable artificial intelligence applications in cyber security: State-of-the-art in research. *arXiv preprint arXiv:2208.14937*, 2022.

[16] Krishna Prakash Kalyanathaya, et al. A literature review and re-search agenda on explainable artificial intelligence (XAI). *International Journal of Applied Engineering and Management Letters*, 6(1):43–59, 2022.

[17] Sourabh Katoch, Sumit Singh Chauhan, and Vijay Kumar. A review on genetic algorithm: Past, present, and future. *Multimedia Tools and Applications*, 80(5):8091–8126, 2021.

[18] Roi Naveiro and Alberto Redondo, David Ríos Insua, Fabrizio Ruggeri, Adversarial classification: An adversarial risk analysis approach. *International Journal of Approximate Reasoning* 113:133–148, 2019. ISSN 0888-613X, https://doi.org/10.1016/j.ijar.2019.07.003

[19] Christian Szegedy, Wojciech Zaremba, Ilya Sutskever, Joan Bruna, Dumitru Erhan, Ian Goodfellow, and Rob Fergus. Intriguing properties of neural networks. In *2nd International Conference on Learning Representations, ICLR 2014 – Conference Track Proceedings*, pages 1–10, 2014.

[20] Ian J. Goodfellow, Jonathon Shlens, and Christian Szegedy. Ex-plaining and harnessing adversarial examples. *arXiv preprint arXiv:1412.6572*, 2014.

[21] Nicholas Carlini and David Wagner. Towards evaluating the robustness of neural networks. In *Proceedings – IEEE Symposium on Security and Privacy*, pages 39–57, 2017.

[22] Nicolas Papernot, Patrick Mcdaniel, Somesh Jha, Matt Fredrik-Son, Z. Berkay Celik, and Ananthram Swami. The limitations of deep learning in adversarial settings. In *Proceedings – 2016 IEEE European Symposium on Security and Privacy, EURO S and P 2016*, pages 372–387, 2016.

[23] Seyed Mohsen Moosavi-Dezfooli, Alhussein Fawzi, and Pascal Frossard. DeepFool: A simple and accurate method to fool Deep Neural Networks. In *Proceedings of the IEEE Computer Society Conference on Computer Vision and Pattern Recognition, 2016 December*, pages 2574–2582, 2016.

[24] Pin Yu Chen, Huan Zhang, Yash Sharma, Jinfeng Yi, and Cho Jui Hsieh. ZOO: Zeroth order optimization based black-box attacks to Deep Neural Networks without training substitute models. In *AISec 2017 – Proceedings of the 10th ACM Workshop on Artificial Intelligence and Security, co-located with CCS 2017*, pages 15–26, November 2017.

[25] Ian J. Goodfellow. NIPS 2016 tutorial: Generative adversarial networks. *CoRR*, abs/1701.00160, 2017.

[26] Zahid Halim, Muhammad Nadeem Yousaf, Muhammad Waqas, Muhammad Sulaiman, Ghulam Abbas, Masroor Hussain, Iftekhar Ahmad, and Muhammad Hanif. An effective genetic algorithm-based feature selection method for intrusion detection systems. *Computers & Security*, 110:102448, 2021.

[27] Yudong Zhang, Shuihua Wang, and Genlin Ji. A comprehensive survey on particle swarm optimization algorithm and its applications. *Mathematical problems in engineering*, 2015:1–39, 2015.

[28] Yanping Xu, Chunhua Wu, Kangfeng Zheng, Xu Wang, Xinxin Niu, and Tianliang Lu. Computing adaptive feature weights with PSO to improve android malware detection. *Security and Communication Networks*, 2017:14 pages, Article ID 3284080, 2017, https://doi.org/10.1155/2017/3284080

[29] Martin Jurecek and Robert Lorencz. Distance metric learning using particle swarm optimization to improve static malware detection. In *ICISSP*, pages 725–732, 2020.

[30] Partha Ghosh, Arnab Karmakar, Joy Sharma, and Santanu Phadikar. CS-PSO based intrusion detection system in cloud environment. In *Emerging Technologies in Data Mining and Information Security*, pages 261–269. Springer, 2019.

[31] Hu Kai-Cheng, Chun-Wei Tsai, Ming-Chao Chiang, and Chu-Sing Yang. A multiple pheromone table based ant colony optimization for clustering. *Mathematical Problems in Engineering*, 2015:11 pages, 2015, Article ID 158632, https://doi.org/10.1155/2015/158632

[32] Oscar Cordon Garcja, Francisco Herrera Triguero, and Thomas Stutzle. A review on the ant colony optimization metaheuristic: Basis, models and new trends. *Mathware & Soft Computing* 9(2[–3]):1–11, 2002.

[33] Ravi Kiran Varma Penmatsa, Akhila Kalidindi, and S. Kumar Reddy Mallidi. Feature reduction and optimization of malware detection system using ant colony optimization and rough sets. *International Journal of Information Security and Privacy (IJISP)*, 14(3):95–114, 2020.

[34] Huijun Peng, Chun Ying, Shuhua Tan, Bing Hu, and Zhixin Sun. An improved feature selection algorithm based on ant colony optimization. *IEEE Access*, 6:69203–69209, 2018.

[35] N. K. Sreelaja. Ant colony optimization based light weight binary search for efficient signature matching to filter ransomware. *Applied Soft Computing*, 111:107635, 2021.

[36] Annu Lambora, Kunal Gupta, and Kriti Chopra. Genetic algorithm – A literature review. In *2019 international conference on machine learning, big data, cloud and parallel computing (COMITCon)*, pages 380–384. IEEE, 2019.

[37] Danial Javaheri, Pooia Lalbakhsh, and Mehdi Hosseinzadeh. A novel method for detecting future generations of targeted and metamorphic malware based on genetic algorithm. *IEEE Access*, 9:69951–69970, 2021.

[38] Nazeeh Ghatasheh, Ismail Altaharwa, and Khaled Aldebei. Modified genetic algorithm for feature selection and hyper parameter optimization: Case of XGBoost in spam prediction. *IEEE Access*, 10:84365–84383, 2022.

[39] Nour Moustafa and Jill Slay. UNSW-NB15: A comprehensive data set for network intrusion detection systems (UNSW-NB15 network data set). In *2015 Military Communications and Information Systems Conference (MILCIS)*, pages 1–6, 2015.

[40] Nickolaos Koroniotis, Nour Moustafa, Elena Sitnikova, and Benjamin Turnbull. Towards the development of realistic botnet dataset in the internet of things for network forensic analytics: Bot-IoT dataset. *Future Generation Computer Systems*, 100:779–796, 2019.

[41] M. Jeyakarthic, P. Pandi Chandran, N. Hema Rajini. Elephant herd optimization with weighted extreme learning machine based PDF malware detection and classification model. *International Journal of Engineering Trends and Technology*, 70(8):216–223, 2022. https://doi.org/10.14445/22315381/IJETT-V70I8P222

[42] Riya Bilaiya and Rajeev Mohan Sharma. Intrusion detection system based on hybrid whale-genetic algorithm. In *2018 Second International Conference on Inventive Communication and Computational Technologies (ICICCT)*, pages 822–825. IEEE, 2018.

[43] Gautam Srivastava, Rutvij H. Jhaveri, Sweta Bhattacharya, Sharnil Pandya, Praveen Kumar Reddy Maddikunta, Gokul Yenduri, Jon G. Hall, Mamoun Alazab, Thippa Reddy Gadekallu, et al. Xai for cybersecurity: State of the art, challenges, open issues and future directions. *arXiv preprint arXiv:2206.03585*, 2022.

[44] Giacomo Iadarola, Fabio Martinelli, Francesco Mercaldo, and Antonella Santone. Towards an interpretable deep learning model for mobile malware detection and family identification. *Computers & Security*, 105:102198, 2021.

[45] Yue Liu, Chakkrit Tantithamthavorn, Li Li, and Yepang Liu. Explainable AI for android malware detection: Towards understanding why the models perform so well? *arXiv preprint arXiv:2209.00812*, 2022.

[46] Kudzai Sauka, Gun-Yoo Shin, Dong-Wook Kim, and Myung-Mook Han. Adversarial robust and explainable network intrusion detection systems based on deep learning. *Applied Sciences*, 12(13):6451, 2022.

[47] Donghai Tian, Qianjin Ying, Xiaoqi Jia, Rui Ma, Changzhen Hu, and Wenmao Liu. MDCHD: A novel malware detection method in cloud using hardware trace and deep learning. *Computer Networks*, 198:108394, 2021.

[48] Preeti Mishra, Vijay Varadharajan, Uday Tupakula, and Em-manuel S. Pilli. A detailed investigation and analysis of using machine learning techniques for intrusion detection. *IEEE communications Surveys & Tutorials*, 21(1):686–728, 2018.

[49] Nicola Capuano, Giuseppe Fenza, Vincenzo Loia, and Claudio Stanzione. Explainable artificial intelligence in cybersecurity: A survey. *IEEE Access*, 10:93575–93600, 2022.

[50] Darshan Tank, Akshai Aggarwal, and Nirbhay Chaubey. A method for malware detection in virtualization environment. In *International Conference on Computing Science, Communication and Security*, pages 263–276. Springer, 2020.

[51] Aditya Kuppa and Nhien-An Le-Khac. Black box attacks on explainable artificial intelligence (XAI) methods in cyber security. In *2020 International Joint Conference on Neural Networks (IJCNN)*, pages 1–8. IEEE, 2020.

[52] Paul Barham, Boris Dragovic, Keir Fraser, Steven Hand, Tim Harris, Alex Ho, Rolf Neugebauer, Ian Pratt, and Andrew Warfield. Xen and the art of virtualization. *ACM SIGOPS: Operating Systems Review*, 37(5):164–177, October 2003.

[53] Mohit Bhatt, Avantika Gaur, Saksham Badoni, and Preeti Mishra. Advanced malware and their impact on virtualization: A case study on hybrid feature extraction using deep memory introspection. In *Proceedings of the 2022 Fourteenth International Conference on Contemporary Computing, IC3-2022*, pages 74–80. Association for Computing Machinery, New York, NY, USA, 2022.

[54] Tamas Lengyel, Steve Maresca, Bryan Payne, George Webster, Se-bastian Vogl, and Aggelos Kiayias. Scalability, fidelity and stealth in the DRAKVUF dynamic malware analysis system. In *Proceedings of the 30th Annual Computer Security Applications Conference (ACSAC '14)*. Association for Computing Machinery, New York, USA, 386–395, 2014. https://doi.org/10.1145/2664243.2664252.

[55] Iyad Lahsen Cherif and Abdesselem Kortebi. On using extreme gradient boosting (XGBoost) machine learning algorithm for home network traffic classification. In *2019 Wireless Days (WD)*, pages 1–6, 2019.

[56] Jitendra Kumar Jaiswal and Rita Samikannu. Application of random forest algorithm on feature subset selection and classification and regression. In *2017 World Congress on Computing and Communication Technologies (WCCCT)*, pages 65–68, 2017.

[57] M. A. Hearst, S. T. Dumais, E. Osuna, J. Platt, and B. Scholkopf. Support vector machines. *IEEE Intelligent Systems and Their Applications*, 13(4):18–28, 1998.

[58] Description of different XAI libraries. https://moez-62905.medium.com/top-explainable-ai-xai-python-frameworks-in-2022-94ff4610b0f5. Accessed: 2022-12-05.

3 Detection of Malicious Activities by Smart Signature-Based IDS

Ramya Chinnasamy and Malliga Subramanian
Kongu Engineering College, Erode, India

CONTENTS

- How an email with an attachment having a known threat (for example, an email with the subject line of "you won a lottery worth $1 million") is identified?
- How a user who tries to log in remotely, which is a clear violation of an organization's policy, is found? [1]

DOI: 10.1201/9781003346340-3

63

3.1 INTRODUCTION: BACKGROUND AND DRIVING FORCES

The answer to the think box is signature-based intrusion detection systems (SIDSs) where the known attacks are called signatures. An attack signature or simply a signature is a familiar pattern of attack that is collected from the previous attack specifications and stored in an attack signature database. An attack signature is also known as Indicators of Compromise (IOCs). A typical IOC includes (i) a particular behavior that normally occurs before a malicious attack, (ii) a malevolent domain, (iii) file hashes, (iv) an email subject heading, and (v) a sequence of bytes.

A SIDS generally surveils the inbound network traffic and compares it with the known list of attack signatures that are stored in the attack signature database [2]. Subsequently, it categorizes the network flow as either normal or malicious. Initially, antivirus developers used the concept of attack signature to monitor the system files for any malicious activity. Clearly, the SIDS is the simplest form of detection as it compares the network flow with an IOC database. It is also called a misuse detection system.

The SIDS identifies the matching pattern in two ways. (i) The patterns may be found within the packet header or packet content that match the malicious pattern or malware that are stored in the attack signature database. (ii) The patterns may be identified in source or destination IP addresses and also with a sequence of packets.

3.2 FLOW DIAGRAM OF SIGNATURE-BASED IDS

The SIDS detects any malevolent activity by comparing the network traffic with the known signature in the IOC database. If there is no match found, then the traffic is categorized as normal flow and is allowed inside the network. On the other hand, if the inbound network flow finds any match in the IOC database, then it is classified as a threat and an alert is generated and sent to the user.

Figure 3.1 shows the basic working principle of SIDS. The IDS contains an attack signature database. Whenever an attacker tries to send any email attachment that contains malicious code with an attractive subject like "Surprise gift is waiting for you" or "you won a lottery worth $1 million", the IDS detects the attack by comparing the subject heading with the signature database. Once the match is found, an alert is sent to the user.

The effectiveness of the SIDS doesn't depend on the number of signatures in the signature database. Instead, it is the flexibility of the signature that identifies the threat. For example, a system with one signature for three different attacks is more efficient than a system that has three separate signatures for three different attacks. The major concern while choosing a SIDS is its flexibility in signatures and the potential to create user-specific signatures.

Obviously, the SIDS has its own pros and cons. They are as follows.

Advantages:
- It detects known threats with high processing speed.
- It detects known attacks with low false positive rates.
- It can process a high volume of network flow effectively.
- Clearly, a SIDS identifies a threat quickly and precisely.
- Best suitable for effectively monitoring inbound network flow.

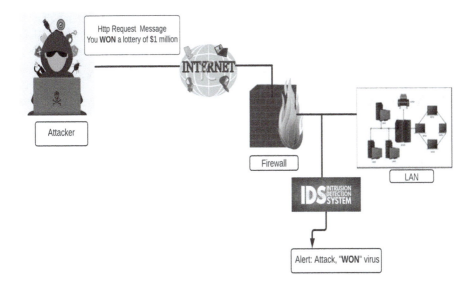

FIGURE 3.1   Flow diagram of signature-based IDS.

Disadvantages:

- The threat can be evaded by simply changing the signature of the attack. For example, the attack signature "SURPRISE" can easily be bypassed by changing it to "AMAZE".
- The IDS may be overloaded if the attack signature database is more advanced as it needs more processing capabilities.
- It cannot detect the "Zero-day attack" in which the attacker uses the system vulnerability before being identified by any detection or prevention systems.
- It can't detect any novel attack other than those defined in the attack signature database.

3.3   CLASSIFICATION OF SIGNATURES

Basically, signatures are of four categories. They are:

i. *Informational*: These are kind of benign signatures that gives some useful information such as the opening or closing of User Datagram Protocol (UDP) and Transmission Control Protocol (TCP) connections, and Internet Control Message Protocol (ICMP) echo requests.

ii. *Reconnaissance*: This kind of signature is triggered by the attacks that try to reach any computer resources or host and check for any vulnerabilities that can be used by attackers. Domain Name System (DNS) queries, ping sweep, and port scanning are perfect examples of reconnaissance attacks.

iii. *Access*: This kind of signature is triggered by attacks related to access issues such as unauthorized access, access to sensitive data, and unauthorized escalation of privileges. A Unicode attack on Microsoft IIS, Back Orifice, and NetBus are perfect examples of access-related attacks.

iv. *Denial of Service (DoS)*: This type of signature is triggered by an attack that tries to reduce the system resource availability or crash the system. A TCP SYN floods, Smurfs, Trinoo, Fraggle, Tribe Flood Network, and the Ping of Death are perfect examples of DoS attacks.

3.4   IMPLEMENTATION OF SIGNATURES

Signatures can be implemented in two ways [3].

i. *Context-specific signature*:
Context-specific signatures check the header of the packet for possible matches. The information that is being checked includes the IP protocol field, IP fragment parameter, IP options, TCP, IP and UDP checksums, TCP flags, IP and TCP port numbers, ICMP message types, and so on.

ii. *Content-specific signature*:
The content-specific signature verifies the packet content for a possible match. It checks the payload of the packet and packet header too for any possible attack. For example, specific URLs or unexpected web server attacks are contained within the payload of the packet.

3.5   SIGNATURE STRUCTURE

Apart from the implementation form, signatures are available in one of the following two structures.

i. *Atomic structure*:
It verifies a single packet for a possible match. For instance, the TCP header segment may be verified for FIN or SYN flags. Since the information is present in the TCP header and within one packet, it is a perfect example of an atomic signature.

ii. *Composite structure*:
It verifies an ensemble of packets for a possible match. For instance, a portion of attacks extends across many packets and among many connections. The composite signature sensor examines an ensemble of packets for a possible match. The sensor that checks for overlapping fragments from an ensemble of fragments from the same connection is a perfect example of a composite structure.

Example 1:   Cisco Signature-based Network-driven IDS

Cisco's network-driven IDS is signature-based. Signatures are of the utmost importance in the scenario of network-based IDSs of Cisco.
Categories of Cisco Signatures
Cisco classifies the signature into the following eight categories [3] as shown in Table 3.1.

TABLE 3.1

Categories of Cisco Signatures [3]

Signature Series	Categories
1000	IP header rule signatures that include IP fragments, IP options, and invalid or bad IP packets.
2000	ICMP packet signatures include ICMP traffic records, Ping sweep, and ICMP attacks.
3000	Signatures on TCP attacks that include TCP applications, TCP host sweeps, TCP port scans, TCP traffic records, email attacks, TCP session hijacking, legacy web attacks, NetBIOS attacks, and TCP SYN floods.
4000	Signatures on UDP attacks that include UDP traffic records, UDP applications, and UDP port scans.
5000	Signatures on web browser and server attacks using Hyper Text Transfer Protocol (HTTP).
6000	Signatures on multiple-protocol attacks include Loki attacks, DNS attacks, distributed DoS attacks, Remote Procedure Call (RPC) attacks, and authentication attacks.
8000	A signature that searches for any possible matching string in TCP applications/sessions.
10,000	Signatures that trigger Access Control List (ACL) violations.

Example 2:   Symantec Attack Signatures

Symantec includes a large-scale database of attack signatures. Each attack signature is explained with five characteristics as shown in Figure 3.2. They are:

Severity: This feature describes the dangerousness of the attack. It is a categorical attribute with values Low, Medium, and High.

Description: This feature gives the details of what is the root cause of the attack. For example, if the user attempts to visit known malicious address, then the description may be given as "You have attempted to visit a known malicious IP address [4]".

Additional Information: This feature presents the details of what to do to avoid these attacks in the future. For example, for the above description of accessing malicious IP address, the additional description may be given as "You have been prevented from accessing a known malicious IP address. It is recommended that you do NOT visit this site".

Affected: This feature explains the details of the various systems and products that are affected by the mentioned attack. As an example, for accessing the malicious IP address, the possible output of the affected field may be "All Products".

Response: This attribute denotes the possible responses for the mentioned attack. As an example, for accessing malicious IP address, the possible response may be "No additional steps are needed. Symantec's Network Threat Protection solution has prevented any potential infection attempts from occurring".

Malicious Site: Malicious Domain Request 15

Severity:Medium

This attack could pose a moderate security threat. It does not require immediate action.

Description

You have attempted to visit a known malicious IP address. Visiting this web site could potentially put you at risk to becoming infected. Symantec's Network Threat Protection solution has prevented any potential infection attempts from occurring. You should not have to take any additional actions and are safe from infection. It is recommended that you do NOT visit this site.

Additional Information

You have been prevented from accessing a known malicious IP address. It is recommended that you do NOT visit this site.

This protection prevents access to potentially malicious IP addresses that are known to be associated with malware, viruses, misleading applications such as fake antivirus or fake codecs. You should not have to take any additional actions as you have been prevented from visiting the malicious IP address. Symantec's Network Threat Protection solution has prevented any potential infection attempts from occurring.

Users can be silently infected just by visiting a web site with attacks known as drive-by downloads or social engineering attacks where misleading applications can attempt to trick users into installing fake antivirus solutions or fake video players.

For more information on social engineering attacks using FakeAV, please see this information.

http://www.symantec.com/business/security_response/writeup.jsp?docid=2007-101013-3606-99

Misleading applications intentionally misrepresent the security status of a computer. Misleading applications attempt to convince the user that he or she must remove potentially malware or security risks (usually nonexistent or fake) from the computer. The application will hold the user hostage by refusing to allow him or her to remove or fix the phantom problems until the 'required' software is purchased and installed. Misleading applications often look convincing - the programs may look like legitimate security programs and often have corresponding websites with user testimonials, lists of features, etc.

Affected

All Products

Response

No additional steps are needed. Symantec's Network Threat Protection solution has prevented any potential infection attempts from occurring.

FIGURE 3.2   An example of Symantec attack signature [4].

Some of these signatures are shown in Figure 3.3.

3.6   SMART INTRUSION DETECTION SYSTEM

The IDSs with less or no human intervention in detecting an attack are termed **smart intrusion detection systems**. The integration of large-scale computing with high performance makes the IDS handle large-scale network flow. Artificial Intelligence (AI) simulates human intelligence by computing systems and is highly recommended for converting information into knowledge. It makes computers advanced and more useful for any kind of application [5]. As a result, AI has been applied to make the IDS smart and accommodate the extensive network flow. Neural networks, Machine Learning (ML), and Deep Learning (DL) algorithms of AI can be used to build an effective IDS. Even though AI techniques can be employed to build any kind of IDS

#-A	B-R	S-Z
Adobe Reader GetIcon BO	Fake App Attack: Fake AV Redirect 15	System Infected: Miner.Bitcoininer Activity 13
Attack : FRITZ!Box Security Bypass	Fake App Attack: Misleading Application Website 7	System Infected: Miner.Bitcoinminer Activity 6
Attack: ADB Malicious APK File Upload	Malicious Site: Malicious Domain Request 15	System Infected: Activity - Bad Application
Attack: Address Space Layout Randomization -	Malicious Site: Malicious Domain Request 16	Reputation Application 4
Invalid Memory Access	Malicious Site: Malicious Domain Request 18	System Infected: Activity - Bad Application
Attack: Aerospike Database RCE CVE-2020-13151	Malicious Site: Malicious Domain Request 19	Reputation Application 5
Attack: Android Metasploit Exploit Download	Malicious Site: Malicious Domain Request 2	System Infected: Adware.DNSUnlocker Activity 2
Attack: Apache APISIX RCE CVE-2020-13945	Malicious Site: Malicious Domain Request 20	System Infected: Adware.Funshion Activity
Attack: Apache APISIX RCE CVE-2022-24112	Malicious Site: Malicious Domain Request 21	System Infected: Adware.Gen Activity 12
Attack: Apache Jetspeed Arbitrary File Upload	Malicious Site: Malicious Domain Request 22	System Infected: Adware.Gen Activity 14
Attack: Apache Jetspeed User Manager Service	Malicious Site: Malicious Domain Request 30	System Infected: Adware.Gen Activity 23
SQL Injection	Malicious Site: Malicious Domain Request 40	System Infected: Adware.Gen Activity 30
Attack: Apache OfBiz RCE CVE-2020-9496	Malicious Site: Malicious Domain Request 52	System Infected: Adware.Gen Activity 31
Attack: Apache OpenOffice Malicious Macro	Malicious Site: Malicious Domain Request 58	System Infected: Adware.Gen Activity 55
Attack: Apache Struts CVE 2017 9805 2	Malicious Site: Malicious Domain Request 59	System Infected: Adware.Gen Activity 7
Attack: Apache Struts CVE-2013-2251 Code	Malicious Site: Malicious Domain Request 62	System Infected: Agent Tesla Infostealer Activity
Execution	Malicious Site: Malicious Domain Request 63	System Infected: Backdoor Mustang Panda Plugx
Attack: Apache Struts CVE-2013-2251 Code	Malicious Site: Malicious Domain Request 64	Activity
Execution 2	Malicious Site: Malicious Domain Request 65	System Infected: Backdoor RedDelta Plugx Activity
Attack: Apache Struts CVE-2013-2251 Code	Malicious Site: Malicious Domain Request 66	System Infected: Backdoor Sogu Activity
Execution 3	Malicious Site: Malicious Domain Request 71	System Infected: Backdoor VBS.Dunihi Activity
Attack: Apache Struts CVE-2016-3087 RCE	Malicious Site: Malicious Domain Request 72	System Infected: Backdoor.Adwind Activity
Attack: Apache Struts CVE-2017-12611 2	Malicious Site: Malicious Domain Request 75	System Infected: Backdoor.Adwind Activity 2
Attack: Apache Struts CVE-2017-5638	Malicious Site: Malicious Domain Request 76	System Infected: Backdoor.Bebsplug Activity 2
Attack: Apache Struts Dynamic Method Invocation	Malicious Site: Malicious Domain Request 78	System Infected: Backdoor.Boda
RCE CVE-2016-3081	Malicious Site: Malicious Domain Request 79	System Infected: Backdoor.Ghostnet Activity 2
Attack: Asuswrt Remote Command Execution CVE-	Malicious Site: Malicious Domain Request 82	System Infected: Backdoor.Ghostnet Activity 3
2014-9583	Malicious Site: Malicious Domain Request 83	System Infected: Backdoor.Gonymdos Activity
Attack: Atlassian JIRA CVE-2019-3402 XSS	Malicious Site: Malicious Domain Request 84	System Infected: Backdoor.Graybird 5
Attack: Atlassian JIRA CVE-2019-8442 Information	Malicious Site: Malicious Domain Request 86	System Infected: Backdoor.Korplug Activity
Disclosure Vulnerability	Malicious Site: Malicious Domains Request	System Infected: Backdoor.Korplug Activity 3
Attack: Atlassian Oauth Plugin CVE-2017-9506	Malicious Site: Malicious IP Address Request	System Infected: Backdoor.Korplug Activity 4
Attack: Attack: MSSQL XP_CmdShell Stored	Malicious Site: SOCKS5 Proxy Onion Connection	System Infected: Backdoor.Matsnu Activity 2
Procedure Execution 2	Malicious Website: Sinkhole Domain Request	System Infected: Backdoor.Nitol Activity
Attack: Attempt to Disable Java Security Manager	Malicious Website: Sinkhole Domain Request 3	System Infected: Backdoor.Ratenjay RAT Activity

FIGURE 3.3   Symantec attack signatures [4].

such as anomaly-based or signature-based, this section describes various AI-based techniques for building an effective smart misuse detection system.

3.7   SMART MISUSE (SIGNATURE-BASED) DETECTION SYSTEM

A high attack detection rate (ADR) and low false alarm rate make a misuse of SIDS, a stable method [6]. However, it doesn't detect new and unknown attacks which makes the IDS lack agility. It is the responsibility of the security administrator to do extensive engineering tasks to make the IDS agile whenever the efficiency drops. Subsequently, this task is tedious and exhaustive by considering the extensive modern network size and huge volume of network flow data. Hence, Artificial Intelligence can be used to build effective SIDS and eventually make it smart. The various AI algorithms that are used for building effective SIDS are (i) self-taught learning, (ii) artificial neural network (ANN), (iii) Bayesian abductive reasoning,

---

input Labeled training set
$$T = \{(x_l^{(1)}, y^{(1)}), (x_l^{(2)}, y^{(2)}), \ldots, (x_l^{(m)}, y^{(m)})\}.$$
Unlabeled data $\{x_u^{(1)}, x_u^{(2)}, \ldots, x_u^{(k)}\}$.

output Learned classifier for the classification task.

algorithm Using unlabeled data $\{x_u^{(i)}\}$, solve the optimization problem (1) to obtain bases b.

Compute features for the classification task to obtain a new labeled training set $\hat{T} = \{(\hat{a}(x_l^{(i)}), y^{(i)})\}_{i=1}^{m}$, where

$$\hat{a}(x_l^{(i)}) = \arg\min_{a^{(i)}} \|x_l^{(i)} - \sum_j a_j^{(i)} b_j\|_2^2 + \beta \|a^{(i)}\|_1.$$

Learn a classifier $\mathcal{C}$ by applying a supervised learning algorithm (e.g., SVM) to the labeled training set $\hat{T}$.

return the learned classifier $\mathcal{C}$.

FIGURE 3.4   Self-taught learning algorithm [7].

(iv) convolutional neural network (CNN), (v) long short-term memory network (LSTM), and (vi) optimizers.

3.7.1   SELF-TAUGHT LEARNING (STL)

Generally, it is tedious and expensive to get labeled data for machine learning and hence the usage of unlabeled data has significant promise in the field of learning methods. Self-taught learning is a supervised classification method that learns from unlabeled data [7]. It is a transfer of learning from unlabeled data. Besides, it formalizes a framework for machine learning and has the ability to make learning cheaper and easier. Further self-taught learning can be implemented using a sparse coding method. Figure 3.4 describes the self-taught learning algorithm.

Papamartzivanos et al. [6] designed a misuse detection system with an ensemble of MAPE-K framework and self-taught learning that is autonomous, self-adaptive, and scalable. This system maintains a high attack detection rate even when there is a drastic and consistent change in network flow. Further, this system extracts the nature of the attack by stemming generalized feature reconstruction from unknown network traffic and unlabeled data. Javaid et al. [8] utilized self-taught learning to build effective and flexible SIDS.

3.7.2   ARTIFICIAL NEURAL NETWORK (ANN)

An ANN or simply Neural Network (NN) simulates neurons of the human brain that help the computer to learn, think, and decide like a human. It contains multiple layers of basic processing components named neurons. Collecting input and generating output are the two major functions of a neuron [9]. Each layer acquires input from many nodes and the output of one layer can also be given as input to more than one layer. An error is the difference between the system output and the desired result. This error information is fed back, and the system adjusts accordingly. Subsequently, the process is repeated until obtaining the desired performance. It is a proven and established method for obtaining accurate classification. There are a variety of ANNs, and each type has its own classification result. Choras et al. [10] proposed a SIDS using optimized ANN. A wide variety of ANNs were checked by altering the number of neurons per layer and the number of hidden layers. The effects of various hyperparameters such as the activation function, the batch size, the optimizer, and the number of epochs on the performance have been evaluated. Bias has been added to deal with data imbalance. Tests were conducted with benchmark data sets CICIDS2017 and NSL-KDD. Finally, it is proved by the test that a small change in the hyperparameter makes a considerable change in the accuracy of the system.

3.7.3 BAYESIAN ABDUCTIVE REASONING

Abductive Reasoning is a method for producing an inference from the given observation based on maximum likelihood. It can be classified into logic-based and probabilistic methods [11]. Traditional abductive reasoning methods using first-order logic cannot handle uncertainty whereas Bayesian abductive reasoning works well with uncertainty but fails to handle the unbounded number of related entities [12]. Snort [13] is a packet sniffer based on libpcap and can be utilized as a lightweight SIDS. It employs rule-based logging to implement content pattern-matching and identify various attacks such as CGI attacks, stealth port scans, buffer overflow attacks, and so on. The major disadvantage of Snort is the rules must be updated frequently by experts which is tedious and time-consuming. Ganesan et al. [11] developed a system with a Bayesian abductive reasoning technique that is augmented with an existing open-source rule-based IDS "Snort" to improve the accuracy of the detection. The proposed system identifies the continuously changing attacks by (i) predicting the rule conditions from existing rules that are likely to occur and (ii) generating new snort rules when the seed rule or start rule is given which in turn lessen the burden on the specialist to frequently update the rules manually.

3.7.4 CONVOLUTIONAL NEURAL NETWORK (CNN)

CNN is a type of ANN that can learn features adaptively and automatically through backpropagation with multiple layers such as convolutional layers, fully connected layers, and pooling layers. It is specialized in processing grid-like topology structured data such as images. The pooling layer is the second layer that is followed by the convolutional layer. Similar to the convolutional layer, there may be one or more pooling layers and finally fully connected layers. Various layers of the CNN will be discussed below.

3.7.4.1 Convolutional Layer

The first layer of CNN is the convolutional layer. There may be one or more convolutional layers. The majority of computations of CNN occur in the convolutional layer and hence is the basic building block of CNN [14]. The components of a convolutional layer are input data, feature map, and filter. For example, a color image that is represented as a three-dimensional matrix with RGB values for height, width, and depth, respectively, can be taken as input. Subsequently, a filter also named a kernel or feature detector moves across the corresponding fields of the image and checks for the relevant feature. This is the convolution process. Feature detector describes part of the image with a two-dimensional array of weights. There are various sizes of feature detectors, but the typical filter is expressed in a 3 × 3 matrix. An area of the image is filtered, and the dot product is computed between the input and the filter. This dot product is sent to an output array. Afterward, the filter is moved slightly and the whole process is repeated again until the filter moved across the complete image. The series of dot products makes the final output known as the activation map, feature map, or convolved feature.

3.7.4.2 Pooling Layer

Pooing layers, also called downsampling, perform dimensionality reduction by decreasing the number of input parameters. Much like the convolution layer, the filter is moved across the entire input but without any weights. An aggregation function has been applied by the kernel to the receptive field values. And fill the output array. There are two kinds of pooling.

Max pooling: If the pixel with the maximum value is dispatched to the output array, while the filter is swept across the input, it is known as max pooling. This is the most commonly used method of pooling.

Average pooling: If the average value of pixels is dispatched to the output array while the filter moves across the input, it is known as average pooling.

Pooling helps to decrease the complexity, increase efficiency, and reduce the overfitting risk.

3.7.4.3 Fully Connected Layer

It is a layer in which each node within an output layer is connected to a node in the previous layer. This layer does the classification task by using the features obtained from previous layers and filters.

The various kinds of CNN architecture include LeNet-5, AlexNet, VGGNet, GoogLeNet, ResNet, and ZFNet. Kim et al. [15] proposed an IDS using CNN architecture, especially for denial-of-service attacks. The performance of the suggested system is evaluated by comparing it with RNN architecture and the results showed that CNN performs better in terms of high accuracy, precision, and low error rate. Duan et al. [16] developed an IDS based on CNN for WiFi networks. First, the detection framework performs data pre-processing. Second, CNN is trained to identify attacks. Third, the risk of network training time and data overfit is reduced using dropout techniques. Finally, investigations were done on various network structures with AWID data set, and the experimental results have shown that the accuracy of the system is greater than 99%.

3.7.5 Long Short-Term Memory (LSTM)

The LSTM architecture has a group of subnets that are recurrently connected called memory blocks [17]. Each block is composed of at least one self-contained memory cell and three multiplicative units such as input, forget gates, and output. LSTM is similar to RNN except that the memory cells replace the summation unit of standard RNN. The LSTM memory cells utilize multiplicative gates for storing and accessing information over extended periods of time and hence avoid the problem of vanishing gradient. Over the years, LSTM has been applied to various classification problems with acceptable performance. LSTM or the ensemble of LSTM with other methods proved efficient in intrusion detection. Kasongo & Sun [18] developed an IDS with deep LSTM (DLSTM) for wireless networks. The results were compared with benchmark systems such as support vector machine (SVM), deep feed-forward neural network, random forest, and Naïve Bayes, and DLSTM outperforms all the methods. Kim et al. [5] developed an AI-based IDS (AI-IDS) using an ensemble of optimal CNN and LSTM (CNN-LSTM). The properties of real-time HTTP traffic have been extracted using spatial feature learning with normalized UTF-8 encoding. AI-IDS distinguishes special attacks such as obfuscated attacks and unknown attacks from normal traffic. AI-IDS has been utilized in improving Snort rules for SIDS. As the model is continuously trained and computing malicious probabilities, it is having the ability to detect any unknown attacks.

3.7.6 OPTIMIZERS

Optimization is the process that alters the hyperparameters to obtain minimized cost function or error. Several optimization techniques are available in the context of artificial intelligence. Some of the optimizers that are useful in IDS are (i) particle swarm optimization, (ii) fruit fly optimization, (iii) multiverse optimization, (iv) crow search optimization, (v) grey wolf optimization (GWO), and (vi) spider monkey optimization.

3.7.6.1 Particle Swarm Optimization

It is a metaheuristic global optimization technique that can be applied to multidimensional, unsupervised, and complex problems to solve them easily when compared to traditional deterministic algorithms [19]. It is based on the social cooperation and flocking behavior of fish schools and birds and the technique derives from the evolutionary properties of these organisms. Ali et al. [20] developed an IDS for a fast learning network using particle swarm optimization and named it PSO-FLN. The system is validated by comparing various performance metrics with extreme learning machines. The results have shown that PSO-FLN outperforms in all the tests. Particle swarm optimization can be applied for dimensionality reduction of the dataset before being applied for classification [21]. An ensemble of PSO and a classifier such as a decision tree or k nearest neighbor improves the performance. The PSO algorithm that is applied to specific features of the dataset reduces the false alarm rate and improves the accuracy and detection rate as compared with the standalone classifiers [22].

3.7.6.2 Fruit Fly Optimization

The fruit fly optimization (FFO) algorithm is a kind of swarm intelligence algorithm used for finding global optimization. It is a fast, easy-to-understand, and easy-to-code metaheuristic algorithm with efficient search capability. Population-based FFO algorithm can be used to optimize the neurons in the hidden layers of autoencoder (AE). This method increased the classification accuracy of the IDS [23].

3.7.6.3 Multiverse Optimization

A multiverse optimization (MVO) is based on the cosmology concepts such as black holes, white holes, and wormholes. The mathematical model is constructed for these three concepts for exploitation, exploration, and local search, respectively. When comparing with various optimization techniques based on performance, MVO performs better than benchmark optimization techniques. An IDS with advanced detection methods has been built by combining ANN with MVO [24]. Since the evolutionary algorithm MVO is combined with ANN, the combination produces Evolutionary Neural Network (ENN).

3.7.6.4 Crow Search Optimization

Crow search optimization (CSO) is a metaheuristic algorithm inspired by swarm intelligence that utilizes some trade-off of randomization and local search. An ensemble of fuzzy inference systems and ANN named ANFIS has used CSO to improve performance [25].

3.7.6.5 Grey Wolf Optimization

GWO is basically, a metaheuristic algorithm, that mimics the cooperative hunting behavior of grey wolfs. An IDS with an ensemble of support vector machines (SVM) and the GWO technique will improve the detection rate and accuracy with minimized processing time [26]. All the acronyms and abbreviations for this chapter are given in Table 3.2.

3.8 IDS PERFORMANCE MEASURES

There are various performance measures available to compute the performance of the IDS. They are calculated based on the confusion matrix given in Table 3.3.

True Positive (TP): The predicted data instances that are correctly categorized as an attack.

False Positive (FP): The data instances that are wrongly predicted as an attack.

True Negative (TN): The data instances that are rightly categorized as normal instances.

False Negative (FN): The data instances that are wrongly categorized as normal instances.

The performance measures using the confusion matrix are the following.

Precision:

The ratio of rightly predicted attacks to all the instances that are predicted as an attack is known as precision.

$$\text{Precision} = \frac{\text{TP}}{\text{TP} + \text{FP}}$$

TABLE 3.2

Acronyms and Their Expansions Used in This Chapter

Acronym	Expansion
IDS	Intrusion Detection System
AI	Artificial Intelligence
DL	Deep Learning
ML	Machine Learning
IOC	Indicators of Compromise
TCP	Transmission Control Protocol
ICMP	Internet Control Message Protocol
UDP	User Datagram Protocol
DNS	Domain Name System
HTTP	Hyper Text Transfer Protocol
RPC	Remote Procedure Call
ACL	Access Control List
AE	Auto Encoder
CNN	Convolutional Neural Network
RNN	Recurrent Neural Network
LSTM	Long Short-Term Memory
PSO	Particle Swarm Optimization
SMO	Spider Monkey Optimization
DoS	Denial of Service
STL	Self-Taught Learning
MAPE-K	Monitor–Analyze–Plan–Execute over a Shared Knowledge
PSO	Particle Swarm Optimization
FLN	Fast Learning Network
FFO	Fruit Fly Optimization
MVO	Multiverse Optimization
CSO	Crow Search Optimization
GWO	Grey Wolf Optimization
SMO	Spider Monkey Optimization

TABLE 3.3

Confusion Matrix

Actual Class	Anticipated Class	
	Breach	Regular
Breach	TP	FN
Regular	FP	TN

Recall:

The ratio of correctly predicted attack with all instances of attack is known as recall or detection rate.

$$\text{Recall} = \text{Detection rate} = \frac{TP}{TP + FN}$$

False Alarm Rate:

The ratio of wrongly predicted attacks to all normal instances is known as the false alarm rate.

$$\text{False Alarm Rate} = \frac{FP}{FP + TN}$$

Accuracy:

The ratio of the right prediction to all the instances is called accuracy.

$$\text{Accuracy} = \frac{TP + TN}{TP + TN + FP + FN}$$

F-Measure:

It is a technique for calculating accuracy using precision and recall.

$$\text{F-measure} = 2 \times \frac{\text{Precision} \times \text{Recall}}{\text{Precision} + \text{Recall}}$$

3.9 SUMMARY

- A **signature** also known as **Indicators of Compromise (IOCs)** is a familiar pattern of attack that is collected from the previous attack specifications and stored in an attack signature database.
- A **signature-based intrusion detection system** also known as a **misuse detection system** generally surveils the inbound network traffic and compares it with the known list of attack signatures that are stored in an attack signature database.
  - *Pros*: High processing speed, low false positive rates.
  - *Cons*: Cannot detect **unknown** attacks and **zero-day** attacks.
  - *Classification of Signatures*: Informational, reconnaissance, access, Denial of Service (DoS).
  - *Implementation of Signatures*: Context-specific signature and content-specific signature.
  - *Signature Structure*: Atomic structure and composite structure.
  - *Smart Intrusion Detection System*: The IDS with less or no human intervention in detecting an attack.

- *Smart Misuse (Signature-Based) Detection System Algorithms*: (i) Self-taught learning, (ii) ANN (iii), Bayesian abductive reasoning, (iv) CNN, (v) LSTM, and (vi) optimizers.
- *IDS Performance Measures*:

$$\text{Precision} = \frac{\text{TP}}{\text{TP} + \text{FP}}$$

$$\text{Recall} = \text{Detection rate} = \frac{\text{TP}}{\text{TP} + \text{FN}}$$

$$\text{False Alarm Rate} = \frac{\text{FP}}{\text{FP} + \text{TN}}$$

$$\text{Accuracy} = \frac{\text{TP} + \text{TN}}{\text{TP} + \text{TN} + \text{FP} + \text{FN}}$$

$$\text{F-measure} = 2 \times \frac{\text{Precision} \times \text{Recall}}{\text{Precision} + \text{Recall}}$$

REFERENCES

[1] ebrary. *How Does Detection Work? Signature-Based Detection*. 2020. Available: https://ebrary.net/26722/computer_science/detection_work#465

[2] M. Rezek. *What is the difference between signature-based and behavior-based intrusion detection systems?* [Web site]. 2020. Available: https://accedian.com/blog/what-is-the-difference-between-signature-based-and-behavior-based-ids/

[3] etutorial.org. *IDS Signatures*. 2021, 29-July-2022. Available: http://etutorials.org/Networking/Router+firewall+security/Part+VII+Detecting+and+Preventing+Attacks/Chapter+16.+Intrusion-Detection+System/IDS+Signatures/

[4] Broadcom. *Symantec Attack Signatures*. 2022. Available: https://www.broadcom.com/support/security-center/attacksignatures

[5] A. Kim, M. Park, and D. H. Lee, "AI-IDS: Application of deep learning to real-time web intrusion detection," *IEEE Access*, vol. 8, pp. 70245–70261, 2020.

[6] D. Papamartzivanos, F. G. Mármol, and G. Kambourakis, "Introducing deep learning self-adaptive misuse network intrusion detection systems," *IEEE Access*, vol. 7, pp. 13546–13560, 2019.

[7] R. Raina, A. Battle, H. Lee, B. Packer, and A. Y. Ng, "Self-taught learning: Transfer learning from unlabeled data," in *Proceedings of the 24th International Conference on Machine Learning*, 2007, pp. 759–766.

[8] A. Javaid, Q. Niyaz, W. Sun, and M. Alam, "A deep learning approach for network intrusion detection system," *EAI Endorsed Transactions on Security and Safety*, vol. 3, p. e2, 2016.

[9] A. Dongare, R. Kharde, and A. D. Kachare, "Introduction to artificial neural network," *International Journal of Engineering and Innovative Technology (IJEIT)*, vol. 2, pp. 189–194, 2012.

[10] M. Choraś and M. Pawlicki, "Intrusion detection approach based on optimised artificial neural network," *Neurocomputing*, vol. 452, pp. 705–715, 2021.

[11] A. Ganesan, P. Parameshwarappa, A. Peshave, Z. Chen, and T. Oates, "Extending signature-based intrusion setection systems with Bayesian abductive reasoning," *arXiv preprint arXiv:1903.12101*, 2019.

[12] R. J. Kate and R. J. Mooney, "RJ: Probabilistic abduction using Markov logic networks," in *IJCAI-09 Workshop on Plan, Activity, and Intent Recognition*, 2009.

[13] M. Roesch, "Snort: Lightweight intrusion detection for networks," in *Lisa*, 1999, pp. 229–238.

[14] I. c. l. hub. *Convolutional Neural Networks*. 2022. Available: https://www.ibm.com/cloud/learn/convolutional-neural-networks

[15] J. Kim, J. Kim, H. Kim, M. Shim, and E. Choi, "CNN-based network intrusion detection against denial-of-service attacks," *Electronics*, vol. 9, p. 916, 2020.

[16] Q. Duan, X. Wei, J. Fan, L. Yu, and Y. Hu, "CNN-based intrusion classification for IEEE 802.11 wireless networks," in *2020 IEEE 6th International Conference on Computer and Communications (ICCC)*, 2020, pp. 830–833.

[17] A. Graves, "Long short-term memory," *Supervised sequence labelling with recurrent neural networks*, pp. 37–45, 2012.

[18] S. M. Kasongo and Y. Sun, "A deep long short-term memory based classifier for wireless intrusion detection system," *ICT Express*, vol. 6, pp. 98–103, 2020.

[19] S. Sengupta, S. Basak, and R. A. Peters, "Particle swarm optimization: A survey of historical and recent developments with hybridization perspectives," *Machine Learning and Knowledge Extraction*, vol. 1, pp. 157–191, 2018.

[20] M. H. Ali, B. A. D. Al Mohammed, A. Ismail, and M. F. Zolkipli, "A new intrusion detection system based on fast learning network and particle swarm optimization," *IEEE Access*, vol. 6, pp. 20255–20261, 2018.

[21] R. O. Ogundokun, J. B. Awotunde, P. Sadiku, E. A. Adeniyi, M. Abiodun, and O. I. Dauda, "An enhanced intrusion detection system using particle swarm optimization feature extraction technique," *Procedia Computer Science*, vol. 193, pp. 504–512, 2021.

[22] N. Kunhare, R. Tiwari, and J. Dhar, "Particle swarm optimization and feature selection for intrusion detection system," *Sādhanā*, vol. 45, pp. 1–14, 2020.

[23] R. Sekhar, K. Sasirekha, P. Raja, and K. Thangavel, "A novel GPU based intrusion detection system using deep autoencoder with Fruitfly optimization," *SN Applied Sciences*, vol. 3, pp. 1–16, 2021.

[24] I. Benmessahel, K. Xie, and M. Chellal, "A new evolutionary neural networks based on intrusion detection systems using multiverse optimization," *Applied Intelligence*, vol. 48, pp. 2315–2327, 2018.

[25] S. Manimurugan, A.-Q. Majdi, M. Mohmmed, C. Narmatha, and R. Varatharajan, "Intrusion detection in networks using crow search optimization algorithm with adaptive neuro-fuzzy inference system," *Microprocessors and Microsystems*, vol. 79, p. 103261, 2020.

[26] M. Safaldin, M. Otair, and L. Abualigah, "Improved binary gray wolf optimizer and SVM for intrusion detection system in wireless sensor networks," *Journal of Ambient Intelligence and Humanized Computing*, vol. 12, pp. 1559–1576, 2021.

4 Detection of Malicious Activities by AI-Supported Anomaly-Based IDS

Akshaya Suresh and Arun Cyril Jose

IIIT-Kottayam, Valavoor, India

CONTENTS

4.1 INTRODUCTION

Modern computer infrastructure must include Network Intrusion Detection Systems (NIDSs) to monitor and detect harmful network activity (such as unauthorized system access or improperly configured systems). The bulk of commercial NIDSs is signature-based, which means that they look for certain patterns in network traffic to establish what constitutes undesired traffic. Despite the fact that such systems are quite

DOI: 10.1201/9781003346340-4

successful against known threats, signature-based detection fails when attack routes are unknown or when existing assaults are updated to circumvent such restrictions.

In addition to having difficulty detecting new or changing threats, signature-based detection in NIDS is commonly afflicted with false positives in real-world circumstances. Detecting malicious shellcode, a high-impact threat vector that allows attackers to gain unrestricted command line access to both traditional computer systems and cyber-physical systems like smart grid infrastructure is particularly challenging because shellcode patterns can be hard to distinguish from benign network traffic.

An intrusion detection system's (IDS) main goal is to spot instances where a suspect is attempting to compromise a system's functionality. In other words, make the system behave in a way that it was not intended to. The system's integrity, confidentiality, and availability, as well as the data it stores and manages, may all be compromised as a result. Systems may include hosts, servers, IoT devices, routers, or other intermediate devices.

Host-based intrusion detection systems (HIDSs) and network-based intrusion detection systems (NIDSs) are the two groups that IDSs typically belong to at the highest level. The former is when a single device detects a breach, whereas the latter is when a compromise is discovered while being transmitted over a network. Anomaly-based systems and signature-based systems are additional categories for NIDS. Commercial NIDSs mostly use signature-based methods, whereas anomaly-based systems are still essentially research ideas with few real-world vendor examples. IDS-generated warnings and other incident data are increasingly being fed into security information and event management (SIEM) systems, where they are combined with other logs and feeds to provide a more comprehensive picture of a possible problem.

4.2 NETWORK SECURITY TOOLS

There are various tools designed to detect network malicious activity. We can use these systems to enforce a variety of security measures against potential threats.

4.2.1 INTRUSION DETECTION SYSTEMS

A system called an intrusion detection system (IDS) watches network traffic for unusual activity and issues warnings when it is seen.

Some IDSs can take action when a malicious activity or anomalous traffic is discovered, like blocking traffic transmitted from suspicious Internet Protocol (IP) addresses. While anomaly detection and reporting are the basic responsibilities of an IDS, some IDSs are also capable of taking further measures when an anomalous activity or suspicious traffic is detected.

4.2.2 WORKING

In order to catch hackers before they seriously harm a network, IDSs are employed to identify anomalies. IDSs can either be host-based or network-based. While an NIDS resides on the network, a HIDS is installed on the client's computer [1].

Systems for detecting intrusions operate by scanning for indications of previously known attacks or changes from routine behavior. The protocol and application layers are moved up the stack to look at these alterations or abnormalities. They are capable of accurately detecting things like Domain Name System (DNS) poisonings and Christmas tree scans.

A network security appliance or a software program running on client hardware can both be used to construct an IDS. To safeguard data and systems in cloud deployments, there are additional cloud-based intrusion detection solutions available.

4.2.3 Types of Intrusion Detection Systems

IDSs come in a variety of flavors and identify suspicious activity using various techniques, such as the following:

- In order to monitor inbound and outbound traffic to and from all the devices on the network, a NIDS is installed at one or more strategically positioned points inside the network.
- Every computer or device connected to the network with direct access to the internet and the company's internal network is running a HIDS. An advantage of a HIDS over an NIDS is that it could be able to identify suspicious network packets coming from within the company or malicious traffic that an NIDS has missed. A HIDS may also be able to detect harmful communication coming from the host itself, such as when the host is infected with malware and tries to propagate to other systems.
- Similar to antivirus software, a signature-based intrusion detection system (SIDS) keeps track of every packet moving through the network and compares it to a database of attack signatures or characteristics of known malicious threats.
- In order to assess what is usual for the network in terms of bandwidth, protocols, ports, and other devices, an anomaly-based intrusion detection system (AIDS) monitors network traffic and compares it against a pre-established baseline. This kind frequently develops a baseline and corresponding security policy using machine learning. Then, it notifies IT personnel of despicable behavior and rules violations. The anomaly-based detection method overcomes the drawbacks of signature-based methods, particularly in the identification of novel threats, by detecting threats using a broad range model rather than specific signatures and features.

Historically, IDSs were classified as either passive or active. When a passive IDS found malicious behavior, it would provide an alert or a log entry but would not take any further action. An active IDS, also known as an intrusion detection and prevention system (IDPS), would create log entries and alerts but could also be set up to perform actions, such as blocking IP addresses or preventing access to restricted resources. Figure 4.1 shows the basic architecture of the IDS. Here, first, network packet analysis is performed and then the training of mode through those packets is performed. And the decision will be made according to the algorithms we choose.

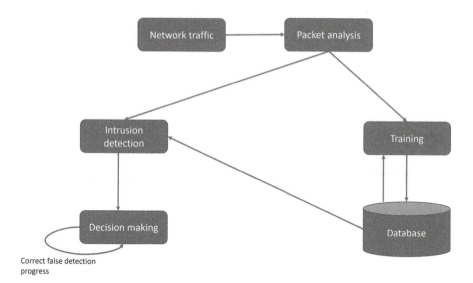

FIGURE 4.1   IDS architecture.

And if there are any changes in the behavior of the network, it will detect the changes by comparing or checking for signatures from the data.

4.2.4 BENEFITS OF INTRUSION DETECTION SYSTEMS

Starting with the ability to recognize security issues, IDSs provide enterprises with a number of advantages. The quantity and variety of attacks can be analyzed with the aid of an IDS. Using this knowledge, organizations can modify their security protocols or put in place better security measures. Companies can find defects or issues with the configuration of their network devices with the use of an IDS. Then, future risks can be evaluated using these metrics [2].

Enterprises can also use IDSs to achieve regulatory compliance. With an IDS, businesses have better network visibility, which makes it simpler to adhere to security standards. Businesses can also utilize their IDS logs as part of the documentation to demonstrate that they are complying with legal standards.

Systems for detecting intrusions can enhance security responses. IDS sensors can identify network hosts and devices, therefore they can also be used to analyze data within network packets and figure out what operating systems are being utilized by the services. It may be considerably more effective to utilize an IDS to gather this data than to manually count all linked systems.

4.3 NETWORK MALICIOUS ACTIVITIES

A network attack is an attempt to enter a company's network unauthorized with the intent of stealing information or carrying out other destructive behavior.

Network attacks generally fall into two categories:

- Passive: Attackers who obtain access to a network can monitor or steal sensitive data while doing so without altering the original material.
- Active: In addition to gaining illegal access, attackers can alter data by deleting, encrypting, or doing other harm.

Malicious activity is something that contains different behaviors that involve unusual access patterns, file and database changes, or any other suspicious activity that could indicate an attack or threat.

When a malicious HTTP request enters your command and controls your servers, your network becomes a part of the attacker's botnets [3]. Cybercriminals who are successful in breaching your network security can observe how many machines your company has. To carry out ransomware attacks or data theft, they might also send out orders and start other hostile activities [3].

Tools for detecting malicious traffic continuously scan network traffic for indications of questionable files, links, or behaviors. The tools evaluate whether the suspicious item is originating from a problematic URL or C2 channels in order to spot fraudulent internet activity.

4.4 ANOMALY-BASED IDS

Anomaly-based detection is based on network behavior. Network behavior is in accordance with some predefined behavior. Network administrators then learn these accepted network behavior.

The main phase in defining network behavior is the IDS engine capability.

The engine must be able to understand the protocol and process them. For detection to occur correctly, the administrators must acquire an in-depth understanding of acceptable network conduct. But once the protocol is established and the rules are clear, anomaly detection systems function effectively.

The main benefit of anomaly-based detection over signature-based engines is the ability to identify fresh attacks for which there is no signature if they deviate from the usual traffic patterns. When the systems discover fresh automated worms, this is seen.

4.5 AI-SUPPORTED ANOMALY-BASED IDS

AI is broadly utilized for intrusion detection purposes. AI-based techniques play an important role in the development of IDS and have many more advantages over other techniques. Artificial Intelligence is the design of intelligent machines through the branch of computer science.

A current trend in development is the implementation of expert systems, along with neural networks, fuzzy logic, and genetic algorithms.

4.5.1 MACHINE-LEARNING-BASED IDS

An anomaly, also known as a variation or an exception, is often something that deviates from the usual. In the context of software engineering, an anomaly is an unusual

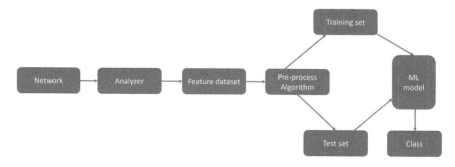

FIGURE 4.2 IDS using ML.

occurrence or event that deviates from the norm and raises suspicion. Examples include sudden bursts or decreases in activity; errors in the text; and sudden rapid drops or increases in temperature.

A software program must function smoothly and predictably; thus any anomaly poses a possible risk to the robustness and security of the program. Normally, you want to detect them all. Anomaly or outlier identification is the process of detecting anomalies.

Why do you need machine learning for anomaly detection? This is a process that is usually conducted with the help of statistics and machine learning tools. The majority of businesses today that require outlier identification operate with enormous volumes of data, including transactions, text, picture, and video material, among other types of data. Another challenge is that the data is frequently unstructured, meaning that it wasn't put in a particular order for the data analysis. Images, emails, and business papers are a few instances of unstructured data. Use technologies that aren't afraid of large amounts of data if you want to be able to gather, clean, organize, analyze, and store data.

The best outcomes for machine learning approaches really occur when big data sets are involved. Figure 4.2 shows the basic architecture of how to identify intrusions using ML algorithms. Here from the network, the packets will get analyzed and it is then fed for the feature extraction process. After using a suitable algorithm the data is fed to a training and testing set, i.e., to train the model and the test set for testing data and then fed to the ML model. Algorithms for machine learning can process the majority of data types. Additionally, you may select the algorithm based on your issue and even mix many methods for the best outcomes. Utilizing machine learning for practical purposes speeds up and conserves resources in the process of anomaly detection. It can take place both post-factum and in the present. For example, fraud detection and cybersecurity are two areas where real-time anomaly detection is used to increase security and resilience.

4.5.2 NEURAL-NETWORKS-BASED IDS

Neural networks can be used to build software behaviors and can make attempts to distinguish between normal and anomalous behavior. An artificial neural network

(ANN) consists of processing units, nodes, and connections between them [4]. The connection between any two units can be used to determine if one is dependent on another because it contains some weight. Each and every node has the ability to connect to another and has its associated weight and threshold. If the output has a value greater than the threshold value then that node is activated and will be sent to the next layer. A Backpropagation network can be used for learning and also helps in learning profiles of the anomalous behavior of the network. Neural networks depend on the training data so as to learn and improve their accuracy over time.

Data are mainly fed to the models to train them and these are the foundations of computer vision, natural language processing, and other neural networks.

Neural networks are classified based on different types of purposes. The perceptron is the oldest neural network which was developed in the year 1958 [4]. It is the simplest form of network and has only one single neuron. Convolutional neural networks (CNNs) are used for image recognition, pattern recognition, and computer vision. Recurrent neural networks (RNNs) are the learning algorithms that are mainly used for the time-series data to make predictions about the future outcomes.

4.5.3 GENETIC-ALGORITHM-BASED IDS

A genetic algorithm(GA) is a combination of computational models that are based on concepts of natural selection and evolution. Genetic algorithm uses chromosomes like data structure and evolves the chromosomes using selection, recombination, etc. [5]. Simple network access rules are defined by the genetic algorithm. These rules can disallow the passage of already known malicious attacks.

A GA is mainly used for search algorithms and is used to solve the optimization and search problems. GA is the subset of the evolutionary algorithms which is used for computation. GA is mainly based on the behavior of the chromosomes and the genetic structure. GA uses the generational cycle for producing high-quality solutions.

The basic phases of GA are as follows: Initial Population, where it is the place where the whole process begins. For each group, there is a different set of individuals. The second phase is the fitness function and it is one of the functions that is used to determine whether they are fit to compete with other individuals. For each individual, they will get a fitness score. Based on the fitness score only most of them are selected for reproduction rely on. In some cases, when the fitness function becomes hard to use, we can use other methods like simulation to find the fitness score. The third phase is the selection which needs to select the best individuals who will create the next generation. As said earlier, each of the individuals is selected based on their fitness score. The fourth phase is the crossover which is the critical phase of the GA. The next phase is a mutation which is defined as the flipping of some of the strings. The sixth phase is the replacement and it is mainly the replacement of the old population with the new child population. This is mainly because the new child population has more fitness scores than the old child population. And finally comes the last phase of the GA, i.e., termination. After the replacement has been done, the termination process is done. The algorithm will terminate once it will achieve the fitness solution [6].

Intrusion is a process of attack that can harm the computer network. The intruder can then have access to the system so that they can steal the information. The training process of GA for IDS is as follows [7]:

- Generate some chromosomes randomly, say, 100.
- Attack recognition between the generated chromosomes and training data.
- To find the fitness score, fitness value is applied.
- Then, data will be sorted according to the highest to lowest fitness value.
- Select top fitness values.
- Create clones which are 5 times that of chromosomes and do the crossover.
- Then do the mutation of the features in the chromosomes.
- Repeat the process until we generate the final population testing process.

Figure 4.3 shows the genetic flow algorithm of how this process is going on, i.e., how the population is generated and how to evaluate and if it reaches its end, it will then produce the best individuals for the results or else the process is repeated by passing through the process of selection, crossover, and mutation. The final population of chromosomes obtained from the training process will be used during the training process. The rate of success will be calculated based on the attack connections that can be recognized during the testing process. The higher the probability, the more positive detection it can produce.

4.5.4 FUZZY-LOGIC-BASED IDS

Fuzzy logic (FL) is most complex when solving complex problems. It consists of a fuzzy set of elements where membership of the element can vary from 0 to 1. In the first step, we map the symbolic valued attributes to numeric attributes. Then features will get scaled linearly to each range. The testing data will then get grouped and fuzzy interference is applied to generate the datasets.

A TCP data packet is subjected to data mining techniques in order to extract parameters that aren't plainly stated in the packet. Once extraction is done, it produces fuzzy sets based on the past inputs and the range over which they will be calculated. Data feeds are calculated over these three characteristics: COUNT, UNIQUENESS, and VARIANCE. There are five fuzzy sets that have been chosen to represent the data elements: LOW, MEDIUM-LOW, MEDIUM, MEDIUM-HIGH, and HIGH.

FL can be said as a method of reasoning that resembles human reasoning. FL can be implemented in various sizes and capabilities that range from small controllers to large, networked, workstation-based control systems. They can be implemented in hardware or software or a combination of both.

FL architecture is mainly divided into four parts [8]:

- Fuzzification Module: It will transform the system inputs into fuzzy sets.
- Knowledge Base: It can store the if-then rule provided by experts.
- Inference Engine: By making inferences on the inputs and if-then rules it can simulate the human reasoning process.
- Defuzzification Module: It will transform the fuzzy set obtained by the inference engine back to the system value.

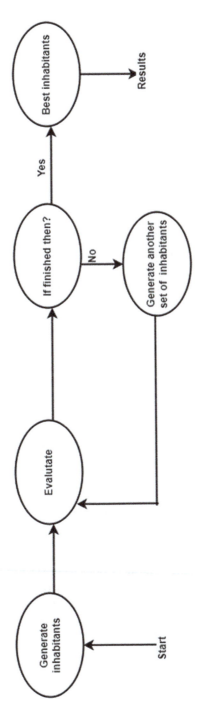

FIGURE 4.3 Genetic algorithm flow.

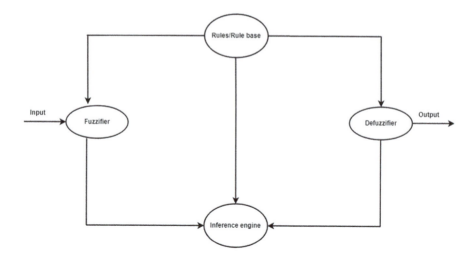

FIGURE 4.4 Fuzzy logic architecture.

When creating expert systems, fuzzy logic helps manage uncertainty by giving users a workspace for word-based computation. It has become now an important and unavoidable part of ML as it can handle any uncertain situation. ML tools are the main ones that are used for intrusion detection models. A fuzzy decision-making module will be used for detection the of intrusions in a particular system.

Using the fuzzy rule learning technique, an effective set of fuzzy rules for the inference approach was found automatically, which are more effective for detecting intrusion in a computer network. The definite rules were originally created by mining the single-length frequent items from both attack and normal data. The fuzzy rules will be then determined by the rules and then these will be fed to the fuzzy system. Figure 4.4 shows the fuzzy logic architecture which is the basic one that gives a set of inputs through the fuzzifier and output is passed through the defuzzifier after passing applying certain rules.

4.6 ANOMALY DETECTION TECHNIQUES

Anomaly detection is based on the host or network. There are many techniques related to the behavioral model: Statistical Model, Operational or Threshold Metric Model, Markov Process or Marker Model, Statistical Moments or Mean and Standard Deviation Model, Univariate Model, Multivariate Model, Time Series Model, Cognition-Based, Finite State Machine Model, Description Script Model, Adept System Model, Machine-Learning-Based Model, Bayesian Model, Genetic Algorithm Model, Neural Network Model, Fuzzy Logic Model, Outlier Detection Model, Computer-Immunology-Based Model, User-Intention-Based Model, etc.

4.6.1 STATISTICAL-MODEL-BASED ANOMALY DETECTION

It entails the acquisition of data pertaining to the behavior of genuine users over time. Here, statistical tests are applied to the observed behavior to determine with a high level of confidence whether the behavior is not genuine or not. There is threshold detection and profile-based detection. In threshold detection, it involves entails creating user-independent criteria for the frequency of occurrence of distinct events. And when it comes to profile-based detection, a profile of each user is used to develop and detect the changes in the behavior [9].

Statistical techniques are also called top-down learning and are employed when the relationship among it is finalized and it can also employ mathematics so that it can aid search. The three basic classes of statistical classes are linear, non-linear, and decision trees. Statistical models are used to assess the data obtained from the system and network for attack analysis. Statistical patterns can be estimated with regard to several time frames, such as the weekday, the month-day, the year-month, and so on.

4.6.1.1   Operational Model or Threshold Metric for Anomaly Detection

If less than "m" or more than "n" events happen over a certain period of time, the alarm will be sounded. This can be seen in Win2K Lock.

Thresholds are defined as the values below which risks are quantifiable and acceptable [10]. The threshold for the analysis mainly uses a logistic regression algorithm. Logistic regression always returns a probability. If the probability for a particular event is 0.995 (say) for a particular event then we can say that it is highly spammed or have highly malicious activity. If in some cases the probability prediction score is 0.0003, then we can say it is very likely not spam or doesn't have that malicious activity [11].

4.6.1.2   Marker Model for Anomaly Detection

In this intrusion detection is found by investigating the system at regular intervals and keeping track of its state. The change of state occurs when an anomaly is detected or a change in behavior is detected in the system. Where command sequences were relevant, the transitions between the commands are determined by anomaly detection.

4.6.1.3   Mean and Standard Deviation Model for Anomaly Detection

In standard deviation, any correlations are called a moment. If the event falls outside the set interval above or below then it is considered anomalous. The system is prone to change as a result of aging data and modifications to the statistical rule database. There are two significant advantages of using an operational model. In order to create restrictions, previous information is not necessary in the first place, and identifying the usual activity depends on observed user data because it differs from user to user. This flexibility is lacking in the threshold model. The main change in the mean and standard deviation model is to give more weight to recent activity.

4.6.1.4   Multivariate Model for Anomaly Detection

The primary distinction between the mean and standard deviation models is based on correlations between two or more measures. If experimental data shows that combining related measures yields higher judicious power than handling them independently.

4.6.1.5 Time Series Model for Anomaly Detection

Interval timers together with event counters or resource measures are major components in this model. If the probability of an occurrence is too low then it is considered an anomaly. The main disadvantage of this model is that it is computationally more expensive.

4.6.2 COGNITION MODEL FOR ANOMALY DETECTION

Cognitive networks are the solution to problems that exist in the current networks. Cognitive networks mainly use network metrics and patterns as input for the decision-making process and it provides output in the form of a set of actions that can be implemented in modifiable network elements. In cognitive networks, learning mainly happens through the following process: Observe, Orient, Decide, and Act loop. This is called the Feature loop. Cognition uses the ML technique and it improves the performance from the gained experience.

4.6.2.1 Finite State Machine for Detection

Finite automation is a model of behavior captured in states, transitions, and actions. An action is defined as an activity description that is performed at a particular moment. There are many types of action, they are entry action, exit action, and transition action.

4.6.2.2 Description Scripts for Detection

There are many proposals for scripting languages that describe the signature of attacks on computers and networks. These scripting languages are capable of identifying the specific events which are indications of attacks.

4.6.2.3 Adept Systems for Detection

Here human expertise is used for solving the problems in adept systems. Here, the uncertainties are solved by experts. These systems are efficient in certain problem domains and are also considered a class of artificial intelligence problems. Adept systems are trained based on expert knowledge of patterns.

4.6.3 INTRUSION PREVENTION SYSTEMS

IPS is considered an expansion of IDSs. Their functionalities and capabilities are all similar but one great importance is that IPS can take action to prevent cyber attacks by blocking suspicious network activities.

IPS can also be referred to as IDPS. IPSs are very effective at detecting and preventing vulnerability exploits. When a vulnerability is found, threat actors often have a window of opportunity to exploit it before a security fix can be implemented. To swiftly stop these sorts of assaults, an IPS is utilized.

An IPS operates by examining all network traffic [12]. An IPS tool will often sit directly behind a firewall to accomplish this, serving as an extra layer to watch events for harmful traffic. IPS instruments are therefore put in direct communication lines between a system and a network, allowing them to evaluate network traffic. Figure 4.5

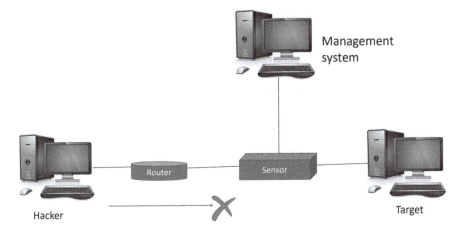

FIGURE 4.5 IPS architecture.

shows the basic IPS architecture when an intrusion occurs, and this is how it manages – when an attack comes from the hacker, the sensor will sense it and doesn't allow it to pass on to the target's computer.

The following are three common approaches for an IPS tool to protect networks:

- Signature-based detection: Here, the IPS tool detects threats and takes action based on previously established attack signatures of known network dangers;
- Anomaly-based detection: If an anomaly is found, the IPS scans for unusual network behavior and restricts access to the host; and
- Policy-based detection: In order to use IPS, administrators must first create security rules – when an event happens that violates a specified security policy, a system administrator alert is delivered.

If threats are found, an IPS program may often provide notifications to the administrator, discard any malicious network packets, and reset connections by reconfiguring firewalls, repackaging payloads, and deleting infected attachments from servers.

The IPS is classified as follows [13]:

- Network-based intrusion prevention system (NIPS): It analyzes protocol behavior to monitor the whole network for suspicious traffic.
- Wireless intrusion prevention system (WIPS): It analyzes wireless networking protocols to detect suspicious traffic on a wireless network.
- Network behavior analysis (NBA): It monitors network traffic in order to detect threats that cause anomalous traffic flows, such as distributed denial of service assaults, certain types of malware, and policy breaches.
- Host-based intrusion prevention system (HIPS): It is a built-in software package that monitors a single host for suspicious behavior by scanning events that occur on that host.

4.6.4 How Do IPS and IDS Differ?

The main difference between Intrusion Prevention System (IPS) with IDSs is that IDS is passive monitoring whereas IPS is active monitoring. IPSs are installed in line and can actively prevent or block suspected invasions [13]. An IPS can raise an alarm, drop discovered malicious packets, reset a connection, or block traffic from the offending IP address. IPS can also rectify cyclic redundancy check (CRC) mistakes, defragment packet streams, resolve TCP sequencing difficulties, and remove unnecessary transport and network layer choices. IDS can record information related to observed malicious events and then they can produce reports against it. IPS is an extension of IDS because they monitor network traffic and system activities of malicious or suspicious activities.

4.7 CONCLUSION

In this chapter, we have mainly studied intrusion detection and its types. Then mainly studied anomaly-based IDS. It briefly describes four main techniques of machine learning, genetic algorithms, fuzzy logic, and neural networks. In several instances, AI methods have been shown to be more effective than conventional methods, which are frequently constrained by the complexity, lack of flexibility, and/or scalability of the deterministic or semi-analytical models on which they are dependent. Then, finally, we have seen the IPS which is used to prevent the attacks that are coming in the near future.

AI can be used for tackling many emerging threats. So, in many cases, AI-based cybersecurity systems can detect more threats more quickly and respond to them more effectively than human experts. Nonetheless, when used correctly, AI can be a perfect weapon to fight against cybercrime.

REFERENCES

[1] Deris Stiawan, Abdul Hanan Abdullah, and Mohd Yazid Idris. The trends of intrusion prevention system network. In *2010 2nd International Conference on Education Technology and Computer*, volume 4, pages V4-217–V4-221, 2010.

[2] What is an intrusion detection system (ids)? Definition from searchsecurity. https://www.techtarget.com/searchsecurity/definition/intrusion-detection-system. (Accessed on 11/26/2022).

[3] Detecting suspicious and malicious activity on your network–demakis. https://demaki stech.com/detecting-malicious-network-activity/. (Accessed on 11/28/2022).

[4] What are neural networks?—India—IBM. https://www.ibm.com/in-en/cloud/learn/neural-networks. (Accessed on 11/28/2022).

[5] Genetic algorithm in artificial intelligence. https://hkrtrainings.com/genetic-algorithm-in-artificial-intelligence. (Accessed on 11/29/2022).

[6] The basics of genetic algorithms in machine learning—engineering education (enged) program—section. https://www.section.io/engineering-education/the-basics-of-genetic-algorithms-in-ml/. (Accessed on 11/29/2022).

[7] Hamizan Suhaimi, Saiful Izwan Suliman, Ismail Musirin, Afdallyna Fathiyah Harun, and Roslina Mohamad. Network intrusion detection system by using genetic algorithm. *Indonesian Journal of Electrical Engineering and Computer Science*, 16:1593–1599, 2019.

[8] Artificial intelligence-fuzzy logic systems. https://www.tutorialspoint.com/artificial_intelligence/artificial_intelligence_fuzzy_logic_systems.htm. (Accessed on 11/29/2022).

[9] K. C. Nalavade. Using machine learning and statistical models for intrusion detection. *International Journal of Computer Applications*, 2020.

[10] Sultan Alhusain. Predicting relative thresholds for object oriented metrics. In *2021 IEEE/ACM International Conference on Technical Debt (TechDebt)*, pages 55–63, 2021.

[11] Classification: Thresholding—machine learning—google developers. https://developers.google.com/machine-learning/ crash-course/classification/thresholding. (Accessed on 11/29/2022).

[12] What is an intrusion prevention system (IPS)? https://www.techtarget.com/searchsecurity/definition/intrusion-prevention. (Accessed on 11/29/2022).

[13] Intrusion prevention system (IPS)—geeksforgeeks. https://www.geeksforgeeks.org/intrusion-prevention-system-ips/. (Accessed on 11/29/2022).

5 An Artificial Intelligent Enabled Framework for Malware Detection

Mahendra Pratap Singh, Hrithik Bhat, Somesh Kartikeya and Shuddhatm Choudhary

NIT Karnataka Mangaluru, India

CONTENTS

5.1 INTRODUCTION

Internet access has risen exponentially, with the number of users rising to 4.9 billion, according to a report by the International Telecommunication Union (ITU). Access to the internet also exposes users to cyber risks such as phishing, data theft, ransomware attacks, and much more. The use of malware is one of the most widely used methods by attackers to gain access to a user's system and launch attacks. Viruses, worms, trojans, adware, and ransomware are various types of malware classified based on their purpose and mode of spreading. The number of systems infected with malware has risen to 812.67 million, from 12.4 million in 2009 [1] as shown in Figure 5.1. The total damage from cyberattacks is estimated to be $6 trillion in 2021, with the number expected to rise to $10.5 trillion by 2025.

DOI: 10.1201/9781003346340-5

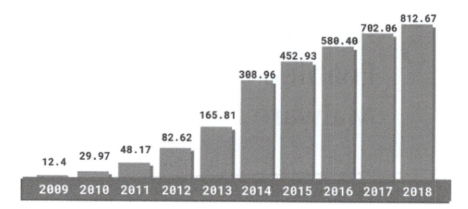

FIGURE 5.1   Malware infection growth rate (in millions) [1].

Once malware is downloaded onto a system or device, it gets converted to executable scripts and causes much damage by slowing down or even crashing the system or device. Malware such as adware and ransomware steal personal data such as bank information, accounts, passwords, etc. Researchers and industry have proposed several approaches to detect malware alike [2–5]. Malware detection is a process of evaluating system or device files and marking them as malicious or benign. Anti-Malware software vendors such as Kaspersky, Avast, and McAfee adopted signature-based malware detection, wherein unique byte strings fingerprint and identify malware files.

The traditional signature-based malware detection approaches were initially effective. But malware authors quickly developed several advanced methods, such as packing, obfuscation, and dynamic polymorphism, which evade malware detection systems easily. The signature-based methods are also slow to respond to new malware, as malware has to be first studied by experts, who then generate a signature to identify the malware. Heuristic algorithms are slow and error-prone, which led to the need for more intelligent malware analysis approaches that can automatically detect malware.

With the rise in access to economical computational power, the development of new and efficient ML algorithms has successfully demonstrated to be capable of learning data patterns and using them to classify data with a high degree of accuracy, depending on the dataset and algorithm used. ML has been widely used in malware detection, which is evident from the literature. Deep learning uses Artificial Neural Networks (ANNs) to learn and classify data. There have been several studies where deep learning, specifically CNNs and ANNs, has been used for malware detection [2, 6–8]. However, deep learning methods could be faster and more interpretable. Interpretability is an essential requirement for malware detection.

This chapter aims to propose an intelligent malware detection framework using ML and AI to classify files as either malware or benign and evaluate their performance. The framework uses an ensemble approach along with SVM, Decision Tree, and Random Forest to pick the best-performing model.

The primary objectives of our work are:

- **To develop an intelligent malware detection framework:** Code obfuscation techniques (such as packing, encryption, and polymorphism) can easily evade the signature-based malware approach. As a result, ML's significance in malware detection becomes increasingly important. We aim to propose an intelligent malware detection framework with a low false-positive rate using AI and ML models.
- **To create a knowledge base to utilize previous results:** To create a knowledge base, we propose an LSH-based embedded AI learner that keeps expanding its knowledge base by utilizing the previous results.
- **To achieve high accuracy and a low false positive rate:** We perform hyper-parameter fine-tuning to get the best performance because our focus is to maximize accuracy while minimizing the false positive rate.

The rest of the chapter is organized as follows. Section 5.2 presents a literature survey for malware detection using ML. The proposed approach is described in Section 5.3. This section also describes the feature selection, AI, and classification modules. Experimental results and analysis have been presented in Section 5.4, including dataset description and feature selection methods, followed by ML models. We conclude our work and present future research directions in Section 5.5.

5.2 LITERATURE SURVEY

This section comprises three subsections that review malware analysis and detection literature. In Section 5.2.1, the literature on malware analysis and feature extraction is reviewed. It contains two subsubsections. Section 5.2.1.1 deals with static analysis. While the second Section 5.2.1.2 reviews literature related to dynamic analysis. Section 5.2.2 covers the literature on malware detection, focusing on ML-based approaches. LSH and its application are described in Section 5.2.3.

5.2.1 MALWARE ANALYSIS AND FEATURE EXTRACTION

Malware detection is a two-stage process that includes feature extraction and classification/ clustering. The former involves studying a malware file and generating relevant features from it [9]. Our work focuses on Windows PE malware. Hence, the majority of the papers reviewed are concentrated in PE files. PE files form most of the malware samples [10]. Feature extraction is mainly of two types: Static Analysis and Dynamic Analysis.

5.2.1.1 Static Analysis

Static analysis of malware consists of analyzing a file without executing it. It is performed on the source code of the target program [11]. Attackers may use packing as a tool for obfuscation, i.e., hiding the code. Such PE files are deobfuscated, and then features are extracted from them. From the decompressed files, data regarding Windows API calls, byte n-grams, strings, opcodes (operational codes), and control flow graphs can be extracted [12]. Application programming interface (API) forms the core of the Windows operating system and can be exploited by malware authors [13]. Windows API calls deal with a program's low-level functioning and can be studied to understand the program's characteristics. Only in malware files the Windows API calls in the "KERNEL32.DLL" of "OpenProcess", "CopyFileA", "CloseHandle", "GetVersionExA", "GetModuleFileNameA", and "WriteFile" are found together and do not occur together in benign files [9].

Watters et al. [14] extracted malicious API calls and proposed a novel framework for building a completely automated API call extraction system. The authors have used an IDA assembler for unpacking, deobfuscating, and disassembling the executable file. They extracted API calls from the machine and mapped them to the MSDN library. API calls are categorized into six categories based on their behavior. Shakarapani et al. [15] explored API calls to generate signatures that can detect obfuscated malware files. They proposed two general malware detection methods, of which the Static Analyzer for Vicious Executables (SAVE) approach uses a Static API call sequence and Static API call set for analysis. Similarly, functions were applied to API call sequences, and classification was done on the scores. A threshold of 70% was set.

A novel approach, using Windows API call sequences and data mining techniques, proposed by Sitaraman et al. [16], uses a dataset of 66,703 executable files consisting of 51,223 malware files. It extracts API calls to generate signatures, compares them with existing ones using data mining techniques, and feeds them into a classifier. Their automated data mining system shows a high true positive (TP) rate of more than 98.5% and a low false positive (FP) rate of less than 0.025%. Das [17] used distinct API call sequences as a feature and applied data mining techniques. They experimented with six data mining classifiers, with the highest accuracy achieved by SVM (98.6%) and the lowest accuracy achieved by ID3 (Decision Tree). Distinct API call sequences based on the odds ratio were selected to constitute a feature vector. n-grams are all N-length substrings in the program code.

Nicholas et al. [12] discovered that assembly n-grams are not a helpful feature and offer poor performance. They proposed a novel approach of using binary opcodes for distinguishing assembly instructions. Using binary opcodes is crucial for generalizing the model. File-level information, e.g., MIME type, size, import libraries, the export table, and file relation graphs, can also provide valuable insight for malware analysis. Unlike dynamic analysis, static analysis can analyze all the different execution paths a program can take without actually executing the program [11].

5.2.1.2 Dynamic Analysis

Dynamic analysis pertains to the execution of malware in a controlled environment to study [9] its behavior. In it, features are extracted by executing the suspicious files on a virtual or controlled machine to study the program's behavior, i.e., information flow tracking and instruction traces, function parameter analysis, and function call monitoring. In dynamic analysis, the system configuration information, such as memory, system configuration details, and registry information, is known, providing an advantage over static analysis. Aman et al. [18] used dynamic malware analysis and extracted features using function call monitoring and information flow tracking.

Information flow tracking (IFT) approaches analyze program behavior from the program's standpoint, i.e., how the program processes and manipulates data. The authors have also compared several existing dynamic analysis tools and highlighted their drawbacks.

M. Ijaz et al. [19] extracted more than 2300 and 92 features using dynamic and static analysis, respectively. The features include registry keys changed, modified directories, API calls, system call sequences, etc. They achieved an accuracy of 94.64% and 99.36% using dynamic malware and static analysis, respectively. Dynamic analysis can rarely capture the malware's behavior as it can ultimately perform actions only upon meeting specific criteria [11].

5.2.2 MALWARE DETECTION APPROACHES

This subsection reviews the literature related to ML-based approaches for classification, and their description is as follows.

Ye et al. [9] presented an in-depth look at the malware industry and the anti-virus software vendors and outlined the main challenges and techniques used. The author's primary focus was on feature extraction and the classification/clustering of malware. The survey gives a brief overview of all the models and approaches used in malware detection and forecasts future trends. ML-based feature hashing can be used to detect malware files much more effectively than traditional signature-based detection systems [5]. Moon et al. [20] experimented with different lengths for the default vector size for feature hashing techniques, as the current vector size used is excessive and inefficient. They reduced the memory space used by more than 70%, significantly improving detection accuracy.

Windows PE header features are one of the most widely studied statically generated features [4, 6, 10]. Azeez et al. [10] proposed an ensemble-based approach that performs the base stage classification through a stacked ensemble of fully connected CNNs and one-dimensional CNNs, and the final type using an ML algorithm. They have explored 15 ML algorithms for the meta-learner, performed dimensionality reduction on the dataset, and selected 55 features. For the baseline model, Random Forest achieved an accuracy of 99.24% and a false positive rate of 2.13%. Using 40 and 50 neurons in the first and second layers, they reached an accuracy of 98.8%. The extra tree was the best meta-learner.

CloudIntell is a scalable cloud architecture-based system proposed in [21] that operates on a rich set of features obtained by static and dynamic analysis and uses 1,50,000 malicious files and 87,000 benign executables of Windows PE format. It contains a classification engine that uses the Random Forest. Another essential feature of this research is its focus on the practical application and scalability of the system. The authors analyzed several deployment techniques based on performance, responsiveness, and scalability. They achieved the best performance by boosting the Decision Tree, generating a 0.9910 area under the ROC curve.

While many researchers focus on large-scale features, such as API n-grams and opcode n-grams, small-scale features are also effective in understanding malware behavior [12]. Chen et al. [22] used features such as import libraries, PE section sizes, section permissions, and content complexities. They achieved the maximum accuracy (99.08%) for Opcode n-grams, with n as 4, and achieved 98.11%, 97.75%, and 97.01% accuracy for content complexity, PE section sizes, and PE section permissions, respectively.

Otherside, Zheng et al. [23] used strings, registry changes, and API sequences to determine whether a given sample is a modified version of a previously seen malware file. They converted each file into feature vectors and applied similarity functions to calculate the similarity values of malware files. This method requires accurate registry changes and captures API call sequences during execution. Capturing this information is only possible through the use of expensive virtual machines. It is the main drawback.

Ensemble Models have been explored and have shown positive results [6, 10]. Researchers experimented with 13 ML methods: Linear SVMs, KNNs, DTs, SGD classifiers, etc. These form a baseline model for a stacked ensemble of dense convolutional neural networks (CNNs), and a meta-learner performs the final classification. A dense CNN ensemble containing 30 and 35 neurons in each of the two layers performed the best with an accuracy of 98.3%, while the ExtraTrees classifier outperformed other models (98.8% accuracy).

The success of deep learning techniques in domains such as Natural Language Processing and Image processing has also inspired a lot of research in applying deep learning to malware detection. Deep learning is computationally expensive and time-consuming. However, it also has certain benefits, including using autoencoders for robust feature extraction, transfer learning, and better performance. Ye et al. [24] proposed a deep learning architecture using the stacked AutoEncoders.

(SAEs) model for malware detection, with the input resting on Windows application programming interface (API) calls extracted from the PE files. It had an accuracy of 96.3% and outperformed other baseline ML models. Datasets containing standard features such as n-grams, opcodes, and Windows API calls can use deep learning.

Rathore et al. [25] studied the application of deep learning using opcode frequency as a feature vector. Opcodes can contain some crucial insight into the payload of executables. For malware classification, the authors used supervised and unsupervised learning and the Malicia Project dataset [26]. Random Forest performed better than ANNs with an accuracy of 97.5% on the feature dimensionality-reduced dataset.

5.2.3 Locality-Sensitive Hashing (LSH)

Locality-sensitive hashing (LSH) is a randomized hashing algorithm for an efficient approximate nearest neighbor (ANN) search in high dimensional space [27]. Unlike a conventional hash, where the entire hash value changes dramatically even if only the contents of a one-bit change, the LSH technique assesses similarity by maximizing the chance of collision of similar data so that similar data have an equal hash value. Representative algorithms include ssdeep, simhash, and TLSH. The LSH scheme indexes all items in hash tables and searches for comparable items via hash table lookup. The hash table is a data structure composed of buckets indexed by a hash code. In [28], the authors surveyed a family of LSH algorithms used for similarity search and provided a theoretical overview of distance metrics and hashing algorithms. They considered various criteria like similarity, hash function, distance measure, and optimization.

LSH can be used in data mining to cluster similar files and extract data from file relation graphs. AESOP [29] is a scalable algorithm that leverages LSH to measure the strength of the inter-file relationships to construct a graph and performs large-scale inference on labeled and unlabeled files. It uses the MinHashing algorithm to calculate the Jaccard similarity between two sets and a dataset consisting of partial listings of the files on PCs to identify close relationships between files that frequently appear together on devices. The voluntary contributions of Norton Security researchers generated the dataset. AESOP accurately labeled 99% of benign and 79% of malicious files earlier than other state-of-the-art algorithms. It had a 99.61% TP rate for detecting malware, at a 0.01% FP rate.

Locality-sensitive hashes were used as input features for a feed-forward neural network to detect Javascript Malware [30]. Four LSH algorithms: Nilsimsa, ssdeep, TLSH, and SDHASH, were tested and evaluated. An accuracy of 98.05% and 97.79% was achieved by Nilsimsa and TLSH, respectively, on a dataset of 1.5 million samples. The succeeding subsections describe two LSH-based hashing algorithms, ssdeep, and TLSH.

5.2.3.1 ssdeep

ssdeep is a context-triggered piecewise hashing algorithm (CTPH) described by Kornblum in [27]. It uses two hashing methods: piecewise and rolling. The first, piecewise hashing, applies an arbitrary algorithm to discrete portions of byte strings rather than the complete file. The Fowler–Noll–Vo hash function, by Fowler et al., is the hashing algorithm used by ssdeep because it is a non-cryptographic hash function focusing on speed. The rolling hash is another hashing method that generates a pseudo-random result based on the input's current context. When a suitable range of bytes of piecewise hashing has happened, the rolling hash is used to trigger appending of the accumulated piecewise hash to a final hash.

5.2.3.2 TLSH

Trend Micro researchers Jonathan Oliver, Chun Cheng, and Yanggui Chen [31] proposed TLSH that can detect and cluster malware. The final hash is a 70-character hexadecimal string created by digesting a byte string with a sliding window of size five and Pearson hash, a fast non-cryptographic hashing technique used to map the relevant values to buckets. The digest body, represented as a hexadecimal text, is then created by separating the bucket array into quartiles q1, q2, and q3 based on the bucket counts. TLSH hash digests were used by Oliver et al. [31] in Hierarchical Agglomerative Clustering (HAC-T) and fast search for similarity in security to build a tree-based index that performs a quick search based on TLSH hash digests. The HAC-T algorithm is used for clustering, which can digest clusters in O(nlogn) time. The purity metric was used to evaluate cluster quality and achieved purity scores of 0.97–0.98 using labels from five major anti-virus vendors on a sample set of size 10 million. Further, the k-means algorithm and HAC-T clustering achieved a 9–12× speedup in [31].

The majority of papers surveyed used features extracted from static analysis. Although Dynamic analysis can be used, it is clear that static analysis is computationally efficient and performs better. ML is highly effective at learning properties from the binary code of malware files, and its performance depends on the dataset used, and the ML algorithm applied. LSH can effectively compare similar files and detect known malware variants, reducing computational costs. Ssdeep and TLSH are the industry standard for malware detection and clustering. In the next section, we present our approach, which overcomes several limitations of the existing approaches.

5.3 PROPOSED APPROACH

This section comprises one subsection and three subsubsections. Section 5.3.1 presents the proposed system architecture, which consists of three modules. These are described in Sections 5.3.1.1 to 5.3.1.3.

5.3.1 SYSTEM ARCHITECTURE

The system architecture comprises three modules: Artificial Intelligence, Feature Extraction and Selection, and Classification, as shown in Figure 5.2. The proposed architecture is robust and computationally efficient. The detailed description of the modules is as follows.

5.3.1.1 Artificial Intelligence Module

The LSH-based similarity and knowledge base form the AI module. This module helps intelligently identify variants of previously seen malware, thereby reducing detection time and improving efficiency. The knowledge base stores metadata (such as file size, code size, MIME type, etc.) regarding previously seen malware files in the form of hashes. The following hashes are calculated to fingerprint the previously seen malware files.

- MD5
- SHA1
- TLSH
- ssdeep

These hashes are referred to perform a database lookup to check whether the file matches known malware. The file can be classified as malware if a match is found. However, malware authors generally modify malware files slightly to escape signature-based detection. So we also hash the file using LSH-based hash algorithms like ssdeep and TLSH. They generate identical hashes for matching files and thus differ from regular hashing, which produces different hashes for similar files.

ssdeep provides a similarity function that calculates the similarity score of two files (hashes) to find how similar they are. The similarity score ranges from 0 to 100, where zero indicates that files are completely different and 100 implies identical

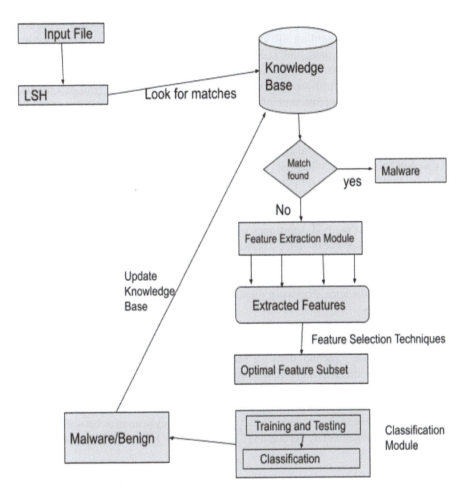

FIGURE 5.2   Proposed system architecture.

files. A knowledge base lookup is performed, and the ssdeep hash is compared to files in the database. An average similarity score is calculated if it exceeds the threshold value of 80. The file is classified as malware. A similarity score using TLSH is also calculated. This score is normalized and combined with the ssdeep similarity score for better performance and robustness. LSH is not very practical for small files; hence, we also use TLSH, which performs well for small file sizes. The knowledge base is updated every time a new malware file is detected.

5.3.1.2   Feature Extraction and Feature Selection Module
Our method analyzes two distinct features: API calls and TPF calls. The information included in the PE-optional header fields represents the TPFs. Therefore, we extract two main sets of features from the binary files, i.e., PE header-based features and API call sequence. PE format is that data structure that informs the Windows OS loader

about the information needed to handle the wrapped executable code. PE headers contain information regarding API export, dynamic library references, import tables, resource management data, and TLS data, among other things. "pefile" is a Python library that helps in extracting PE header information. We created a Python module that uses "pefile", a third-party multiplatform Python module, to read and interact with PE files and extract different information. For API calls, this extraction approach is based on a static examination of the IAT, and for TPFs, the PE-optional header.

We created a dataset based on these API calls and TPF headers as features. For a particular executable file, the column value for an API or TPF header feature is one if that API call is found; otherwise, it is 0. We use a feature selection technique to find the most optimal features for classification that reduces the dimensionality and over-fitting issues.

Feature selection is based on the Chi-square hypothesis test, a well-known statistical approach. This method determines whether two qualitative variables have a substantial relationship. The distance d between an observed frequency o and an expected frequency e, representing perfect independence between the variables, expresses this relationship. As a result, the strength of the correlation between two variables is proportional to the distance d between them. So, we looked at the relationship between the two variables.

To begin, there is a variable "Feature", which has two modalities: "present" and "not present". This variable indicates the presence or absence of a feature (TPF and API) in the "pefile". Second, there's a variable "PE-cat" which has both "malware" and "benign" modes and helps in distinguishing between "malware" and "benign" PE files. We began a Chi-square test by defining the two hypotheses HT0 (null hypothesis) and HT1 (alternative hypothesis), one of which will be accepted and the other will be rejected. The independence and dependency scenarios between the two variables are represented by HT0 and HT1, respectively. HT0 and HT1 are defined as follows:

- **HT0:** A feature's existence (API, TPF) is unaffected by the kind of PE file.
- **HT1:** A feature's existence (API, TPF) is linked to the kind of PE file.

After computing the Chi-square values for the retrieved features, we decide which of the two hypotheses, HT0 or HT1, would be accepted or rejected for each feature. To do so, we compared each feature's obtained Chi-square values (D2) to a threshold, which reflects the theoretical Chi-square value (2), and HT0 was approved (HT1 was refused) for every feature with D2.

According to the Chi-square hypothesis test, the features for which HT0 is accepted are considered irrelevant and will be progressively deleted. The Chi-square value is calculated by determining the degree of freedom (DF) and then selecting a significance level representing the likelihood of rejecting a hypothesis even if it is true.

The Chi-square score is normalized using the Phi coefficient. The importance of a characteristic (API or TPF) is proportional to its value, which runs between 0 and 1. As a result, we identified three subsets, including characteristics with values of 0.25,

0.5, and 0.75, respectively. Our goal was to determine the ideal amount of characteristics required to achieve the best level of accuracy while also reducing detection time.

5.3.1.3   Classification Module

The classification module is built using a supervised ML-based ensemble model. The ensemble model consists of three base learners, e.g., Support Vector Machine (SVM), Decision Tree, and Random Forest, which are described below:

- **Support Vector Machine:** It is a supervised learning algorithm that uniquely classifies the data points by identifying a hyperplane in an n-dimensional space, where n is the total number of features. For non-linearly separable data, the SVM kernel, which is a function that takes low-dimensional space as input and transforms it into higher-dimensional output space, is used.
- **Decision Tree:** A Decision Tree classifier creates a list of rules that can categorize data for a given set of attributes and their classes. The main advantages of Decision Trees are that they are easy to comprehend and visualize, require minimal data preparation, and can handle numerical and categorical data.
- **Random Forest:** The Random Forest classifier is a meta-prediction method that fits many decision trees on different subsets of datasets and utilizes the average method to improve the model's accuracy of prediction and control over-fitting.

The malware detection is modeled as a binary classification problem, and the binary executables are passed as input to the classification module, classifying them as malware or benign.

5.4   EXPERIMENTAL DESIGN AND ANALYSIS

This section presents experimental details and results and an analysis of the proposed approach. Section 5.4.1 describes the experimental setup, whereas the libraries and third-party software are covered in Section 5.4.2. The dataset is described in Section 5.4.3, While results are presented and analyzed in Section 5.4.4.

5.4.1   System Specification

To train and test the model, the following system configuration was created on the Google Colab platform.

- **Google Colab Platform (a.k.a Colab or "Collaboratory"):** It allows users to write and execute scripts in the browser, with
  - No configuration,
  - Free access to GPUs, and
  - Easy sharing

The specification includes:
- Disk: 107.72 GB
- RAM: 12.69 GB
- CPU: Intel(R) Xeon(R) CPU @ 2.20 GHz (1 core, 2 threads)
- GPU: 1xTesla K80, compute 3.7, having 2496 CUDA cores, 12 GB GDDR5 VRAM

5.4.2 FRAMEWORK & LIBRARIES USED

To extract features and build the ML models, we used the following libraries/ frameworks:

- **exifTool:** It is a free, open-source software program for reading, writing, and updating metadata in various files, including PDF, audio, video, and pictures.
- **ssdeep:** ssdeep is a program for computing piecewise hashes activated by context (CTPH). CTPH, also known as fuzzy hashes, can match inputs with homologies. Such inputs contain sequences of identical bytes in the same order. However, the content and length of the bytes between these sequences may differ.
- **TLSH:** TLSH is a library for fuzzy matching and generates a hash value from a file (minimum 50 bytes) that can be used for similarity comparisons. Similar files will have identical hash values, allowing similar objects to be identified by comparing their hash values.
- **sklearn:** This is for model implementation, splitting the dataset, calculating precision, recall, accuracy, and generating classification summaries.
- **numpy:** It is for matrix/array operations.
- **pandas:** It is for data frame management and related operations.
- **matplotlib:** It is for graph plotting.

5.4.3 DATASET DESCRIPTION AND GENERATION

In this subsection, we describe the dataset and define the generation of subsets using the feature selection approach. We provide examples of PE header features and depict feature selection using tables.

5.4.3.1 Dataset Description

We collected 439 malware binary executables from the GitHub repository maintained by the "zoo". It is a repository of live malware files. This set of malware files is diverse, containing viruses, worms, Trojans, and RATs. A total of 239 Windows OS executables were used as benign files.

These files were cross-verified using Virus Total. API calls and TPF headers are extracted from the following files.

Optional Header

- **MajorLinkerVersion**: It is an unsigned integer that identifies the state of the image file. The most common number is 0×10B, identifying it as a normal executable file.
- **MajorLinkerVersion**: It stores the linker major version number.
- **MinorLinkerVersion**: It captures the linker minor version number.
- **SizeOfCode**: It stores the size of the code (text) section or the sum of all code sections if there are multiple sections.
- **SizeOfInitializedData**: It captures the size of the initialized data section or the sum of all such sections if there are multiple data sections.
- **SizeOfUninitializedData**: It is the size of the uninitialized data section (BSS) or the sum of all such sections if there are multiple BSS sections.
- **AddressOfEntryPoint**: It stores the address of the entry point relative to the image base when the executable file is loaded into memory.
- **BaseOfCode**: When the beginning-of-code section is loaded into memory, this address is relative to the image base.
- **ImageBase**: The preferred address of the first byte of the image, when loaded into memory, must be a multiple of 64 K. The default for DLLs is 0×10000000.
- **SectionAlignment**: It is used to store the alignment (in bytes) of sections when loaded into memory.
- **FileAlignment**: It is used to capture the alignment factor (in bytes) used to align the raw data of sections in the image file.
- **MajorOperatingSystemVersion**: It stores the major version number of the required operating system.
- **MinorOperatingSystemVersion**: It captures the operating system's minor version **number**.
- **MajorImageVersion**: It captures the image's major version number.
- **MinorImageVersion**: It is used to store the image's minor version number
- **MajorSubsystemVersion**: It captures the subsystem's major version number.
- **MinorSubsystemVersion**: It stores the subsystem's minor version number.
- **SizeOfImage**: It stores the image's size (in bytes), including all headers, as it is loaded into memory.
- **SizeOfHeaders**: An MS-DOS stub, PE header, and section headers were rounded up to a multiple of FileAlignment.
- **CheckSum**: It captures the image file checksum. The following are checked for validation at load time: drivers, any DLL loaded at boot time, and any DLL that is loaded into a critical Windows process.
- **Subsystem**: The subsystem that is required to run this image.
- **SizeOfStackReserve**: It shows the size of the stack reserve. Only SizeOfStackCommit is committed; the rest is made available one page at a time until the reserve size is reached.
- **SizeOfStackCommit**: It shows the size of the stack to commit.

- **DllCharacteristics**:
  - **SizeOfHeapReserve**: It shows the size of the local heap space reserve. Only SizeOfHeapCommit is committed; the rest is made available one page at a time until the reserve size is reached.
  - **SizeOfHeapCommit**: It captures the size of the local heap space to commit.
  - **LoaderFlags**: It is reserved and must be zero.
  - **NumberOfRvaAndSizes**: It captures the number of data-directory entries in the remainder of the optional header. Each describes a location and size.

After collecting binary executables belonging to both malware and benign classes, we extracted 5945 API calls and 1461 TPF (PE file header features) from them. We generated a dataset using a Python library called "pefile" and also calculated the Chi-square and PHI values for API and TPF features shown in Tables 5.1 and 5.2, respectively.

TABLE 5.1

Overview of Obtained CHI-Square and PHI Values for Selected APIs

No	API's	CHI_SQUARE	PHI
1	RtlVirtualUnwind	339.577109	0.707708
2	RtlLookupFunctionEntry	339.577109	0.707708
3	RtlCaptureContext	339.577109	0.707708
4	__C_specific_handler	332.464435	0.700257
5	memset	277.203758	0.639418
....	....	....	....
5941	___p___fmode	0.001832	0.001644
5942	CharLowerW	0.001318	0.001394
5943	InvalidateRgn	0.001318	0.001394
5944	OpenProcessToken	0.000141	0.000456
5945	CoGetClassObject	0.000014	0.000144

TABLE 5.2

Overview of Obtained CHI-Square and PHI Values for Selected TPFs

No	TPF's	CHI_SQUARE	PHI
1	ImageBase5368709120	350.595235	0.719098
2	MajorImageVersion10	330.627615	0.69832
3	MajorOperatingSystemVersion10	328.790795	0.696378
4	SizeOfStackCommit8192	314.096234	0.680639
5	DllCharacteristics49504	314.096234	0.680639
....	....	....	....
1459	SizeOfCode45056	0.004832207	0.002669672
1460	SizeOfImage241664	0.004832207	0.002669672
1461	SizeOfInitializedData189952	0.004832207	0.002669672

Additionally, we removed the irrelevant features with a Chi-square value of less than 2.5 and obtained a list of 2891 API and 249 TPF features.

We divided those features into groups (subsets) according to their PHI values. At the end of the feature selection phase, we obtain three subsets of API calls, A1, A2, and A3, and three subsets for TPFs, H1, H2, and H3. The latter three subsets correspond to the PHI values, PHI ≥ 0.7, PHI ≥ 0.5, and PHI ≥ 0.25. We obtained 4, 16, and 265 APIs in A1, A2, and A3. We got 1, 9, and 35 TPF in H1, H2, and H3, respectively. We also used a fourth subset of APIs (A4) and TPFs (H4) that contained all of the extracted features (2891 API and 249 TPF). The goal of using the latter two subsets was to see if the proposed feature selection method improved the performance of our system.

5.4.4   Experimental Results

This subsection presents the experiments' results and also evaluates them using performance metrics such as accuracy, detection rate, and false positivity rate.

5.4.4.1   Results and Evaluation

We divided each of the datasets into training and testing datasets with a ratio of 80:20. Then we ran our testing data on our models and found classification accuracy (CA), Detection Rate (DR), and False Positivity Rate (FP).

Accuracy: Accuracy defines the percentage of files correctly classified and is given by the following formula:

$$AC = \left(\text{Number of correctly classified files/Total number of files}\right) \times 100$$

Detection Rate: Detection rate defines the percentage of malware files correctly classified among the set of malware files and is given by the following formula:

$$DR = \left(\text{Number of detected malware/Total number of malware}\right) \times 100$$

False Positivity Rate: The false Positivity rate defines the percentage of actual malware files wrongly classified as benign files and is given by the following formula:

$$FA = \left(\text{No. of malware files classified as benign/Total no.of malware files}\right) \times 100$$

Table 5.3 shows the results obtained on API subsets A1, A2, A3, and A4 for all four ML models.

The SVM classifier obtains the highest accuracy, which is **97.18%**.

Similarly, Table 5.4 shows the results obtained on TPF subsets H1, H2, H3, and H4 for all four ML models. The Decision Tree obtains the highest accuracy on the H4 dataset, which is **98.31%**.

Table 5.5 shows the results obtained on all 16 subsets, which are the combination of TPF and API subsets. The highest accuracy obtained by Random Forest and Voting ensemble classifiers on six subsets is **99.02%**.

TABLE 5.3

Experimental Results Using API Subsets. Best Performance Is in Bold

Subset	PHI	API Counts	Classifier	AC (%)	DR (%)	FP (%)
A1	≥0.70	4	Random Forest	94.35	98.31	1.69
			Decision Tree	94.35	98.31	1.69
			SVM	93.22	98.31	1.69
			Voting Ensemble	94.35	98.31	1.69
A2	≥0.5	16	Random Forest	94.92	96.61	3.69
			Decision Tree	94.92	96.61	3.69
			SVM	94.92	96.61	3.69
			Voting Ensemble	94.92	96.61	3.69
A3	≥0.25	265	Random Forest	96.05	98.31	1.69
	—		Decision Tree	94.92	96.61	3.69
			SVM	96.05	98.31	1.69
			Voting Ensemble	96.05	98.31	1.69
A4	—	2891	Random Forest	96.61	98.31	1.69
			Decision Tree	96.05	97.46	2.54
			SVM	**97.18**	**100**	**0**
			Voting Ensemble	96.61	98.31	1.69

TABLE 5.4

Experimental Results Using TPF Subsets

Subset	PHI	TPF Counts	Classifier	AC (%)	DR (%)	FP (%)
H1	≥0.70	1	Random Forest	93.22	98.31	1.69
			Decision Tree	93.22	98.31	1.69
			SVM	93.22	98.31	1.69
			Voting Ensemble	93.22	98.31	1.69
H2	≥0.5	9	Random Forest	94.92	98.31	1.69
			Decision Tree	94.92	98.31	1.69
			SVM	93.79	100	0
			Voting Ensemble	94.92	98.31	1.69
H3	≥0.25	35	Random Forest	97.18	97.46	2.54
	—		**Decision Tree**	**98.31**	**98.31**	**1.69**
			SVM	96.05	100	0
			Voting Ensemble	97.74	98.31	1.69
H4	—	249	Random Forest	97.74	98.31	1.69
			Decision Tree	**98.31**	**98.31**	**1.69**
			SVM	96.61	100	0
			Voting Ensemble	97.74	98.31	1.69

TABLE 5.5

Experimental Results Using Combinations of API + TPF Subsets. Best Performance Is Represented in Bold

Subset	Classifier	AC (%)	DR (%)	FP (%)
A1 + H1	Random Forest	94.12	98.53	1.47
A1 + H2	Random Forest	96.08	98.53	1.47
A1 + H3	Voting_Ensemble	98.53	98.53	1.47
A1 + H4	**Random Forest**	**99.02**	**98.53**	**1.47**
A2 + H1	Decision_Tree	95.1	97.06	2.94
A2 + H2	Random_Forest	96.08	98.53	1.47
A2 + H3	Voting_Ensemble	98.53	98.53	1.47
A2 + H4	**Random_Forest**	**99.02**	**98.53**	**1.47**
A3 + H1	Random_Forest	96.08	98.53	1.47
A3 + H2	Random_Forest	96.08	98.53	1.47
A3 + H3	**Random_Forest**	**99.02**	**98.53**	**1.47**
A3 + H4	**Random_Forest**	**99.02**	**98.53**	**1.47**
A4 + H1	SVM	97.06	100	0
A4 + H2	SVM	97.06	100	0
A4 + H3	**Voting_Ensemble**	**99.02**	**98.53**	**1.47**
A4 + H4	**Random_Forest**	**99.02**	**98.53**	**1.47**

TABLE 5.6

Result Analysis and Comparison with Different Papers

Paper	Machine Learning Algorithm	Accuracy (%)	False positivity Rate (%)	Features used
Azeez et al. [10]	Ensemble, Random Forest, CNNs	99.24 (RF)98.8 (CNN)	2.13	PE header features
Ali mirza et al. [21]	Random Forest	99.10	0.25	Static and Dynamic features
Robertas et al. 2021 [6]	CNN, Extra Trees, KNN, SVM	99.8	0.15	PE header features
Rathore et al. [25]	Random Forests, Deep Neural Networks	99.78	0.67	Opcode frequency
Sahu et al. [4]	Random Forest	89.47	—	N-gram Opcode

Table 5.6 shows the result analysis of different papers and is used to compare with the results obtained by our proposed approach.

From the graphs shown in Figures 5.3–5.5 and Table 5.6, we can see the accuracy of TPF and API features on increasing Phi values. In the graphs, the blue line indicates the accuracy of TPF features, and the orange line shows the accuracy of API

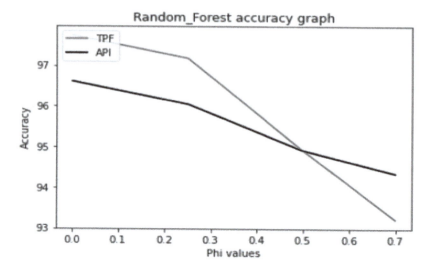

FIGURE 5.3   Accuracy graph for random forest classifier.

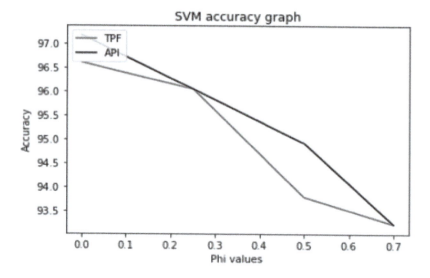

FIGURE 5.4   Accuracy graph for SVM.

features. As the Phi value increases, the total number of features on which the model has been trained decreases; thus, the model's accuracy decreases. We can understand the importance of feature selection by analyzing the obtained results. The model trained on a lesser but most relevant feature (A1 + H4) also gives us the highest accuracy, along with the model trained on all features (A4 + H4). Thus reducing the number of features reduces complexity and achieves the same optimal results (Figure 5.6).

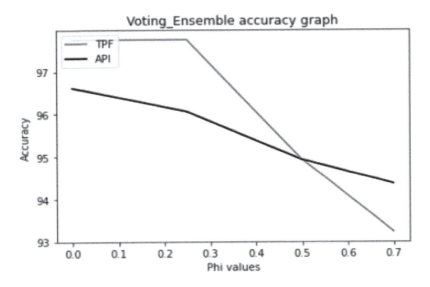

FIGURE 5.5 Accuracy graph for voting classifier.

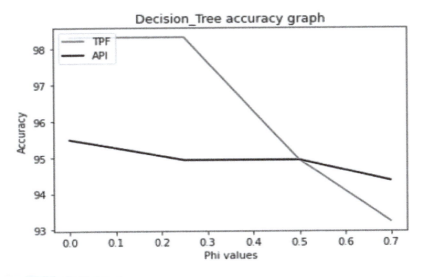

FIGURE 5.6 Accuracy graph for Decision Tree.

5.5 CONCLUSION AND FUTURE WORK

We proposed an Intelligent Malware detection framework using ML that used a dataset consisting of PE header features and API call sequence and performed feature selection using the Chi-square method. We used the ensemble approach and achieved the highest accuracy of 99.02% with a low false positivity rate of 1.47% using the Random Forest Algorithm.

As the dataset size is relatively small, future work will focus on training the model on a larger dataset. Additional features such as n-grams, opcodes, and file headers can be another scope of future work.

REFERENCES

[1] Purplesec Security. 2021 Cyber security statistics. https://purplesec.us/resources/cyber-security-statistics/. May 2021.

[2] Sanjay K. Sahay, Hemant Rathore, Swati Agarwal, and Mohit Sewak. Malware detection using machine learning and deep learning. arXiv:1904.02441, 2019.

[3] N. Udayakumar, T. Subbulakshmi, A. Mishra, S. Mishra, and P. Jain. Malware category prediction using KNN and SVM classifiers. *International Journal of Mechanical Engineering and Technology*, 10:787–797, 2019.

[4] Amit Sahu, Prachi Parwar, and Deepak Agrawal. A realistic approach to detect malware using binary analysis and machine learning. *International Journal for Science and Advance Research in Technology*, 5(9):112, 2019.

[5] Nishidh Shekhawat and Rejo Mathew. A review of malware classification methods using machine learning. *SSRN Electronic Journal*, 2021, 776–784.

[6] Robertas Damaševičius, Algimantas Venčkauskas, Jevgenijus Toldinas, and Šarūnas Gri-galiūnas. Ensemble-based classification using neural networks and machine learning models for windows PE malware detection. *Electronics*, 10(4), 2021.

[7] Xinjun Pei, Long Yu, and Shengwei Tian. Amalnet: A deep learning framework based on graph convolutional networks for malware detection. *Computers and Security*, 93:101792, 2020.

[8] Muhammad Furqan Rafique, Muhammad Ali, Aqsa Saeed Qureshi, Asifullah Khan, and Anwar Majid Mirza. Malware classification using deep learning based feature extraction and wrapper based feature selection technique, *arXiv preprint arXiv:1910.10958*, 2019.

[9] Yanfang Ye, Tao Li, Donald Adjeroh, and S. Sitharama Iyengar. A survey on malware detection using data mining techniques. *ACM Computer Survey*, 50(3), 1–40, 2017.

[10] Nureni Ayofe Azeez, Oluwanifise Ebunoluwa Odufuwa, Sanjay Misra, Jonathan Oluranti, and Robertas Damaššević. Windows pe malware detection using ensemble learning. *Informatics*, 8(1), 2021.

[11] Yanfang Ye. Research on intelligent malware detection methods and their applications. *Journal in Computer Virology*, 4, 2010.

[12] Richard Zak, Edward Raff, and Charles Nicholas. What can n-grams learn for malware detection? In *2017 12th International Conference on Malicious and Unwanted Software (MALWARE)*, Fajardo, PR, USA, pages 109–118, 2017. doi: 10.1109/MALWARE.2017.8323963

[13] Madhu Shankarapani, Subbu Ramamoorthy, R. Movva, and Srinivas Mukkamala. Malware detection using assembly and API call sequences. *Journal in Computer Virology*, 7:107–119, 2011.

[14] Mamoun Alazab, Sitalakshmi Venkataraman, and Paul Watters. Towards understanding malware behaviour by the extraction of API calls. In *2010 Second Cybercrime and Trustworthy Computing Workshop*, pages 52–59, 2010.

[15] Madhu Shankarapani, Subbu Ramamoorthy, R. Movva, and Srinivas Mukkamala. Malware detection using assembly and API call sequences. *Journal in Computer Virology*, 7:107–119, 05 2011.

[16] Mamoun Alazab, Sitalakshmi Venkatraman, Paul Watters, and Moutaz Alazab. Zero-day malware detection based on supervised learning algorithms of API call signatures. In *Proceedings of the Ninth Australasian Data Mining Conference – Volume 121*, AusDM'11, pages 171–182, Australian Computer Society, Inc, AUS, 2011.

[17] Om Samantray, Susant Das, and Satya Tripathy. A data mining based malware detection model using distinct API call sequences. *International Journal of Innovative Technology and Exploring Engineering*, 8:896–902, 2019.

[18] Waqas Aman. A framework for analysis and comparison of dynamic malware analysis tools. *Computing Research Repository (CoRR)*, abs/1410.2131, 2014.

[19] Muhammad Ijaz, Muhammad Hanif Durad, and Maliha Ismail. Static and dynamic malware analysis using machine learning. In *2019 16th International Bhurban Conference on Applied Sciences and Technology (IBCAST)*, pages 687–691, 2019.

[20] Damin Moon, JaeKoo Lee, and MyungKeun Yoon. Compact feature hashing for machine learning based malware detection. *ICT Express*, 2021.

[21] Qublai K. Ali Mirza, Irfan Awan, and Muhammad Younas. CloudIntell: An intelligent malware detection system. *Future Generation Computer Systems*, 86:1042–1053, 2018.

[22] Zhenshuo Chen, Eoin Brophy, and Tomas Ward. Malware classification using static disassembly and machine learning. *Computing Research Repository*, abs/2201.07649, 2022.

[23] Zhenshuo Chen, Eoin Brophy, and Tomas Ward. Malware classification using static disassembly and machine learning. *ArXiv*, abs/2201.07649, 2021.

[24] Shifu Hou, Yanfang Ye, William Hardy, Lingwei Chen, and Xin Li. Deep4MalDroid: A deep learning framework for android malware detection based on linux kernel system call graphs. *2016 IEEE/WIC/ACM International Conference on Web Intelligence Workshops (WIW)*, Omaha, NE, USA, pages 104–111, 2016. doi: 10.1109/WIW.2016.040

[25] Hemant Rathore, Swati Agarwal, Sanjay K. Sahay, and Mohit Sewak. Malware detection using machine learning and deep learning. In *Big Data Analytics*, pages 402–411. Springer International Publishing, 2018.

[26] Antonio Nappa, M. Zubair Rafique, and Juan Caballero. The MALICIA dataset: Identification and analysis of drive-by download operations. *International Journal of Information Security*, 14(1):15–33, 2015. doi: 10.1007/s10207-014-0248-7

[27] Piotr Indyk and Rajeev Motwani. Approximate nearest neighbors: towards removing the curse of dimensionality. In *ACM Symposium on Theory of Computing '98*, 1998.

[28] Jingdong Wang, Heng Tao Shen, Jingkuan Song, and Jianqiu Ji. Hashing for similarity search: A survey, *arXiv preprint arXiv:1408.2927*, 2014.

[29] Acar Tamersoy, Kevin Roundy, and Duen Horng Chau. Guilt by association: Large scale malware detection by mining file-relation graphs, In Proceedings of the *20th ACM SIGKDD international conference on Knowledge discovery and data mining (KDD '14)*, Association for Computing Machinery, New York, NY, USA, pages 1524–1533, 2014, doi: 10.1145/2623330.2623342

[30] Stefan Peiser, Ludwig Friborg, and Riccardo Scandariato. *JavaScript Malware Detection Using Locality Sensitive Hashing*, pages 143–154, 2020.

[31] J. Oliver, C. Cheng and Y. Chen, TLSH – A locality sensitive hash, *2013 Fourth Cybercrime and Trustworthy Computing Workshop*, Sydney, NSW, Australia, pages 7–13, 2013. doi: 10.1109/CTC.2013.9

6 IDS for Internet of things (IoT) and Industrial IoT Network

Rashi Makwana

Christ University (Deemed to be University), Bangalore, India

CONTENTS

6.1 INTRODUCTION

The IoT has fantastic opportunities to simplify our everyday life. The adoption of the IoT gives diverse infrastructures with the integration of rapid and constant records analytics. The IoT allows related tracking structures, sensor units, and miniature detectors which could trap actual-time facts to deliver greater multifarious and devoted offerings for complex structures (Barbosa et al., 2020; Cherifi et al., 2017). While those machines have many use subjects, they additionally bring protection and privateness situations because of the shortage of standardization in evolution, restrained assets, lack of upkeep, bobbing up IoT malware, negative layout standards, and manufacturer mistakes (Charyyev, Mansouri, and Gunes, 2021).

The IoT paradigm has newly been utilized in making clever environments, including smart towns and clever homes, with diverse software domains and related services. The goal of making such clever environments is to create human existence more powerful and comfy by way of solving demanding situations related to the residing environment, energy intake, and commercial needs (Kafle, Fukushima, and Harai, 2016). This goal is without delay reflected in the large growth within the acknowledged IoT-based total offerings and applications throughout numerous networks.

Smart environments include sensors that depict, and at the same time, manipulate operations. Wireless sensors, Wi-Fi verbal exchange strategies, and IPv6 help in the development of clever environments. Such environments are huge-ranging, from clever towns and smart houses to clever healthcare and smart services. The integration of IoT systems and clever environments makes smart items more realistic. For more than two decades, IDSs have stood as essential devices for the safety of networks and records systems. However, concerning traditional IDS strategies in the IoT is difficult because of its unique functions inclusive of limited-useful resource gadgets, particular protocol stacks, and requirements. An intrusion detection machine (IDS) is a protection device that works, in particular, inside the network of an IoT machine. An IDS deployed for an IoT method should be successful to look at packets of information and generate solutions in real-time, analyzing data packets in diverse layers of the IoT community with exclusive protocol accumulations, and adapt to exceptional technology inside the IoT environment (Gendreau and Moorman, 2016). An IDS this is designed for IoT-primarily based clever environments ought to picture beyond extreme conditions of low processing capacity, speedy reaction, and high-volume statistics processing. Therefore, conventional IDSs won't be fully suitable for IoT environments. IoT safety is a non-stop and serious issue; consequently, an updated model of the protection vulnerabilities of IoT systems and the effect of corresponding alleviation systems are required.

6.2 OBJECTIVES

This study will focus on the following:

1. Creation of IDS design for IoT model.
2. How can an IoT IDS be developed for the IoT paradigm?
3. Challenges presented by the IoT while still providing high detection capabilities expected of modern IDS solutions.

6.3 IoT PARADIGM

The IoT idea has been proven because of the founding of the Auto-ID Center at the Massachusetts Institute of Technology (MIT) in 1999. The Auto-ID Center created the electronic product code (EPC) numeral, which counted on radio frequency identification (RFID), in 2003. This concept is the generation of the IoT (IEEE Institute, Special Report: The Internet of Things, 2017).

However, the IoT is a nicely set up paradigm, and it is described in several methods from diverse perspectives. Thiesse and Michahelles (2006) defined the IoT as inclusive of hardware items and digital information streams based on RFID tags. The IoT functions and architectures delivered with the aid of exceptional requirements and industrial groups are explained in what follows.

The Institute of Electrical and Electronics Engineers (IEEE) describes the IoT as a set of objects with sensors that create a grid connected to the Internet (Minerva, Biru, and Rotondi, 2015). The International Telecommunication Union (ITU) describes the IoT in three dimensions, as a web that is unrestricted anywhere, anytime, and by using whatever and all people (SPU, 2005). The European Telecommunications Standards Institute (ETSI), instead of making use of the phrase "Internet of Things (IoT)", defines gadget-to-machine (M2M) contacts as an automatic transmissions system that makes judgments without forthright mortal intervention (Krčo, Pokrić, and Carrez, 2014).

The Coordination and Support Action for Global RFID-Related Activities and Standardisation (CASAGRAS) assignment has developed a new vision of the IoT that incorporates perspectives: the relationship of bodily entities with digital objects over an international network with no human intervention to maximum extent capability (Ray, 2018) and the splendid increase in IoT programs within conventional webs because of the significance of IoT trade (Ray, 2018).

Moreover, Cisco, a commercial association, works on IoT generation underneath the identity of the Internet of Everything (IoE). Cisco has translated the IoE belief as a community that consists of people, facts, matters, and methods. Thus, communication and sports are created in and pushed through this grid (Bradley et al., 2013).

6.4 IoT SYSTEM ARCHITECTURES

The scope of this challenge is to symbolize the IoT domain names and the diverse packages in these environments (IEEE, 2015). This IoT structure is separated into three layers: the software layer, the networking and facts communications layer, and the sensing layer.

According to Bandyopadhyay and Sen (2011), Han et al. (2013), and Khan et al. (2012), the available structure of the IoT is split into five layers that transit three domain names, specifically, the application domain, the network domain, and the physical area; as a consequence, the IoT can be custom-designed to suit the requirements of various clever environments. The software domain incorporates control and usage. The network surroundings are accountable for information transmission. The bodily area is answerable for knowledge collection. The capability of the different layers is discussed in what follows (Figure 6.1).

The perception layer is a hardware layer that consists of detectors and physical gadgets in diverse paperwork. These hardware components deliver identification, record storage, data collection, and fast processing. The data resulting from this layer is transmitted to the following layer (the network layer) to be despatched to the processing machine.

The network layer is a communication layer that transmits the information from physical gadgets or detectors to the processing device over confident traces working

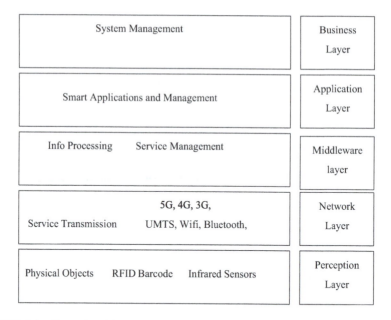

System Management	Business Layer
Smart Applications and Management	Application Layer
Info Processing Service Management	Middleware layer
Service Transmission 5G, 4G, 3G, UMTS, Wifi, Bluetooth,	Network Layer
Physical Objects RFID Barcode Infrared Sensors	Perception Layer

FIGURE 6.1 General architecture of the IoT. It consists of five layers according to Khan, Khan, Zaheer, and Khan (2012) Future Internet.

a conversation machine. The info output from this residue is despatched to the next layer (the middleware layer).

The middleware layer is accountable for service manipulation over IoT devices to finish connections between IoT gadgets that supply the identical provider. Moreover, the middleware layer holds the details coming back from the grid layer in a database to allow selection-making primarily based on information processing operations.

The application layer is responsible for the global management of IoT applications. The utility layer is based on the details processed in the middleware layer. Moreover, the software layer counts on the specifics of the numerous enforced IoT packages, along with clever industry and construction, metropolis, and fitness applications.

The business layer is likewise answerable for the worldwide control of IoT programs as well as carrier manipulation over IoT appliances. The enterprise layer bureaucracy is a commercial enterprise model that relies on the facts processed in the implemented layer and takes a look at the outcomes of those data processing operations.

6.5   CLOUD COMPUTING AND THE IoT

IoT structures consists of a massive number of contraptions and sensors buying and selling a considerable quantity of records and assisting an exquisite number of offerings. The control and research of this information pose precise unique situations, along with powerful processing, big storage, and excessive-speed networking abilities (Rao et al., 2012).

Cloud computing offers high computational electricity, great garage capability, and configurable resources with virtualization capabilities for exploiting huge portions of facts accumulated from IoT-based clever environments. With the integration of cloud computing systems and IoT-based totally smart environments, clever things may be accessed and achieved without difficulty, at any time and region, and higher offerings may be brought via the IoT version (Khan, Kiani, and Soomro, 2014).

According to Al-Fuqaha et al. (2015), one of the great challenges in working with a cloud computing system for the IoT is the synchronization between various cloud providers. A second project is gaining compatibility between regarded cloud carrier environments and IoT requirements. Security challenges are the fundamental element delaying the adoption of cloud computing by way of businesses and government establishments (Charif and Awad, 2014). Thus, the capacity to understand the specified safety restraints to satisfy the necessities of the IoT in a cloud computing forum is an important requirement. A strong and green safety answer such as an IDS is one viable alternative. Moreover, standardization, enhancement, and control for the deployment of IoT structures and their association with the cloud are additional challenges that must be accepted for proper solutions.

6.6   IoT AND SMART ENVIRONMENTS

The goal of smart environments is to create more-at-ease and more efficient human lifestyles by using detectors. IoT-primarily based smart environments facilitate the practical finishing touch of smart objects. Employing an IoT community, sensors may be monitored and managed remotely. According to Navigant Research, the global clever metropolis offerings call for is anticipated to boom by 93%, i.e., from 5 billion in 2017 to 9 billion US dollars by 2026 (Citron, Maxwell, and Woods, 2017).

Ahmed et al. (2016) mentioned that "The period clever refers to the capacity to autonomously attain and practice know-how, and the period environment refers to the environment". A clever metropolis is one sort of clever surrounding. The second issue of a clever city is incorporated expertise middle-operated by the IoT provider company, which provides expertise on offerings consisting of electricity, water, and gasoline.

Smart health, smart enterprise, clever buildings, and clever houses are different varieties of clever environments. The cause of such clever environments is to grant help through smart techniques based on the information accrued by IoT-enabled sensors (Figure 6.2).

Smart environments founded on the IoT paradigm have certain unique features, and therefore, unique necessities arise in the deployment of such environments. For example, faraway tracking and remote management abilities are had to permit clever gadgets to organize technique statistics and carry out operations remotely. Moreover, the functionality to make judgments is a crucial feature of this sort of system. A smart object must be certified to make thoughtful choices without human intervention via the usage of information mining and different techniques for dragging useful records.

Under these characteristics, clever environments provide specific capabilities that may be utilized to enhance the Quality of Service (QoS) of person programs. Real-time details are any such factor. Smart gadgets can organize and interpret facts and

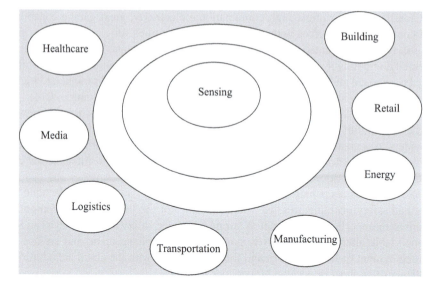

FIGURE 6.2   IoT-based smart environments. The architecture of the IoT and the extent of the IoT market according to Minerva, Biru, and Rotondi D (2015).

make intelligent judgments in real-time. Moreover, the fee-effectiveness of cloud packages may be operated to enhance the QoS of smart environment packages. The integration of clever IoT environments affords further possibilities concerning the QoS of services and packages.

6.7   IoT TECHNOLOGY FOR DEVELOPING SMART CITIES

Many national governments are running at the strands and communication genera-tion (ICT) infrastructure to decode the problems involved in conventional public management affairs. One of the countless modern-day and realistic solutions is to inaugurate a smart metropolis (Zanella et al., 2014). The clever metropolis imagina-tion and prescient are one aspect of the concept of smart environments.

There are many advantages to reworking fashionable public offerings and aids into a layout that takes gain of the smart town idea, which includes increasing the charge of public services and decreasing the running prices of public administration (Schaffers et al., 2011). However, the control and implementation of public services in a smart metropolis require an effective community, along with an IoT network.

Additionally, there are many boundaries to the area of an IoT-based clever town. The wonder, complexity, and technical demanding situations of IoT structures pose the greatest difficulty. Furthermore, with the lack of widely mentioned definitions for clever town features, political and economic boundaries manipulate the smart town's imagination and prescient from being efficaciously carried out.

The Padova Smart City in Italy is a thriving illustration of a clever town that has overcome these obstacles. The most important purpose of selecting the Padova Smart

City is to lay out ICT answers for public management structures using various varieties of records and eras.

The overall performance of the IoT paradigm for growing clever environments, mainly smart cities, faces numerous technical demanding situations. Among these, accuracy, latency, and fashionable bandwidth have sizeable consequences in many smart environments, together with business and healthcare environments. Because of the need to hold an increasing number of users and smart gadgets in IoT networks and the related technology of increasingly massive portions of records, scalable computing systems, together with cloud computing, are important. Such media can enhance the implementation of records management assistance in IoT structures and the QoS of smart environment packages (Taherkordi and Eliassen, 2016).

6.8 SECURITY CHALLENGES IN IoT-BASED SMART ENVIRONMENTS

The protection of IoT structures is extremely difficult due to the increasing range of benefits and customers in IoT networks. The integration of IoT techniques and clever environments creates smart gadgets more successfully. However, the consequences of IoT security exposures are extraordinarily risky in vital clever environments utilized in areas that include medication and industry. In IoT-primarily based clever environments without robust protection systems and programs may be in danger. Confidentiality, integrity, and availability are three crucial protection principles of applications and offerings in IoT-based totally smart environments; for this reason, to manage those situations, information security in IoT systems needs extra attention. For example, IoT-based totally smart homes face safety- and privacy-demanding situations that tour all layers of the IoT architecture (Ali and Awad, 2018).

The layout of clever environments in real international encounters two amazing obstacles: a) the security of IoT systems and b) the complexity and compatibility of IoT environments. Attacks including DoS or DDoS attacks on IoT networks impact IoT offerings and consequently affect the offerings added by using smart environments.

Researchers have been looking at the safety challenges of the IoT from many diverse points of view, one among which is the protection vulnerability of IoT transmission protocols (Granjal, Monteiro, and SáSilva, 2015). This survey concentrates on IDSs for the IoT paradigm, independent of any exact protocol; as a consequence, this becomes one of the security challenges confronting IoT structures based entirely on the IEEE definition and the unrestricted IoT structure.

The security challenges in IoT systems are connected to safety problems taking place within the numerous IoT layers. Physical harm, hardware failure, and strength barriers are demanding situations encountered in the physical layer. DoS attacks, gasping, gateway attacks, and unauthorized access are challenges applicable to the community layer. Hostile code attacks, software exposures, and software bugs are challenges encountered in utility (Kumar, Vealey, and Srivastava, 2016).

According to Liu et al. (2017), the safety-related problems of any IoT system can be categorized into four types: authentication and bodily threats, confidentiality dangers, facts integrity problems, and privacy troubles.

The authentication-related problem and bodily dangers are the first challenges that affect an IoT device. The belief layer contains several IoT gadgets, which include sensors, that rely upon their safety systems; for that reason, they may be liable to bodily assaults.

Confidentiality-related risks emerge among IoT instruments and the gateways in the community layer. The aid-restrained essence of the low-level machines in IoT structures poses an indirect project regarding the confidentiality of facts communicated in IoT networks (Trappe, Howard, and Moore, 2015).

One-third elegance of safety challenges includes the integrity of the facts between blessings and programs. Data integrity crises rise while imitating attacks or when noise influences an IoT gadget. DoS, DDoS, and probe attacks are incidental assaults that can damage IoT applications and services.

The demanding situations of the fourth kind are related to privateness. Information privacy is a crucial element of safety in IoT structures. Different IoT members use various styles of entity identity technologies; for that reason, each entity has its label tag, which maintains personal, vicinity, and motion details. Managing and gazing at the programs and services in an IoT device approach figure out know-how privateness at hazard; for instance, the usage of a machine learning in a deep packet inspection method for authorized functions inside an IoT device is meant to be a breach of information. Any invasive access to the coping system without consent jeopardizes the records and privacy of IoT customers.

Real-world applications of IoT systems face multiple open demanding situations. The open safety challenges concerning IDS features are recognized with the aid of Bandyopadhyay and Sen (2011), Khan et al. (2012), Kumar, Vealey, and Srivastava (2016), and Jing et al. (2014).

A smart environment that includes IoT technology is meant to be a complex method as it includes numerous developments from distinct companies primarily based on diverse technology that don't speak a common language. Therefore, standardization is yet another important element of safety in IoT techniques. Creating a common IoT architecture installed on one non-unusual generation for all providers and producers might improve the interoperability of the safety functionalities of all entities and detectors in an IoT gadget. The fulfillment of this integration will lean on cooperation among businesses to expand. Such standardization will significantly lessen IoT network protection.

A single rich penetration of one or more home equipment can jeopardize the protection of a whole IoT machine and induce damage to its packages and offerings, particularly from a commercial point of view (Forsström et al., 2018). Thus, the overall performance of an important protection device in an IoT system is based on the energy of the security for man or woman IoT devices, which in turn counts on energy and remembrance elements. Consequently, power and memory constraints are believed to pose averting protection-demanding situations in IoT systems. To handle those challenges, lightweight security answers and lightweight encryption and decryption processes are required. These answers and methods must be appropriate in exceptional IoT domain names and should meet the security situations without influencing the QoS.

6.9 IDSs: A HISTORICAL OVERVIEW

Monitoring and interpreting consumer knowledge, grids, and offerings via stagnant visitor exhibitions and research are precious instruments for operating grids and uncovering protection exposures right away (Rubio-Loyola, Sala, and Ali, 2008a). An IDS is a tool for looking at traffic statistics to recognize and shield against intrusions that endanger the confidentiality, integrity, and availability of an information device (Ghorbani, Lu, and Tavallaee, 2010) (Figure 6.3).

The features of an IDS can be split into three phases. The first is the monitoring degree, which depends on network-primarily based or host-based detectors. The second phase is the evaluation stage, which depends on feature extraction strategies or layout name techniques. The final level is the detection degree, which relies upon anomaly or mishandling intrusion detection. An IDS grabs a duplicate of the statistics of visitors into an intake gadget after which it explores this replica to look for potential dangerous moves (Anwar et al., 2017).

The image of an IDS as a data safety system has evolved significantly over the past 30 years. During those years, investigators have supplied one-of-a-kind approaches and strategies for covering diverse types of systems using IDSs. In 1987, Denning proposed an intrusion detection version that might resemble malicious invasion behavior against the ordinary version for the device of the declaration (Denning, 1987).

In 2000, Axelsson (Stefan, 2000) analyzed 20 research tasks on IDSs. He recorded 14 IDSs depending on host-primarily based procedures, IDSs relying on community-based processes, and three IDSs leaning on both host-based totally and network-primarily based strategies. However, the IDS model used in the research may became outdated and concentrated more on the local device than on network visitors.

In 2013, Ganapathy et al. (2013) brought up a survey on intelligent strategies for feature selection and class-based intrusion detection in networks. This survey evaluated fuzzy techniques, neural networks, genetic algorithms, neuro-genetic algorithms, particle swarm intelligence, and difficult units for Internet protection and

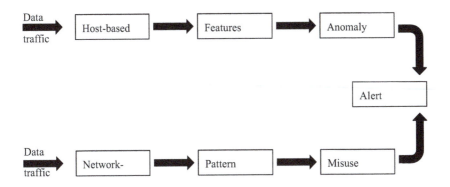

FIGURE 6.3 IDS operations. IDS operations can be divided into the monitoring stage, the analysis stage, and the detection stage.

QoS enhancement. Moreover, these writers presented a new function section and classification algorithms. In their research, they employed 19 flow-primarily based capabilities incorporating primary features, packet content material features, and traffic capabilities.

In 2014, Mitchell and Chen (2014) analyzed 60 papers on IDSs advanced for Wi-Fi environments. Their survey established the strengths and weaknesses of IDS processes for Wi-Fi local vicinity networks (WLANs), Wi-Fi mesh networks (WMNs), Wi-Fi personal area networks (WPANs), wireless sensor networks (WSNs), cyber-physical systems (CPSs), advert hoc networks, and mobile telephony. They confirmed that an anomaly-based IDS is a drastically suitable strategy for mobile telephony strategies. However, such IDSs face demanding situations in terms of their extended fake high-quality tempo and computational intricacy. High fake rates decrease the QoS of a cell network gadget. If any person's bundle is settled via blunders, the user will suffer billing errors, and the person's bundle might be postponed. Anomaly-based IDSs additionally face challenges concerning illegal studies techniques, which include packet-based methods, that infringe on consumer privacy. This survey advised detection latency as an important metric for use in destiny research.

Also in Butun et al. (2014), surveyed 18 papers focusing on cellular ad hoc networks (MANETs) and 17 papers concentrating on WSNs in their survey on IDSs in WSNs. These writers were involved in the feasibility of the usage of techniques evolved for MANETs in WSNs. The capability security attacks in opposition to WSNs had been separated into two categories: passive attacks and active assaults. These authors showed that IDSs are very crucial for the security of WSNs and that an IDS invented for a WSN should have unique special traits, which include low electricity intake. A WSN is a useful resource-limited surrounding, so the significance of an IDS in a WSN is predicated on its impact on the strength intake of the community.

Button et al. (2014) cautioned the use of a hierarchical IDS model to crack the power intake problem in WSNs. Following the suitable utility necessities, Butun et al. endorsed the usage of a dispersed IDS gadget for mobile applications, a centralized IDS gadget for stationary packages, and a hierarchical IDS approach for cluster-based total programs.

6.10   INTRUSION DETECTION SYSTEM (IDS): CLASSIFICATION

An IDS is a system that video-displays units' network traffic for suspicious hobbies and triggers an alert when such motion is found. It is software that monitors a network or a way for dangerous action or policy breaching. Any adverse incident or violation is usually registered either to an administrator or accrued centrally using a security information and event management (SIEM) system. A SIEM device integrates outcomes from more than one asset and makes use of alarm-filtering strategies to differentiate malicious movement from false alarms.

Although intrusion detection structures test grids for probably opposed activity, they're also disposed to faulty alarms. Hence, communities need to fine tune their IDS products when they first deploy them. Intrusion prevention structures also screen network programs inbound the machine to prevent malicious activities imposed by it and send caution messages right away.

6.10.1 Classification of Intrusion Detection System

IDS are classified into five types as follows.

1. **Network Intrusion Detection System (NIDS):** Network intrusion detection systems (NIDS) are located at an organization within the network to analyze site visitors from all machines on the network. It serves as a statement of handing visitors at the entire subnet and checks the gridlock that is handed by the organization of recognized attacks. Once an attack is recognized or atypical conduct is observed, a signal may be sent to the administrator. An example of a NIDS is establishing it at the subnet in which firewalls are placed to see if anyone is trying to crack the firewall.

2. **Host Intrusion Detection System (HIDS):** Host intrusion detection systems (HIDS) operate on independent hosts or appliances in the community. A HIDS scans the incoming and outgoing packages from the device most effectively and will caution the administrator if the suspect or malicious interest is observed. It takes a shot of current machine documents and compares them with the sooner snapshot. If the analytical gadget documents were revised or deleted, an alert is transferred to the administrator to explore.

3. **Protocol-Based Intrusion Detection System (PIDS):** Protocol-primarily based intrusion detection machine (PIDS) contains a technique or agent that could still stay on the front end of a server, managing and analyzing the protocol among a person/device and the server. It is trying to relax the web server by frequently looking at the HTTPS protocol flow and receiving the associated HTTP protocol. As HTTPS is encrypted and contents are unreadable, this is less susceptible to attacks.

4. **Application Protocol-Based Intrusion Detection System (APIDS):** An Application Protocol-Based Intrusion Detection System (APIDS) is a system or agent that generally rooms within a set of servers. It determines the intrusions by tracking and studying the transmission of utility-specific protocols. For example, this would examine the SQL protocol to the middleware because it transacts with the database in the Internet server.

5. **Hybrid Intrusion Detection System:** Hybrid intrusion detection device is created by the combination of two or more techniques of intrusion detection gadgets. In the hybrid intrusion detection approach, host agent or device data are included with community understanding to create a comprehensive view of the network device. A hybrid intrusion detection device is more realistic in the evaluation of the alternative IDS. The prelude is an instance of hybrid IDS.

6.11 DETECTION METHOD OF IDS

1. **Signature-Based Method:** Signature-based IDS witnesses the invasions primarily based on particular strategies together with several bytes or digits of ones or a variety of zeros in the community site visitors. It is additionally observed primarily based on the already known opposing coaching

collection this is utilized by the malware. The detected practices in the IDS are known as signatures. Signature-based IDS can efficaciously come across the attacks whose pattern (signature) already exists in the device, but it is pretty hard to trap the new malware episodes as their pattern (signature) isn't always acknowledged.

2. **Anomaly-Based Method:** Anomaly-primarily based IDS is used to detect zero day attacks as new malware is created unexpectedly. In anomaly-based IDS, these IDSs use normal class to train the machine learning model, and when a deviation is seen during testing, it is considered to be suspicious. The gadget getting to know the primarily based method has a better-generalized impact on the assessment of signature-based IDS as those measures may be skilled and consistent with the packages and hardware configurations.

6.12   COMPARISON OF IDS WITH FIREWALLS

Both IDSs and firewalls are connected for network protection but an IDS differs from a firewall in that a firewall examines outwardly for intrusions to prevent them from taking place. Firewalls restrict access among networks to control intrusion and if a seizure is from within the network, it doesn't trigger an alarm. An IDS describes a meant intrusion once it has transpired after which it indicates an alarm.

6.13   DISCUSSION

Integrity, confidentiality, and availability are three crucial elements in IoT systems. In most cases, applications that use well-known IoTs are imagined to be important, along with industrial and medical programs. On the one hand, these programs may be actual-time applications; for that reason, network uncertainty and latency instantly influence their performance. On the other hand, assaults which include DoS, DDoS, probing, and RPL invasions can impair the usability of those packages. Thus, protection problems may be regarded as an existence-threatening state of affairs in e-fitness systems, for instance. Therefore, effective protection standards are wished for in IoT networks. Such a security mechanism should defend the IoT network and its aids without affecting the device's execution or consumer privacy.

Moreover, IoT-based smart environments encompass a large spectrum of contraptions, sensors, and IoT entities from numerous carriers and are installed on diverse IoT systems. Thus, interoperability issues manage the emergence of IoT generation at a massive rate. Interoperability and standardization troubles must be taken into consideration in growing IDSs for IoT-primarily based clever environments.

IoT network's efficiency concerns; for that reason, a lightweight IDS that needs only a small digit of computational techniques is wanted. In a HIDS, the IoT gadgets need to concurrently achieve the critical computational approaches for the IDS and IoT offerings. Thus, power assets and battery life should be regarded in HIDS designs. Because of the energy and memory constraints of IoT systems, the electricity consumption, processing time, and overall performance overhead of an IDS are critical overall performance metrics. Thus, these metrics need to be evaluated when growing IDSs for IoT-based totally smart environments. These troubles should acquire a full-size awareness inside the analysis of HIDSs for such instances.

Privacy is yet another vital detail in IoT systems. Deep packet evaluation techniques have been deemed to be a breach of privacy. Such methods and different techniques with comparable functions are consequently avoided. Moreover, the blockade of ordinary information applications issues IoT programs and benefits. This effect could be very dangerous, particularly for important and actual-time packages, such as commercial and medical programs. Therefore, a smart machine without a deep packet examination assumes that methods inside the IoT device will manage any unauthorized entry to IoT entities. A new IDS design with a considerably low FPR and increased detection precision is needed for utility in critical and real-time programs due to the fact that traditional IDSs cannot fulfill those conditions.

IDS placement is also an extreme hassle that needs to be taken into consideration while making any type of IDS, whether or not it is a NIDS or a HIDS. The placement of the IDS inside the IoT community will affect the winning performance of the IDS. There are two to-be-had IDS placement techniques: centralized and allotted. The centralized strategy not only indicates the benefit of centralized management but can also guide design processing overload, which may additionally involve the QoS in IoT networks. The distributed method has the blessings of decreasing the amount of monitored gridlock and improving processing functionality. However, executing an IDS in distinct elements of an IoT community is a venture due to the related handling troubles.

Finally, there's necessity for a stable database that is up to date and combined with IoT packages and services. These databases might be very beneficial for straining diverse IDS types and strategies in IoT environments. The capacity to gain success and influential IDS comparisons will depend on these databases.

6.14 CONCLUSION

As the quantity of IoT users, offerings, and programs grow, a pressing requirement for a robust and mild protection decision that is suitable for use in IoT domain names is present. Furthermore, IoT networks are the foundation of clever environments; as a result, any flaw within the safety of these IoT networks will instantly affect the smart environments wherein they're established. Attacks including DoS, DDoS, probing, and RPL attacks problem the advantages and packages proposed in IoT-based clever environments; therefore, the safety of IoT environments is an extremely serious hassle. An IDS is one capability solution for this issue. This chapter offered a survey of IDSs for IoT environments. Suggestions for designing a robust and lightweight IDS have been additionally benefits.

In this survey, several papers had been analyzed. These papers specifically examine the introduction and overall performance of IDSs for providers inside the IoT paradigm that can be worried in smart environments. The traits of all IDS strategies provided in these papers have been interpreted. Moreover, this chapter presented a few pointers that need to be evaluated while growing an IDS for the IoT, consisting of the requirement for a strong and light system with a proper placement method that does not adversely impact the integrity, confidentiality, and availability of the IoT area. This takes a look at found out that there may be a need to develop an included IDS that can be provided in IoT-based totally smart environments. This method will need to be examined on a unified IoT database. The query of the positioning strategy ought to be taken into consideration in this design.

Future creation will discover the advent of an excessive-performance hybrid IDS especially designed for IoT-based clever environments primarily based on the pointers of this analysis. Moreover, the security exposures of IoT-permitting technology and protocols can be evaluated in the IDS design. In addition, the IDS can be achieved on programmable reconfigurable hardware appliances, inclusive of FPGAs, to facilitate adaptation to IoT-based totally smart environments. The strategy needs to be suitable for both distributed and centralized placement systems and should feature the capacity to glimpse into exceptional sorts of assaults.

REFERENCES

Ahmed E, Yaqoob I, Gani A, Imran M, Guizani M (2016) Internet-of-things-based smart environments: State of the art, taxonomy, and open research challenges. *IEEE Wirel Commun* 23(5):10–16.

Al-Fuqaha A, Guizani M, Mohammadi M, Aledhari M, Ayyash M (2015) Internet of things: A survey on enabling technologies, protocols, and applications. *IEEE Commun Surv Tutor* 17(4):2347–2376.

Ali B, Awad AI (2018) Cyber and physical security vulnerability assessment for IoT-based smart homes. *Sensors* 18(3):1–17.

Anwar S, Mohamad Zain J, Zolkipli MF, Inayat Z, Khan S, Anthony B, Chang V (2017) From intrusion detection to an intrusion response system: Fundamentals, requirements, and future directions. *Algorithms* 10(2):1–24.

Bandyopadhyay D, Sen J (2011) Internet of things: Applications and challenges in technology and standardization. *Wirel Pers Commun* 58(1):49–69.

Barbosa H, Gomez-Gardenes J, Gonçalves B, Mangioni G, Menezes R, Oliveira M. *Complex Networks XI: Proceedings of the 11th Conference on Complex Networks CompleNet 2020*. Springer Nature, 2020.

Bradley J, Loucks J, Macaulay J, Noronha A (2013) *Internet of Everything (IoE) value index*. Technical report, Cisco.

Button, M., Nicholls, C. M., Kerr, J., Owen, R. (2014) Online frauds: Learning from victims why they fall for these scams. *Aust NZ J Criminol* 47(3):391–408.

Butun I, Morgera SD, Sankar R (2014) A survey of intrusion detection systems in wireless sensor networks. *IEEE Commun Surv Tutor* 16(1):266–282.

Charif B, Awad AI (2014) Business and government organizations' adoption of cloud computing. In Corchado E, Lozano JA, Quintián H, Yin H (eds) *Intelligent Data Engineering and Automated Learning – IDEAL 2014*, 492–501. Springer, Cham.

Charyyev B, Mansouri M, Gunes MH (2021) Modeling the adoption of internet of things in healthcare: A systems approach. In *2021 IEEE International Symposium on Systems Engineering (ISSE)*, 1–8.

Cherifi C, Cherifi H, Karsai M, Musolesi M (2017) *Complex Networks & Their Applications VI: Proceedings of Complex Networks 2017*. In *The Sixth International Conference on Complex Networks and Their Applications*, vol. 689. Springer.

Citron R, Maxwell K, Woods E (2017) Smart City services market. Technical report, Navigant Research.

Denning DE (1987) An intrusion-detection model. *IEEE Trans Softw Eng* SE-13(2):222–232.

Forsström S, Butun I, Eldefrawy M, Jennehag U, Gidlund M (2018) Challenges of securing the industrial internet of things value chain. In *2018 Workshop on Metrology for Industry 4.0 and IoT*, 218–223. IEEE, Brescia.

Ganapathy S, Kulothungan K, Muthurajkumar S, Vijayalakshmi M, Yogesh P, Kannan A (2013) Intelligent feature selection and classification techniques for intrusion detection in networks: A survey. *EURASIP J Wirel Commun Netw* 2013(1):1–16.

Gendreau AA, Moorman M (2016) Survey of intrusion detection systems towards an end-to-end secure internet of things. In *2016 IEEE 4th International Conference on Future Internet of Things and Cloud (FiCloud)*, 84–90. IEEE, Vienna.

Ghorbani AA, Lu W, Tavallaee M (2010) *Network Intrusion Detection and Prevention, Advances in Information Security*, vol. 47. Springer, US.

Granjal J, Monteiro E, SáSilva J (2015) Security for the internet of things: A survey of existing protocols and open research issues. *IEEE Commun Surv Tutor* 17(3):1294–1312.

Han C, Jornet JM, Fadel E, Akyildiz IF (2013) A cross-layer communication module for the internet of things. *Comput Netw* 57(3):622–633.

IEEE (2015) Standards, Internet of Things, IEEE P2413. http://standards.ieee.org/develop/project/2413.html. Accessed 8 Jan 2017.

IEEE Institute, Special Report: The Internet of Things. http://theinstitute.ieee.org/static/special-report-the-internet-of-things. Accessed 8 Jan 2017.

Jing Q, Vasilakos AV, Wan J, Lu J, Qiu D (2014) Security of the internet of things: perspectives and challenges. *Wirel Netw* 20(8):2481–2501.

Kafle VP, Fukushima Y, Harai H (2016) Internet of things standardization in ITU and prospective networking technologies. *IEEE Commun Mag* 54(9):43–49.

Khan R, Khan S, Zaheer R, Khan S (2012) Future internet: The internet of things architecture, possible applications and key challenges. In *2012 10th International Conference on Frontiers of Information Technology*, 257–260. IEEE, Islamabad.

Khan Z, Kiani SL, Soomro K (2014) A framework for cloud-based context-aware information services for citizens in smart cities. *J Cloud Comput* 3(1):14.

Krčo S, Pokrić B, Carrez F (2014) Designing IoT architecture(s): A European perspective. In *2014 IEEE World Forum on Internet of Things (WF-IoT)*, 79–84. IEEE, Seoul.

Kumar S, Vealey T, Srivastava H (2016) Security in internet of things: Challenges, solutions and future directions. In *2016 49th Hawaii International Conference on System Sciences (HICSS)*, 5772–5781, Koloa.

Liu X, Zhao M, Li S, Zhang F, Trappe W (2017) A security framework for the internet of things in the future internet architecture. *Future Internet* 9(3) 1–10.

Minerva R, Biru A, Rotondi D (2015) Towards a definition of the internet of things (IoT). Technical report, IEEE, Internet of Things.

Mitchell R, Chen I-R (2014) A survey of intrusion detection in wireless network applications. *Comput Commun* 42:1–23.

Rao BBP, Saluia P, Sharma N, Mittal A, Sharma SV (2012) Cloud computing for the internet of things & sensing based applications. In *2012 Sixth International Conference on Sensing Technology (ICST)*, 374–380. IEEE, Kolkata.

Ray PP (2018) A survey on Internet of Things architectures. *J King Saud Univ Comput Inform Sci* 30(3):291–319.

Rubio-Loyola J, Sala D, Ali AI (2008a) Accurate real-time monitoring of bottlenecks and performance of packet trace collection. In *2008 33rd IEEE Conference on Local Computer Networks (LCN)*, 884–891. IEEE, Montreal.

Rubio-Loyola J, Sala D, Ali AI (2008b) Maximizing packet loss monitoring accuracy for reliable trace collections. In *2008 16th IEEE Workshop on Local and Metropolitan Area Networks*, 61–66. IEEE, Chij-Napoca.

Schaffers H, Komninos N, Pallot M, Trousse B, Nilsson M, Oliveira A (2011) *Smart Cities and the Future Internet: Towards Cooperation Frameworks for Open Innovation*. Springer, Berlin.

SPU (2005) The internet of things executive summary. Technical report, The ITU Strategy & Policy Unit (SPU).

Stefan A (2000) Intrusion detection systems: A survey and taxonomy. Technical report, Chalmers University of Technology Göteborg, Sweden.

Taherkordi A, Eliassen F (2016) Scalable modeling of cloud-based IoT services for smart cities. In *2016 IEEE International Conference on Pervasive Computing and Communication Workshops (PerCom Workshops)*, 1–6. IEEE, Sydney.

Thiesse F, Michahelles F (2006) An overview of EPC technology. *Sens Rev* 26(2):101–105.

Trappe W, Howard R, Moore RS (2015) Low-energy security: Limits and opportunities in the internet of things. *IEEE Secur Priv* 13(1):14–21.

Zanella A, Bui N, Castellani A, Vangelista L, Zorzi M (2014) Internet of things for smart cities. *IEEE Internet Things J* 1(1):22–32.

7 An Improved NIDS Using RF-Based Feature Selection Technique and Voting Classifier

Pankaj Kumar Keserwani
NIT Sikkim, Ravangla, India

Mridul Mittal
Navi Bengaluru, Bangalore, India

Mahesh Chandra Govil
NIT Sikkim, Ravangla, India

CONTENTS

DOI: 10.1201/9781003346340-7

7.1   INTRODUCTION

The Internet and workplace networks are strongly intertwined with global economic and business innovations. In daily life, common people communicate through the Internet and retain their personal information and business information in computer networks more than ever before [1]. The network administrators are responsible for any problems such as flash crowds, network factors failures, mistakes with configurations, malicious assaults, and more, in order to protect the information of different users [2, 3]. Government and private businesses need systems that can safeguard their information assets from unauthorized or unwanted access as well as prevent and detect intrusions in the network [4]. A network-based intrusion detection system (NIDS) refers to the process of monitoring and categorizing network flows to determine whether they are typical behaviors that occur frequently in a network or movements that could damage the security of information systems. Machine learning (ML) techniques are used in the field of intrusion detection systems. Machine learning is a methodology of data analysis that uses artificial intelligence to create analytical models [5, 6]. ML-based techniques have revolutionized in the last two decades [7]. Researchers can use ML-based techniques to deal with a variety of data sources, such as medical imaging, history, medical notes, video data, network flow, and so on. As a result, various themes and applications with remarkable performance outcomes in disease prediction, such as illnesses and heart difficulties, are introduced, as inference in Covid-19 research. Intrusion detection is one of the most trending topics in the current and future research areas, involved by both educational and industry sectors. A NIDS is an intrusion detection system to detect intrusions at the targeted network from the network flow. Its detection focuses on the network and host systems. The managed network is the only design that fits and functions with NIDS. The advantage of adopting NIDS is that it is less expensive and responds faster since no sensor tuning is required at the network or host level. The monitoring of traffic is almost real-time, and NIDS can detect assaults as they happen. It does, however, have the following limitations. There is no efficient way to detect the type of attack by analyzing encrypted network traffic [8, 9]. Furthermore, in a big or busy network, the traditional NIDS are facing a lot of problems in catching all packets. As a result, an assault initiated during a moment of heavy traffic may go undetected. It is extremely difficult and time intensive to discern between intrusion and typical network traffic activity. Malicious software (malware) has emerged as a significant threat to the development of intrusion detection systems (IDSs). As malware producers utilize numerous strategies to escape secret information and avoid detection by IDS, cruel attacks have become more complex and a huge problem to identify anonymous and unknown malware. Moreover, safety worries as well as zero-day assaults intended to target network users have accelerated. In 2016, more than 3 billion zero-day attacks were recorded [10], 9 billion records were misplaced or stolen by hackers [11], etc. According to a Symantec survey, nowadays, security breaches are becoming more common [12]. A huge number of cyber thieves are motivated to steal information, earn unlawful funds, and find new targets all around the world. Malware is developed with the intent of compromising computer systems and exploiting any vulnerability that may exist. With the usage of information technology, information protection has become very essential. An effective IDS for detecting complex malware is required. The goal of an IDS is to quickly identify different types of malware, which is impossible to do with a standard firewall. The development of powerful IDSs has become increasingly vital as the amount of computer malware is growing.

Machine learning has been optimized by the research community to quantify intrusion detection over the last few decades, and there is currently a demand for a modern, comprehensive taxonomy and testing for this latest activity. The traditional IDS that rely on known attack signatures has a low detection accuracy in real environments due weakness to detect novel attacks. To improve the findings in an IDS, many researchers have employed classic machine learning models, in-depth learning models, or hybrid models. Based on the placement IDS is of two types: Host-Based IDS (HIDS) and Network-Based IDS (NIDS).The HIDS is placed into the host to identify the malicious activities of the host. The NIDS is placed in a network to identify the network intrusions. To determine the sequence of intrusion on the network connection, an analyst must evaluate all of the data that are huge and wide. As a result, it requires a method to identify network intrusion and reflect current network activity. In this regard, a Hybrid NIDS has been proposed in this chapter. The proposed NIDS model uses a feature selection technique based on random forest (RF) to produce a feature subset of relevant features. The relevant feature subset is input to various state-of-the-art ML algorithms (such as random forest, k-Nearest Neighbor [k-NN], and Support Vector Machine [SVM]) and their output is applied to voting classifiers for better intrusion detection. The proposed model is evaluated using an NLS-KDD dataset to detect Denial of Service (DoS), Probe, Remote to User (R2L), and User to Root (U2R) attacks efficiently.

The main contributions of this work are:

- Development of an adopting the Hybrid NIDS model named RF-FS-Voting NIDS model where the output of classic machine learning approaches – RF, Decision Tree k-NN, and SVM – have been used as the input for the voting classifier.
- Evaluation of the developed and proposed NIDS model on the NSL-KDD dataset.
- In the evaluation, the proposed NIDS model has outperformed for anomaly detection as DoS, Probe, R2L, and U2R assaults.
- The proposed NIDS model has achieved better accuracy in comparison to other recent approaches for DoS, Probe, R2L, and U2R assaults or intrusions.

7.2 BACKGROUND STUDY AND RELATED SURVEY

7.2.1 BACKGROUND STUDY

In this section, the intrusion and intrusion detection techniques have been discussed:

7.2.1.1 Intrusion
The intrude is the act of forcing oneself in without invitation, permission, or welcome as defined by Merriam-Webster Online Search [13]. In computer networks,

the terminology "intrusion" is described as an unauthorized entry into a computer system or network. While the physical incursion into a location or circumstance differs from a technological trespass, the implications are the same. An intrusion is the collection of behaviors that tries to damage a resource's confidentiality, integrity, or availability (CIA) [14]. Confidentiality is an important pillar of the CIA; it validates user access to the information so that only the authorized user can access the particular information. Integrity ensures the quality and completeness of the information in the context of data security. Integrity-focused security procedures are intended to prevent information from being modified or unwanted use by an unauthorized system or user. It refers to the consistency and reliability of data across its full life cycle. Availability refers to the ability for authorized users to access information. It ensures that the information belonging to the authorized user is available for that user at the time of requirement. The availability is often connected with system uptime and reliability, which could be influenced by unwanted issues such as hardware disasters, unplanned software program downtime, and physical error, as well as malicious ones such as cyber attacks and insider threats.

Evasion, Insertion, Port Scanning, DoS attacks, U2R attacks, and R2L attacks are all well-known or common types of intrusions. Evasion attack is one of the most popular attack types which incurred during adversarial settings of system operations such as evading the detection approach by confusing spam emails content and malware code. In an insertion attack, the intruder investigates assault signatures of the IDS and uses the shielding method by inputting the data to avoid the IDS. In port scanning, the intruder glances over the ports of a network by sending a message to all of the network's ports to find out the open ports. The open ports are then used to break into the system or the network. This is accomplished by sending a message to all of the network's ports. By doing so, the intruder can determine whether ports are busy, already in use, and available to perform further attacks. In a DoS attack, the legitimate (authorized) user is prevented from accessing system resources such as blocking access to emails and specific websites. In a U2R attack, a local user (intruder) tries to gain root access illegally to a machine by exploiting various user vulnerabilities. In an R2L attack, an intruder tries to get unauthorized local access to a machine or workstation for exploiting its vulnerabilities.

7.2.2 INTRUSION DETECTION SYSTEM (IDS)

The recent technological advancements have encouraged users to share their information massively. Some fields such as medicine and military use cryptography to share their sensitive and critical data over the Internet. In cryptography, a secret key is used to encrypt messages so that only authenticated receivers can decrypt them and the message's authenticity is preserved. But the intruders, on the other hand, are not interested in decrypting messages. They are employing sophisticated tools to assault a network host and gain access to critical information. IDS is a lifesaver in this situation. Monitoring, detecting, and responding to unwanted actions are three critical security services provided by IDS [15, 16]. An IDS is able to identify attacks and deny or halt unauthorized access and act as the solution to attack classification problems. Observing and analyzing host and network activity, auditing system configurations, and evaluating the integrity of key information by calculating aberrant actions are the three services it normally performs. The IDS can be classified on the basis of placement and on the basis of detection.

Based on the placement, it is categorized into two types: Host-Based IDS (HIDS) and Network-Based IDS (NIDS).

1. HIDS: The IDS which is applied on the individual host or device in which it is placed is known as a host-based intrusion detection system (HIDS) [17]. It analyzes the incoming and outgoing packets of the device or host by logging them. The host agent keeps an eye on intruders and protects the system's security policies. One can use it to detect and respond to malicious or unusual behaviors that occur in the surroundings but it is not giving a complete view of a security posture on its own. To provide a complete view, its log data must be able to be correlated with other essential security data as well as recent real-world threat information, which is a complex and difficult task. Antivirus and HIDS serve various purposes. Antivirus is supposed to monitor all activities inside the system, but it doesn't care about buffer overflow attacks on system memory or malicious behavior of operating system processes. HIDS, on the other hand, checks and collects system data such as the File System, network events, and system calls to see if any inconsistencies have occurred.

2. NIDS: It is generally used to monitor network traffic on a network [18]. In general, the NIDS system works by detecting attacker signatures within the network. Occasionally, network professionals will inquire, "What can NIDS accomplish that a Firewall can't?" The firewall functions similarly to a perimeter security fence and a guard post at the front gate. However, the firewall is unable to detect what is going on inside [19]. Tunneling attacks and application-based assaults are the most common types of attacks on firewalls. In the daily lives of the people, communication systems are unavoidable. Business data processing, education and learning, cooperation, large-scale data collecting, and entertainment, all benefit from computer networks. The current computer network protocol stack was created with the goal of being transparent and user-friendly. This imposes computer network monitoring and protection on a continuous basis. The NIDS automates the monitoring process using ML-based learning.

Based on detection, the IDS can be classified basically into three types: Signature-Detection-Based IDS, Anomaly-Detection-Based IDS, and Hybrid-Detection-Based IDS.

1. **Signature-Detection-Based IDS:** This IDS uses fingerprints of known threats. Once malware or other hazardous content has been discovered, a signature is created and put to the IDS solution list to verify incoming data. The IDS may achieve a higher level of risk detection without false positives because all warnings are based on the identification of risky content. Signature-Detection-Based IDS is only confined to known attacks and cannot identify zero-day threats.

2. **Anomaly-Detection-Based IDS:** This IDS solution gives the protected to the network or a system by profiling itself based on normal behavior during its training. All subsequent actions are compared to the trained model, and any discrepancies are flagged as potential danger through an alert. While this approach can detect novel or zero-day threats, the difficulty of creating an accurate model of "normal" behavior means that these systems must equate false positives (negative warnings) which decreases its performance in the real environment.

3. **Hybrid-Detection-Based IDS:** In this IDS, both Signature-Detection-Based and Anomaly-Detection-Based IDS beneficial properties are utilized. As a result, it may detect potential assaults with a lower level of error.

7.2.3 RELATED SURVEY

In the related survey, it was observed that most of the intrusion detection techniques in a network follow signature-based methods. Due to the difficulty in finding training samples expressing the system or network behavioral dynamics and the endurance of built models, it is difficult to implement the anomaly-based detection NIDS model. In the implementation of network security, the research community is facing two primary challenges: first, continuously increasing network traffic data and, second, the increase in the number of connected users. To address the mentioned issues, it is necessary that the NIDS should analyze the network traffic speedily, effectively, and efficiently. The proposed NIDS utilizes an RF-based feature selection technique to produce a feature subset of relevant features to increase the speed of data processing for the detection. The relevant feature subset is input to various state-of-the-art ML algorithms: RF, k-NN, and SVM, and then their outputs are validated on the voting classifier for effective and efficient intrusion detection. Some of the related works are as follows.

Dhaliwal et al. [20] explored the Xgboost algorithm for designing network intrusion on the NSL-KDD dataset and compared it with the models trained using SVM, NB, and RF. The hyper parameter tuning of the Xgboost model made the Xgboost-based NIDS model better. Tang et al. [21] have used a deep learning approach based on self-taught learning (STL) for designing NIDS. Mansour Sheikhan and Amir Khalili [22] proposed a method for developing IDS and classifying intrusion patterns. For comparison of the performance of their model with other models created with machine learning algorithms, they used the multi-layer perception (MLP) with output weight optimization–hidden weight optimization (OWO-HWO) training algorithm using selected inputs based on the conclusions of a feature significance analysis. The IDS based on DCS rule extraction performed better at differentiating hard detectable attack categories, such as U2R, and had a lower false alarm rate (FAR). MLP outperformed other machine learning algorithms in terms of detection rate (DR) and cost per example (CPE), using only 25 input characteristics instead of the 41 standard features established by the knowledge discovery and data mining group (KDD). Kyaw Khaing [23] proposed a more desirable SVM version that used Recursive feature removal and the k-NN technique to perform the version's function ranking and choice. Recursive feature elimination (RFE) reduced redundant and recursive features, whereas KNN picked more appropriately than classical SVM. The incursion dataset, the KDD Cup 1999 dataset, turned into used for experiments and comparisons. The model used RFE to grade the features of intrusion detection records, and it also applied k-NN to growth class accuracy. For the KDD Cup dataset, it becomes proposed that the model was effective. Notwithstanding the fact that the model's fake terrible fees have been decreasing than the ones of traditional SVM, the version's precision degrees were now not significantly different. Furthermore, compared to an ordinary SVM, the time it took to detect an incursion in the version was notably shorter. It also had the advantage of requiring less time to run because of the usage of fewer capabilities for categorization. To create a multiclass intrusion detection system, Snehal et al. [24] suggested a decision-tree-based approach. SVMs were the first classifiers developed for binary classification. Classification applications could be used to solve multiclass challenges. A decision-tree-based SVM that combines SVMs and decision trees (DTs) could be a good way to address multiclass problems. This method could help the system run more efficiently by reducing training and testing time. The various methods for constructing binary trees divide the data set into two compartments from root to leaf, with each subset containing only one class. The binary-tree-building order has a significant impact on categorization performance. MeeraGandhi et al. [25] looked at how well four supervised machine learning algorithms performed in detecting four different types of attacks: DoS, R2L, Probe, and U2R. In comparison to naïve Bayes, the C4.5 decision tree classifier performs better in prediction accuracy. The algorithms were evaluated based on the number of false alarms, accuracy, and detection of four different types of attacks. They discovered that the decision tree (J48) method beats the other two algorithms in these tests. The Mininet and floodlight platforms were used to simulate a detection system based on DDoS assault characteristics using the SVM algorithm [26]. The proposed technique divides the characteristics into six tuples based on packet network calculations. The speed of the source IP (SSIP), the speed of the source port, the standard deviation of flow packets, the standard deviation of flow bytes (SDFB), the speed of flow entries, and the ratio of pair-flow are all examples of these properties. The current network state is normal or attack, based on the estimated statistics from the SVM classifier's six features. To attain an average accuracy of 95%, attack flow (AF), DR, and FAR were used.

7.3 PROPOSED APPROACH

The proposed approach for network intrusion detection is demonstrated in Figure 7.1. The modules of the proposed approach are data analysis and pre-processing, Random forest-based feature selection, training and testing phases of classical machine learning algorithms, and result generation using a voting classifier.

7.3.1 Data Analysis and Pre-Processing

The statistics pre-processing module numericizes text features and standardizes numerical functions, and authentic intrusion records are typically one-dimensional

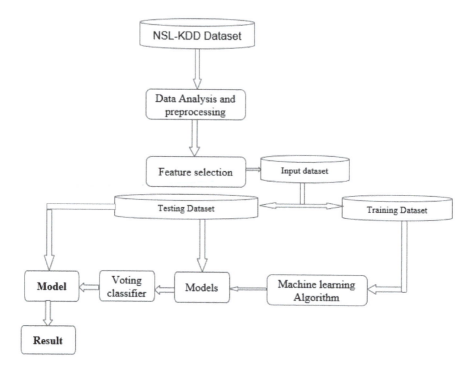

FIGURE 7.1   Proposed model.

vector facts that must be transformed into more than one-dimensional static. Now we have to first convert categorical data that are present in the dataset into numerical. This is because most of the machine learning algorithms do not work on categorical data. It is possible to employ one Hot Encoding or label encoding. The increased features improve detection accuracy by increasing the information capacity of the data sample, increasing the distance between different categories of data in the sample space, and increasing the distance between distinct categories of data in the sample space.

- **Label Encoding**: It is a popular encoding method for handling categorical data. In this method, each categorical label is assigned a distinct integer based on alphabetical ordering.
- **One Hot Encoding**: It refers to the process of dividing a column containing numerical categorical data into multiple columns based on the number of categories in that column. Each column has a value "0" or "1" based on where it was placed.

7.3.2   FEATURE SELECTION

Feature selection technique makes the IDS more efficient and fast on large datasets by selecting the relevant feature subset. In this way, it reduces the data dimension and complexity for training a classifier. Filter and wrapper are the two basic kinds of feature selection techniques [27]. The filter approach works without using any of the induction algorithm's information. Filter technique finds the optimal feature set based on prior information such as the feature should have a strong association with the target class or feature should be uncorrelated to each other. Alternatively, the wrapper technique searches over the space of feature subsets and evaluations using a specified induction procedure to identify a subset of features with the highest evaluation. As the wrapper technique contains a specialized induction algorithm to improve feature selection, the process of feature selection operates as if it were "wrapped around" an induction algorithm; it frequently produces a better classification accuracy result than the filter approach. The wrapper technique takes longer than the filter method because it is tightly tied to an induction process, which is called frequently to evaluate the performance of each subset of features. As a result, using a wrapper method to choose features from a big dataset with many features and instances becomes impractical.

In this proposed approach, RFE as a wrapper method with the help of random forest algorithm is utilized for feature selection. It requires the number of features to be selected and the choice of algorithm. Both hyper parameters are explored for better output. The random forest is considered here as the guidance method for selecting the relevant feature subset. The random forest is a decision-tree-based supervised machine learning technique for classification, regression, and solving other problems [28]. The random forest tree generates a collection of decision trees using subsets of the training data that are randomly chosen. It consists of a series of DTs drawn from a randomly selected subset of the training set, which are then voted on to determine the final prediction.

7.3.3 Supervised Machine Learning (ML) Algorithms

Supervised machine learning algorithms are applied to the dataset for classification. The dataset has a target variable and the independent variables that are given to the ML to determine and learn the significance of each sample in the training phase. The learned trained or ML algorithm is known as a model. The model is tested with testing samples in testing phase. The model can be implemented in a real context after the values of the considered parameters are satisfactory. Examples of supervised learning algorithms are DT, RF, SVM, k-NN, stacking, bagging, boosting, Artificial Neural Networks (ANNs), and other classical or state-of-the-art popular supervised algorithms. The state-of-the-art ML algorithms used in the proposed approach are RF, k-NN, SVM, and voting classifier described further.

7.3.3.1 Random Forest (RF)

The random forest has evolved from the concept of ensemble learning where more than one decision tree is participating in obtaining the decision for the data sample of an unknown class. The decision tree contains roots, branches, and leaves in its structure where each node represents a feature or attribute, each branch represents a decision or rule and each leaf represents an outcome in the form of categorical or continuous value [29]. Random forest provides better prediction performance. In this, a bootstrap-based sample technique is used for training each tree. It can handle larger datasets easily and is also able to handle categorical features. The hyper parameters of random forest are:

- **n estimators**: This parameter specifies the number of trees in the forest. It's a whole number. It has a default value of 100.
- **n jobs (int, default: None)**: This variable indicates how many jobs are running in parallel. The trees are parallelized for fitting, prediction, decision paths, and application. Unless in the context of joblib. parallel backend, none means 1. −1 indicates that all processors are being used.
- **Max_depth**: It specifies the most depth of the trees. If none is special, the nodes might be enlarged till all leaves are pure or until all leaves have fewer than min samples split samples. It helps to avoid the overfitting situation.
- **min_samples_split**: To split an internal node, it provides the number of samples required. If the value "int" is stored, the minimum range is used to break up the samples. If "go with the flow" is preserved, min samples cut up is a fragment, and ceil (min samples split * n samples) is the smallest number of samples for each breakup.
- **min samples leaf**: It specifies the minimum variety of samples that ought to be gift at a leaf node. If a cut-up point leaves at least min leaf education samples in each of the left and right branches, irrespective of intensity, it is going to be considered. This has the capability to clean out the version, especially in terms of regression. If int is stored, min samples leaf is taken as the minimum range. If ceil (min samples leaf * n samples) is genuine, then min samples leaf is a fragment and ceil(min samples leaf * n samples) is the least number of samples in keeping with node.

7.3.3.2   Support Vector Machine (SVM)

SVM uses an optimal hyper plane for classification, which is a line for 2D space, a plane for 3D space, and so on. In other words, the SVM maximizes the margins between classes during its training phase by creating the hyper planes. The cost function between the hyper plane and nearest training data points must be minimized mathematically to provide the ideal solution.

$$\text{Minimize} \frac{1}{2}\|w\|^2 + C\left(x+a\right)^n = \sum_{i=1}^{n} \in^2$$

subject to

$$y_i\left(w^T x_i + b\right)^3 \geq 1 - \in_i \text{ where } \in_i \geq 0$$

where $w^T \in R^2$, $\|w\|^2 = w^T w$ C refers to the trade-off parameter between margin and error, $\in_i$ denotes the measures of training data, and y_i is the class label for ith data sample. SVM is applicable for linear and nonlinear data classification. The hyper parameters of SVM are as follows.

- **kernel**: This parameter indicates the type of kernel used in the algorithm. It must be one of the following: linear, rbf, sigmoid, precomputed, or a callable. If no value is specified, "rbf" will be used instead. If a callable is specified, it will be used to pre-compute the kernel matrix using data matrices. The callable should be of the shape (n samples, n samples).
- **C**: It is a regularization parameter. It is a control on your fitting parameters. As the value of the fitting parameters increases, there will be increasingly penalty on the cost function. It must be strictly positive and float value and the default value of C is 1.0
- **Random state**: It regulates the creation of pseudo random numbers for shuffling data for probability estimates. When the probability is false, it is ignored. For consistent output across several function calls, pass an int.

7.3.3.2.1 k-Nearest Neighbor (k-NN)

k-NN is a supervised machine learning approach that is simple and gets trained fairly well on large training datasets. It follows the assumption that data points with similar characteristics reflect similar outcomes. k-NN method predicts an unknown data sample based on the majority neighbors among k-neighbors. It's resistant to noisy training data and works well with a large number of training samples. The distance between each instance and all training data samples takes longer to compute [30]. The hyper parameters of k-NN are as follows.

- **n_neighborsint**: It tells the algorithm to use in the algorithm. Its default value is 5.
- **radiusfloat**: It decides the range of parameter space for use in the algorithm. By default, its value is 1.
- **algorithm {'auto', 'ball_tree', 'kd_tree', 'brute'}**: It tells the algorithm by which method the nearest neighbors can be computed. By default, "auto" is used which decides the method to be used automatically based on the passed values to be fitted in the algorithm1. For sparse input brute force method is used.
- **leaf_sizeint**: When all Tree or k-Decision Tree is selected, it accepts the number of leaf node depending on the nature of the problem. By default, it is 30. This hyper parameter plays a very important role in deciding the speed of tree construction and memory space for storing the tree.
- **Metrics or callable**: By default, the Minkowski formula is used for which $p = 2$ known as Euclidean distance.
- **n_jobsint**: This hyper parameter determines the number of parallel jobs to search run for neighbors. By default, it is none which means 1.

7.3.3.3 Voting Classifier

A voting classifier is a system learning version that learns from an ensemble of models to predict the output based on the best chance of the ensemble models. It sums up the results of each classifier into a balloting system and forecasts the output quality based on which class received the most votes. The idea is that rather than creating separate devoted models and locating the accuracy for each of them, a single NIDS model is created. The single NIDS model trains with the aid of classifiers and predicts the output based on their blended majority of vote casting for each output. The voting hyper parameter is fed classifiers and voting criteria: hard or soft.

a) **Hard Voting**: The projected output class in hard voting is the one with the most votes, that is, the one with the highest likelihood of being predicted by each of the classifiers. Assume that three classifiers predicted the output class (A, A, B), and the majority of them anticipated A as the result. As a result, the ultimate forecast will be A.

b) **Soft Voting**: The output class in soft voting is the prediction based on the average probability assigned to that class. Assume that the prediction probability by the three models are class A = (0.43, 0.67, 0.23) and class B = (0.29, 0.92, 0.70). So, with an average of 0.443 for class A and 0.637 for class B, class B is clearly the winner because it had the highest probability averaged by each classifier.

7.4 EXPERIMENT AND RESULTS

This section presents the description of the experimental setup, considered metrics to evaluate the results, used dataset, results of conducted experiments, and comparison of results from other similar recent approaches.

7.4.1 EXPERIMENTAL SETUP

The work was carried out on a computer configured with Ubuntu 20.04 operating system with Anaconda environment and Python 3.8 as the programming language, with a Dell laptop, 8 Gigabyte of RAM, and a 1 TB HSD.

7.4.2 PERFORMANCE METRICS

This work undertakes a variety of network intrusion classification tests, with a normal (negative) sample and a combination of attacks that means positive samples in each dataset. The number of classes marked in each dataset varies. The information regarding actual and predicted classes is kept in this confusion matrix. The confusion matrix yields four major results: true positives (TPs), true negatives (TNs), false positives (FPs), and false negatives (FNs). These four outcomes, unlike the two classification techniques, may have slightly different interpretations in multiclass classification tasks. To begin with, TN is an accurate predictor of a normal outcome.

Formula (7.1) can be used to determine FP, where N is the number of attack classes and FP_i denotes the typical number of samples of the ith attack class. The total number of assault samples is equal to TP. In multiclass classification tasks, these outcomes have slightly different implications than the two classification methods. To begin with, TN is an accurate predictor of a normal sample. TP_i is the exact predictor of the ith attack category, and it is the sum of all assault samples that are really identified as their respective attack category using Formula (7.2). Finally, FN is the total number of assault samples that have been incorrectly classified into normal classes. Formula (7.3) may be used to compute FN, where FN_i is the number of samples of the attack class that were misunderstood as normal. Formula (7.4) may be used to compute FP, where FP_i is the number of samples of the normal class that were misunderstood as attacks.

$$FP = \sum_{i=1}^{N} FP_i, \tag{7.1}$$

$$TP = \sum_{i=1}^{N} TP_i, \tag{7.2}$$

$$FN = \sum_{i=1}^{N} FN_i \tag{7.3}$$

$$FP = \sum_{i=1}^{N} FP_i \tag{7.4}$$

These four effects are then combined to provide five assessment indicators, allowing us to assess the version's overall performance on the dataset. Some equations have been altered to conform to the previously stated terminology definition of the multiclass NIDS system. The following is the definition of the assessment indicator and the equation that goes with it.

- Accuracy tells about the success of the model on the test dataset:

$$Accuracy = \frac{TP + TN}{TP + TN + FP + FN} \tag{7.5}$$

- Precision refers to the classifier's accuracy:

$$Precision = \frac{TP}{TP + FP} \tag{7.6}$$

- The classifier's integrity, is known as recall:

$$Recall = \frac{TP}{TP + FN} \tag{7.7}$$

- The F-score can be thought of as the harmonic mean of the precision (P) and recall (R) indicators; that is, the F-score is the harmonic mean of the precision (P) and recall (R) indications.

$$F\text{-core} = \frac{2 \times P \times R}{P + R} \qquad (7.8)$$

- The error alert rate reveals that for every attack category, every normal data in the test set are not classified as normal sample rates. In other words, it is also called false positive rate (FPR):

$$FPR = \frac{FP}{FP + TN} \qquad (7.9)$$

7.4.3 USED DATASET

NSL-KDD is a dataset developed to address the issues with the KDD Cup 1999 data-set. No matter the reality that this new version of the KDD information set nevertheless has some troubles, we agree with it could nevertheless be used as a beneficial benchmark statistic set to help researchers examine extraordinary intrusion detection techniques because of the dearth of publicly available statistics sets for network-primarily based IDSs. Furthermore, the NSL-KDD train and test sets have an inex-pensive amount of data. This advantage makes it feasible to execute the experiments at the entire set without having to pick out a tiny sample at random. As a result, the assessment results of diverse studies tasks can be consistent and comparable. Originally, the NSL-KDD dataset had 43 different features. This dataset was used by many researchers in the past and is a kind of "hello world" for a researcher who has started research in the field of intrusion detection. It is a very wide dataset which covers almost all the things that are required for a researcher as a beginner. Of the 43 features, not all are participating in the building of the intrusion detection system. Some of the features are overhead for building the model of intrusion detection. That's why there is a need for feature selection and feature extraction. There has been a lot of research on feature extraction and feature selection so that a useful feature can be used for building the model.

Python is used to implement the proposed method. The proposed technique for estimating the performance of the NSL-KDD dataset is extremely difficult because of its vast scale – for training, 90% of data samples and for testing, 10% of data samples of the NSL-KDD dataset are considered using the train test validation method. Precision, Recall, F-score, and Accuracy are used to evaluate the proposed technique's achievement.

7.4.4 OBTAINED RESULTS ON NSL-KDD DATASET

7.4.4.1 Test Result of Random Forest
Confusion matrices are as follows (Tables 7.1–7.21).

TABLE 7.1
Confusion Matrix of DoS

	Predicted YES	Predicted NO
Actual YES	9674	37
Actual NO	23	7437

TABLE 7.2
Confusion Matrix of Probe

	Predicted YES	Predicted NO
Actual YES	9683	28
Actual NO	13	2408

TABLE 7.3
Confusion Matrix of R2L

	Predicted YES	Predicted NO
Actual YES	9681	28
Actual NO	125	2760

TABLE 7.4
Confusion Matrix of U2R

	Predicted YES	Predicted NO
Actual YES	9705	6
Actual NO	19	48

TABLE 7.5
Accuracy, Precision, Recall, F-measure

Attacks Name	Accuracy	Precision	Recall	F-measure
DoS	99.76	99.86	99.55	99.70
Probe	99.25	99.18	98.76	98.86
R2L	97.21	97.14	96.76	97.11
U2R	99.73	94.57	87.84	90.21

7.4.4.2 Test Result for k-NN

TABLE 7.6
Confusion Matrix of DoS

	Predicted YES	Predicted NO
Actual YES	9672	39
Actual NO	27	7423

TABLE 7.7
Confusion Matrix of Probe

	Predicted YES	Predicted NO
Actual YES	9687	22
Actual NO	25	2396

TABLE 7.8
Confusion Matrix of R2L

	Predicted YES	Predicted NO
Actual YES	9587	123
Actual NO	69	2816

TABLE 7.9
Confusion Matrix of U2R

	Predicted YES	Predicted NO
Actual YES	9703	8
Actual NO	21	46

TABLE 7.10
Accuracy, Precision, Recall, F-measure

Attacks Name	Accuracy	Precision	Recall	F-measure
DoS	99.71	99.67	99.66	99.67
Probe	99.07	98.60	98.50	98.55
R2L	96.73	95.31	95.48	95.38
U2R	99.70	93.28	84.83	87.75

7.4.4.3   Test Results for SVM

TABLE 7.11
Confusion Matrix of DoS

	Predicted YES	Predicted NO
Actual YES	9680	31
Actual NO	67	7393

TABLE 7.12
Confusion Matrix of Probe

	Predicted YES	Predicted NO
Actual YES	9653	58
Actual NO	15	2406

TABLE 7.13
Confusion Matrix of R2L

	Predicted YES	Predicted NO
Actual YES	9583	126
Actual NO	61	2824

TABLE 7.14
Confusion Matrix of U2R

	Predicted YES	Predicted NO
Actual YES	9699	12
Actual NO	20	61

TABLE 7.15
Accuracy, Precision, Recall, F-measure

Attacks Name	Accuracy	Precision	Recall	F-measure
DoS	99.37	99.10	99.45	99.27
Probe	98.45	96.90	98.36	97.61
R2L	96.79	94.85	96.26	95.52
U2R	99.65	91.98	83.98	85.91

7.4.4.4   Test Result of Voting Classifier When Hyper Parameter Is "Soft"

TABLE 7.16
Confusion Matrix of DoS

	Predicted YES	Predicted NO
Actual YES	9678	33
Actual NO	21	7439

TABLE 7.17
Confusion Matrix of Probe

	Predicted YES	Predicted NO
Actual YES	9686	25
Actual NO	13	2408

TABLE 7.18
Confusion Matrix of R2L

	Predicted YES	Predicted NO
Actual YES	9690	121
Actual NO	65	2820

TABLE 7.19
Confusion Matrix of U2R

	Predicted YES	Predicted NO
Actual YES	9705	6
Actual NO	18	63

TABLE 7.20
Accuracy, Precision, Recall, F-measure

Attacks Name	Accuracy	Precision	Recall	F-measure
DoS	99.80	99.86	99.67	99.77
Probe	99.28	98.77	98.93	98.80
R2L	97.26	95.85	96.38	96.12
U2R	99.75	91.98	83.98	85.91

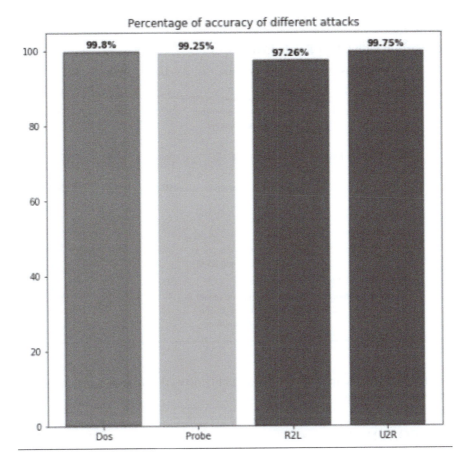

Percentage of accuracy of different attacks

TABLE 7.21

Analysis of Voting Classifier on the Basis of Hyper Parameter

Hyper Parameter	DoS	Probe	R2L	U2R
soft	99.80	99.28	97.26	99.75
hard	99.77	99.25	97.26	99.74

7.4.5 COMPARATIVE ANALYSIS

In Table 7.22, we compare the previously build NIDS model using different machine learning algorithms with our NIDS model which is built using RF-based feature selection and voting classifier (takes model built by random forest, SVM, and k-NN as input). Also, we compare the model with respect to the hyper parameter of the random classifier that is soft and hard. We find that the calculated matrices using a "soft" hyper parameter are more accurate than matrices calculated using a "hard"

TABLE 7.22
Comparison with Other Related Work

S. No	Target Class	Algorithm	Dos	Probe	R2L	U2R
1	Wang et al. [31]	k-NN	94.34	98.17	97.56	70.83
2	Elme R C. Mat El [32]	GA-IFS Genetic algorithm with improved feature selection	97.17	95.11	94.89	98.22
3	Bhumgara and Pitale [33]	J48 Decision tree	98.10	97.60	97.70	97.50
4	Bhumgara and Pitale [33]	Support vector machine	97.50	97.10	93.70	93.40
5	Uikey and Gyanchandani [34]	Random forest	99.58	98.43	52.17	95.48
6	Zhang and Pan [35]	Hybrid intrusion detection based on FCM and SVM	98.40	95	90	65
7	El Mrabet et al. [36]	Decision tree	92	82	93	98
8	Proposed Approach	Voting classifier on model generated from decision tree, SVM, k-neighbors	99.80	99.25	97.26	99.75

hyper parameter. The model's ability to identify network intrusion is determined by how well its evaluation indicators are tuned.

7.5   CONCLUSION

We know that network intrusion detection is very challenging in the aspect of network security. In this work, a multiclass network intrusion detection model based on RFE with random forest for feature selection and voting classifier for prediction is used. For evaluation, NSL-KDD dataset is used in Anaconda Navigator surroundings. The trial results show that the recommended network intrusion detection version improves accuracy and recall, decreases the fake fine charge, and provides better detection results for unknown attacks.

The accuracy of the version proposed method must be improved in classification trials; specifically, the categorization effects of unknown fantastic assault types also have room for improvement, which must be examined in future work. The dataset that was used in this mission's test was individually analyzed and refined. The subsequent datasets can be investigated in destiny studies: to affirm the technique proposed in this assignment attempt, the newly developing dataset for community intrusion detection will extract the essential records from actual network visitors' features. These performance tests can be effectively completed with the use of acceptable test criteria and a suitable dataset. While many IDS systems employ Snort rules as security policies, others, such as Sax2 IDS, employ alternative policies. As a result, this study offers a lot of potential for examining security policies (rules).

REFERENCES

[1] Tsai, C. F., Hsu, Y. F., Lin, C. Y., & Lin, W. Y. (2009). "Intrusion detection by machine learning: A review," *Expert Sys. Appl.*, vol. 36(10), pp. 11994–12000.

[2] J. Zhang, H. Li, Q. Gao, H. Wang, and Y. Luo, "Detecting anomalies from big network traffic data using an adaptive detection approach," *Inf. Sci. (Ny).*, vol. 318, pp. 91–110, 2015.

[3] G. Fernandes Jr, L. F. Carvalho, J. J. P. C. Rodrigues, and M. L. Proença Jr, "Network anomaly detection using IP flows with principal component analysis and ant colony optimization," *J. Netw. Comput. Appl.*, vol. 64, pp. 1–11, 2016.

[4] S. Naseer et al., "Enhanced network anomaly detection based on deep neural networks," *IEEE Access*, vol. 6, pp. 48231–48246, 2018.

[5] D. E. Denning, "An intrusion-detection model," *IEEE Trans. Softw. Eng.*, vol. SE-13, no. 2, pp. 222–232, 1987.

[6] S. Vieira, W. H. L. Pinaya, and A. Mechelli, "Using deep learning to investigate the neuroimaging correlates of psychiatric and neurological disorders: Methods and applications," *Neurosci. & Biobehav. Rev.*, vol. 74, pp. 58–75, 2017.

[7] Hijazi, A., El Safadi, A., & Flaus, J. M. (2018, December). A Deep Learning Approach for Intrusion Detection System in Industry Network. In *BDCSIntell* (pp. 55–62).

[8] J. Ye, X. Cheng, J. Zhu, L. Feng, and L. Song, "A DDoS attack detection method based on SVM in software defined network," *Secur. Commun. Netw.*, vol. 2018, 2018. pp. 1–11.

[9] S. Singh and P. Gupta, "Comparative study ID3, cart and C4. 5 decision tree algorithm: A survey," *Int. J. Adv. Inf. Sci. Technol.*, vol. 27, no. 27, pp. 97–103, 2014.

[10] Yan, S., Ren, J., Wang, W., Sun, L., Zhang, W., & Yu, Q. (2022). A Survey of Adversarial Attack and Defense Methods for Malware Classification in Cyber Security. *IEEE Communications Surveys & Tutorials*.

[11] Thales Group, url: "2017 Data Breach Level Index.", report, 2017.

[12] Broadcom, url: "Symantec Security Center." report, Jul. 2021.

[13] Merriam, url: "Intrude | Definition of Intrude by Merriam-Webster." report, Sep. 2021.

[14] E. O. Yeboah-Boateng, *Cyber-Security Challenges with SMEs in Developing Economies: Issues of Confidentiality, Integrity & Availability (CIA)*. Institut for Elektroniske Systemer, Aalborg Universitet, 2013.

[15] G. Bruneau, "The history and evolution of intrusion detection," *SANS Inst.*, vol. 1, 2001. pp. 1–9.

[16] D. Wang, D. S. Yeung, and E. C. C. Tsang, "Weighted mahalanobis distance kernels for support vector machines," *IEEE Trans. Neural Netw.*, vol. 18, no. 5, pp. 1453–1462, 2007.

[17] P. Deshpande, S. C. Sharma, S. K. Peddoju, and S. Junaid, "HIDS: A host based intrusion detection system for cloud computing environment," *Int. J. Syst. Assur. Eng. Manag.*, vol. 9, no. 3, pp. 567–576, 2018.

[18] P. K. Keserwani, M. C. Govil, and E. S. Pilli, "An effective NIDS framework based on a comprehensive survey of feature optimization and classification techniques," *Neural Comput. Appl.*, pp. 1–21, 2021.

[19] Rebecca, B. (2009). An introduction to intrusion detection & assessment. In *Proceedings of the International Conference on Software Architecture (ICSA)* (pp. 89–96).

[20] S. S. Dhaliwal, A.-A. Nahid, and R. Abbas, "Effective intrusion detection system using XGBoost," *Information*, vol. 9, no. 7, p. 149, 2018.

[21] T. A. Tang, L. Mhamdi, D. McLernon, S. A. R. Zaidi, M. Ghogho, and F. El Moussa, "DeepIDS: Deep learning approach for intrusion detection in software defined networking," *Electronics*, vol. 9, no. 9, p. 1533, 2020.

[22] M. Sheikhan and A. Khalili, "Intrusion detection based on rule extraction from dynamic cell structure neural metworks," *Majlesi J. Electr. Eng.*, vol. 4, no. 4, 2010.

[23] K. T. Khaing, "Enhanced features ranking and selection using recursive feature elimination (RFE) and k-nearest neighbor algorithms in support vector machine for intrusion detection system," *Int. J. Netw. Mob. Technol.*, vol. 1, no. 1, pp. 1832–6758, 2010.

[24] S. A. Mulay, P. R. Devale, and G. V. Garje, "Article: Intrusion detection system using support vector machine and decision tree," *Int. J. Comput. Appl.*, vol. 3, no. 3, pp. 40–43, 2010.

[25] G. MeeraGandhi, K. Appavoo, and S. Srivasta, "Effective network intrusion detection using classifiers decision trees and decision rules," *Int. J. Adv. Netw. Appl.* vol. 2, 2010. pp. 1–13.

[26] S. K. Dey et al., "Effects of machine learning approach in flow-based anomaly detection on software-defined networking," *Symmetry (Basel).*, vol. 12, no. 1, p. 7, 2020.

[27] Y. B. Wah, N. Ibrahim, H. A. Hamid, S. Abdul-Rahman, and S. Fong, "Feature selection methods: Case of filter and wrapper approaches for maximising classification accuracy," *Pertanika J. Sci. & Technol.*, vol. 26, no. 1, 2018.

[28] Rakhra, M., Soniya, P., Tanwar, D., Singh, P., Bordoloi, D., Agarwal, P., … & Verma, N. (2021). Crop price prediction using random forest and decision tree regression:-a review. *Materials Today: Proceedings.* pp. 1–6.

[29] H. H. Patel and P. Prajapati, "Study and analysis of decision tree based classification algorithms," *Int. J. Comput. Sci. Eng.*, vol. 6, no. 10, pp. 74–78, 2018.

[30] L. Peterson, "K-nearest neighbor,". Scholarpedia (2009)." 1883.

[31] H. Wang, B. Han, J. Su, and X. Wang, "A high-performance intrusion detection method based on combining supervised and unsupervised learning," in *2018 IEEE SmartWorld, Ubiquitous Intelligence & Computing, Advanced & Trusted Computing, Scalable Computing & Communications, Cloud & Big Data Computing, Internet of People and Smart City Innovation (SmartWorld/SCALCOM/UIC/ATC/CBDCom/IOP/SCI)*, 2018, pp. 1803–1810.

[32] N. Mishra and S. Mishra, "On the NSL-KDD dataset, a survey of machine learning-based intrusion detection systems," *J. Huazhong Univ. Sci. Technol. ISSN*, vol. 1671, p. 4512.

[33] A. Bhumgara and A. Pitale, "Detection of network intrusions using hybrid intelligent systems," in *2019 1st International Conference on Advances in Information Technology (ICAIT)*, 2019, pp. 500–506.

[34] R. Uikey and M. Gyanchandani, "Survey on classification techniques applied to intrusion detection system and its comparative analysis," in *2019 International Conference on Communication and Electronics Systems (ICCES)*, 2019, pp. 1451–1456.

[35] Z. Zhang and P. Pan, "A hybrid intrusion detection method based on improved fuzzy c-means and support vector machine," in *2019 International Conference on Communications, Information System and Computer Engineering (CISCE)*, 2019, pp. 210–214.

[36] Z. El Mrabet, H. El Ghazi, and N. Kaabouch, "A performance comparison of data mining algorithms based intrusion detection system for smart grid," in *2019 IEEE International Conference on Electro Information Technology (EIT)*, 2019, pp. 298–303.

8 Enhanced AI-Based Intrusion Detection and Response System for WSN

A Kathirvel

Sri Krishna College of Engineering and Technology, Coimbatore, India

C P Maheswaran

Karunya Institute of Technology and Sciences, Coimbatore, India

CONTENTS

DOI: 10.1201/9781003346340-8

8.1   OVERVIEW

A wireless sensor network (WSN) is highly sophisticated than an ad hoc wireless network. Ad hoc wireless networks are mostly affected by different resources such as high processing energy, storage capabilities, and battery backup. The open nature, poor infrastructure, quick deployment practices, and conflict environments make them susceptible to a wide range of attacks. Recently, network attacks have been affecting the performance of networks such as network lifetime, throughput, delay, energy consumption, and packet loss. Conventional security mechanisms like intrusion detection systems (IDSs) of network security are not enough for these networks. In this chapter, we introduce an AI-based enhanced intrusion detection and response (EIDR) system using two tire processes. The first contribution of the proposed EIDR system is optimal cluster formation and is performed by the chaotic ant optimization (CAO) algorithm. The second contribution is to calculate the trust value of each sensor node using the multi-objective differential evolution (MODE) algorithm. The computed trust value is used to design the intrusion response action (IRA) system, which offers additional functions and exhibits multiple characteristics of response to mitigate intrusion impacts. The simulation results display that the proposed EIDR system has a better detection rate and false positive rate without affecting the network performance.

8.2   INTRODUCTION TO AI AND IDS

Wireless sensor networks (WSNs) are distributed volatile sensors to monitor physical or environmental conditions like temperature, pressure, and sound, and synchronize their data with the network. Due to the continued development of wireless sensor networks, the need for more effective security mechanisms is also increasing. The security issues of the sensor network should be addressed by the beginning of the design of the system because the sensor networks interact with sensitive data and generally work in hostile unpredictable environments. Wireless Sensor Networks require a detailed understanding of the capabilities and limitations of each basic technology for secure work. At each end of the WSN, the design should be designed to provide the main sources of synchronization of the combined topology package, which is strict energy consumption. The protection of the connection to the group that requires the delivery of packages from one or more of the senders is a major objective (Bleda et al., 2017; Wu et al., 2016; Jokhio et al., 2013).

An intrusion detection system (IDS) attempts to detect insecure conditions of networks due to malicious attacks. Intrusion is a set of events that can lead to unofficial access or a change of wireless networking system (Valeur et al. 2004). IDS methods can detect cruel intruders from those anomalies and monitor the system's behavior, identify the existing intrusions in the network, alert the users after the intrusion has been identified, and re-enter the network if this is possible Mishra et al. (2004). Generally, the neighbors of a malicious node are the first to learn those abnormal behaviors. Therefore, it is easy to let every node control its neighbors in such a way that the IDS mechanism can be activated as soon as possible Ye et al. (2004). IDS observes and analyzes the maximum security problems in the network system, track unusual events and is used to monitor the network. The principal approaches for IDS are classified into two: misuse detection and anomaly detection. The misuse detection technique compares the behavior observed with known attack signatures. Action patterns that cause security threats should be defined and stored in the system. The advantage of this technique is that it can detect instances of known attacks accurately and efficiently, But it does not have the ability to detect unknown types of attacks (Ye et al., 2004). Anomaly detection is based on the general behavior of a system and it compares normal activities against the events observed for identifying important deviations (Erbacher et al., 2002).

In recent years, many IDS are proposed for WSN. IDS employed as a second line of defense is mandatory to provide a high-security information system and it can effectively identify intruders and thus provides intensive security Hoyle et al. (2015). The intrusion detection models are single-sensing detection and multi-sensing identification used to detect intrusion in both homogeneous and heterogeneous WSN by showing the probability of intrusion detection with distance and network parameters Sun et al. (2007).

Artificial Intelligence (AI) is the ability of a digital computer or computer-controlled robot to perform tasks commonly associated with intelligent beings. The term is frequently applied to the project of developing systems endowed with the intellectual processes characteristic of humans, such as the ability to reason, discover meaning, generalize, or learn from past experience. Since the development of the digital computer in the 1940s, it has been demonstrated that computers can be programmed to carry out very complex tasks—as, for example, discovering proofs for mathematical theorems or playing chess—with great proficiency. Still, despite continuing advances in computer processing speed and memory capacity, there are as yet no programs that can match human flexibility over wider domains or in tasks requiring much everyday knowledge. On the other hand, some programs have attained the performance levels of human experts and professionals in performing certain specific tasks, so artificial intelligence in this limited sense is found in applications as diverse as medical diagnosis, computer search engines, and voice or handwriting recognition.

8.2.1 INTELLIGENCE

Even the simplest human behavior is ascribed to intelligence, while even the most complicated insect behavior is never taken as an indication of intelligence. What is the difference? Consider the behavior of the digger wasp, *Sphex ichneumoneus*. When the female wasp returns to her burrow with food, she first deposits it on the threshold, checks for intruders inside her burrow, and only then, if the coast is clear, carries her food inside. The real nature of the wasp's instinctual behavior is revealed if the food is moved a few inches away from the entrance to her burrow while she is inside: on emerging, she will repeat the whole procedure as often as the food is displaced. Intelligence—conspicuously absent in the case of *Sphex*—must include the ability to adapt to new circumstances.

Psychologists generally do not characterize human intelligence by just one trait but by the combination of many diverse abilities. Research in AI has focused chiefly on the following components of intelligence: learning, reasoning, problem-solving, perception, and using language.

- **Learning**
  There are a number of different forms of learning as applied to artificial intelligence. The simplest is learning by trial and error. For example, a simple computer program for solving mate-in-one chess problems might try moves at random until mate is found. The program might then store the solution with the position so that the next time the computer encountered the same position it would recall the solution. This simple memorizing of individual items and procedures—known as rote learning—is relatively easy to implement on a computer. More challenging is the problem of implementing what is called generalization. Generalization involves applying past experience to analogous new situations. For example, a program that learns the past tense of regular English verbs by rote will not be able to produce the past tense of a word such as jump unless it previously had been presented with jumped, whereas a program that is able to generalize can learn the "add ed" rule and so form the past tense of jump based on experience with similar verbs.

- **Reasoning**
  To reason is to draw inferences appropriate to the situation. Inferences are classified as either deductive or inductive. An example of the former is, "Fred must be in either the museum or the café. He is not in the café; therefore he is in the museum," and of the latter, "Previous accidents of this sort were caused by instrument failure; therefore this accident was caused by instrument failure." The most significant difference between these forms of reasoning is that in the deductive case, the truth of the premises guarantees the truth of the conclusion, whereas in the inductive case, the truth of the premise lends support to the conclusion without giving absolute assurance. Inductive reasoning is common in science, where data are collected and tentative models are developed to describe and predict future behavior—until the appearance of anomalous data forces the model to be revised. Deductive reasoning is common in mathematics and logic, where elaborate structures of irrefutable theorems are built up from a small set of basic axioms and rules.

  There has been considerable success in programming computers to draw inferences, especially deductive inferences. However, true reasoning involves more than just drawing inferences; it involves drawing inferences relevant to the solution of a particular task or situation. This is one of the hardest problems confronting AI.

- **Problem-solving**

  Problem-solving, particularly in artificial intelligence, may be characterized as a systematic search through a range of possible actions in order to reach some predefined goal or solution. Problem-solving methods are divided into special purpose and general purpose. A special-purpose method is tailor-made for a particular problem and often exploits very specific features of the situation in which the problem is embedded. In contrast, a general-purpose method is applicable to a wide variety of problems. One general-purpose technique used in AI is means-end analysis—a step-by-step, or incremental, reduction of the difference between the current state and the final goal. The program selects actions from a list of means—in the case of a simple robot, this might consist of PICKUP, PUTDOWN, MOVEFORWARD, MOVE-BACK, MOVELEFT, and MOVERIGHT—until the goal is reached.

  Many diverse problems have been solved by artificial intelligence programs. Some examples are finding the winning move (or sequence of moves) in a board game, devising mathematical proofs, and manipulating "virtual objects" in a computer-generated world.

- **Perception**

  In perception, the environment is scanned by means of various sensory organs, real or artificial, and the scene is decomposed into separate objects in various spatial relationships. The analysis is complicated by the fact that an object may appear different depending on the angle from which it is viewed, the direction and intensity of illumination in the scene, and how much the object contrasts with the surrounding field.

  At present, artificial perception is sufficiently well advanced to enable optical sensors to identify individuals, autonomous vehicles to drive at moderate speeds on the open road, and robots to roam through buildings collecting empty soda cans. One of the earliest systems to integrate perception and action was FREDDY, a stationary robot with a moving television eye and a pincer hand, constructed at the University of Edinburgh, Scotland, during the period 1966–1973 under the direction of Donald Michie. FREDDY was able to recognize a variety of objects and could be instructed to assemble simple artifacts, such as a toy car, from a random heap of components.

- **Language**

  A language is a system of signs having meaning by convention. In this sense, language need not be confined to the spoken word. Traffic signs, for example, form a minilanguage, it being a matter of convention that "⚠" means "hazard ahead" in some countries. It is distinctive of languages that linguistic units possess meaning by convention, and linguistic meaning is very different from what is called natural meaning, exemplified in statements such as "Those clouds mean rain" and "The fall in pressure means the valve is malfunctioning."

  An important characteristic of full-fledged human languages—in contrast to birdcalls and traffic signs—is their productivity. A productive language can formulate an unlimited variety of sentences.

It is relatively easy to write computer programs that seem able, in severely restricted contexts, to respond fluently in a human language to questions and statements. Although none of these programs actually understands language, they may, in principle, reach the point where their command of a language is indistinguishable from that of a normal human. What, then, is involved in genuine understanding, if even a computer that uses language like a native human speaker is not acknowledged to understand? There is no universally agreed-upon answer to this difficult question. According to one theory, whether or not one understands depends not only on one's behavior but also on one's history: in order to be said to understand, one must have learned the language and have been trained to take one's place in the linguistic community by means of interaction with other language users.

An EIDR system is proposed using two tier processes: optimal clustering and trust computation. The IDS module classifies the type of malicious present in the network and the IRS module is responsible to make the response action of a particular malicious problem in the data transmission path. The main objective is to maximize the detection rate and minimize the false positive rate without affecting the network performance such as network lifetime, throughput, end-to-end delay, energy consumption, and packet loss.

8.3   WHY IS ARTIFICIAL INTELLIGENCE IMPORTANT?

AI is important because it can give enterprises insights into their operations that they may not have been aware of previously and because, in some cases, AI can perform tasks better than humans. Particularly when it comes to repetitive, detail-oriented tasks like analyzing large numbers of legal documents to ensure relevant fields are filled in properly, AI tools often complete jobs quickly and with relatively few errors.

This has helped fuel an explosion in efficiency and opened the door to entirely new business opportunities for some larger enterprises. Prior to the current wave of AI, it would have been hard to imagine using computer software to connect riders to taxis, but today Uber has become one of the largest companies in the world by doing just that. It utilizes sophisticated machine learning algorithms to predict when people are likely to need rides in certain areas, which helps proactively get drivers on the road before they're needed. As another example, Google has become one of the largest players for a range of online services by using machine learning to understand how people use their services and then improving them. In 2017, the company's CEO, Sundar Pichai, pronounced that Google would operate as an "AI first" company.

8.3.1   Strong AI vs. Weak AI

AI can be categorized as either weak or strong.

- **Weak AI**, also known as narrow AI, is an AI system that is designed and trained to complete a specific task. Industrial robots and virtual personal assistants, such as Apple's Siri, use weak AI.

- **Strong AI**, also known as artificial general intelligence (AGI), describes programming that can replicate the cognitive abilities of the human brain. When presented with an unfamiliar task, a strong AI system can use fuzzy logic to apply knowledge from one domain to another and find a solution autonomously. In theory, a strong AI program should be able to pass both a Turing Test and the Chinese room test.

8.4 TYPES OF ARTIFICIAL INTELLIGENCE

Arend Hintze, an assistant professor of integrative biology and computer science and engineering at Michigan State University, explained in a 2016 article that AI can be categorized into four types, beginning with the task-specific intelligent systems in wide use today and progressing to sentient systems, which do not yet exist. The categories are as follows:

Type 1: **Reactive machines**. These AI systems have no memory and are task-specific. An example is Deep Blue, the IBM chess program that beat Garry Kasparov in the 1990s. Deep Blue can identify pieces on the chessboard and make predictions, but because it has no memory, it cannot use past experiences to inform future ones.

Type 2: **Limited memory**. These AI systems have memory, so they can use past experiences to inform future decisions. Some of the decision-making functions in self-driving cars are designed this way.

Type 3: **Theory of mind**. Theory of mind is a psychology term. When applied to AI, it means that the system would have the social intelligence to understand emotions. This type of AI will be able to infer human intentions and predict behavior, a necessary skill for AI systems to become integral members of human teams.

Type 4: **Self-awareness**. In this category, AI systems have a sense of self, which gives them consciousness. Machines with self-awareness understand their own current state. This type of AI does not yet exist.

8.5 EXAMPLES OF AI TECHNOLOGY AND HOW IS IT USED TODAY?

AI is incorporated into a variety of different types of technology. Here are six examples:

- **Automation**. When paired with AI technologies, automation tools can expand the volume and types of tasks performed. An example is robotic process automation (RPA), a type of software that automates repetitive, rules-based data processing tasks traditionally done by humans. When combined with machine learning and emerging AI tools, RPA can automate bigger portions of enterprise jobs, enabling RPA's tactical bots to pass along intelligence from AI and respond to process changes.

- **Machine learning**. This is the science of getting a computer to act without programming. Deep learning is a subset of machine learning that, in very simple terms, can be thought of as the automation of predictive analytics. There are three types of machine learning algorithms:
  - **Supervised learning**. Data sets are labeled so that patterns can be detected and used to label new data sets.
  - **Unsupervised learning**. Data sets aren't labeled and are sorted according to similarities or differences.
- **Reinforcement learning**. Data sets aren't labeled but, after performing an action or several actions, the AI system is given feedback.
- **Machine vision**. This technology gives a machine the ability to see. Machine vision captures and analyzes visual information using a camera, analog-to-digital conversion, and digital signal processing. It is often compared to human eyesight, but machine vision isn't bound by biology and can be programmed to see through walls, for example. It is used in a range of applications from signature identification to medical image analysis. Computer vision, which is focused on machine-based image processing, is often conflated with machine vision.
- **Natural language processing (NLP)**. This is the processing of human language by a computer program. One of the older and best-known examples of NLP is spam detection, which looks at the subject line and text of an email and decides if it's junk. Current approaches to NLP are based on machine learning. NLP tasks include text translation, sentiment analysis, and speech recognition.
- **Robotics**. This field of engineering focuses on the design and manufacturing of robots. Robots are often used to perform tasks that are difficult for humans to perform or perform consistently. For example, robots are used in assembly lines for car production or by NASA to move large objects in space. Researchers are also using machine learning to build robots that can interact in social settings.
- **Self-driving cars**. Autonomous vehicles use a combination of computer vision, image recognition, and deep learning to build automated skills at piloting a vehicle while staying in a given lane and avoiding unexpected obstructions, such as pedestrians.

8.6 APPLICATIONS OF AI

Artificial intelligence has made its way into a wide variety of markets. Here are nine examples.

- **AI in healthcare**. The biggest bets are on improving patient outcomes and reducing costs. Companies are applying machine learning to make better and faster diagnoses than humans. One of the best-known healthcare technologies is IBM Watson. It understands natural language and can respond to questions asked of it. The system mines patient data and other available data sources to form a hypothesis, which it then presents with a confidence scoring schema. Other AI applications include using online virtual health assistants and chatbots to help patients and healthcare customers find medical information, schedule appointments, understand the billing process and complete other administrative processes. An array of AI technologies is also being used to predict, fight, and understand pandemics such as COVID-19.

- **AI in business**. Machine learning algorithms are being integrated into analytics and customer relationship management (CRM) platforms to uncover information on how to better serve customers. Chatbots have been incorporated into websites to provide immediate service to customers. Automation of job positions has also become a talking point among academics and IT analysts.

- **AI in education**. AI can automate grading, giving educators more time. It can assess students and adapt to their needs, helping them work at their own pace. AI tutors can provide additional support to students, ensuring they stay on track. And it could change where and how students learn, perhaps even replacing some teachers.

- **AI in finance**. AI in personal finance applications, such as Intuit Mint or TurboTax, is disrupting financial institutions. Applications such as these collect personal data and provide financial advice. Other programs, such as IBM Watson, have been applied to the process of buying a home. Today, artificial intelligence software performs much of the trading on Wall Street.

- **AI in law**. The discovery process—sifting through documents—in law is often overwhelming for humans. Using AI to help automate the legal industry's labor-intensive processes is saving time and improving client service. Law firms are using machine learning to describe data and predict outcomes, computer vision to classify and extract information from documents, and natural language processing to interpret requests for information.

- **AI in manufacturing**. Manufacturing has been at the forefront of incorporating robots into the workflow. For example, the industrial robots that were at one time programmed to perform single tasks and separated from human workers, increasingly function as cobots: Smaller, multitasking robots that collaborate with humans and take on responsibility for more parts of the job in warehouses, factory floors, and other workspaces.

- **AI in banking**. Banks are successfully employing chatbots to make their customers aware of services and offerings and to handle transactions that don't require human intervention. AI virtual assistants are being used to improve and cut the costs of compliance with banking regulations. Banking organizations are also using AI to improve their decision-making for loans, and to set credit limits and identify investment opportunities.

- **AI in transportation**. In addition to AI's fundamental role in operating autonomous vehicles, AI technologies are used in transportation to manage traffic, predict flight delays, and make ocean shipping safer and more efficient.

- **Security**. AI and machine learning are at the top of the buzzword list security vendors use today to differentiate their offerings. Those terms also represent truly viable technologies. Organizations use machine learning in security information and event management (SIEM) software and related areas to detect anomalies and identify suspicious activities that indicate threats.

By analyzing data and using logic to identify similarities to known malicious code, AI can provide alerts to new and emerging attacks much sooner than human employees and previous technology iterations. The maturing technology is playing a big role in helping organizations fight off cyber attacks.

8.7 AUGMENTED INTELLIGENCE VS. ARTIFICIAL INTELLIGENCE

Some industry experts believe the term artificial intelligence is too closely linked to popular culture, and this has caused the general public to have improbable expectations about how AI will change the workplace and life in general.

- **Augmented intelligence**. Some researchers and marketers hope the label augmented intelligence, which has a more neutral connotation, will help people understand that most implementations of AI will be weak and simply improve products and services. Examples include automatically surfacing important information in business intelligence reports or highlighting important information in legal filings.
- **Artificial intelligence**. True AI, or AGI, is closely associated with the concept of the technological singularity—a future ruled by an artificial superintelligence that far surpasses the human brain's ability to understand it or how it is shaping our reality. This remains within the realm of science fiction, though some developers are working on the problem. Many believe that technologies such as quantum computing could play an important role in making AGI a reality and that we should reserve the use of the term AI for this kind of general intelligence.

8.7.1 Cognitive Computing and AI

The terms AI and cognitive computing are sometimes used interchangeably, but, generally speaking, the label AI is used in reference to machines that replace human intelligence by simulating how we sense, learn, process, and react to information in the environment.

The label cognitive computing is used in reference to products and services that mimic and augment human thought processes.

8.7.1.1 AI as a Service

Because hardware, software, and staffing costs for AI can be expensive, many vendors are including AI components in their standard offerings or providing access to artificial intelligence as a service (AIaaS) platforms. AIaaS allows individuals and companies to experiment with AI for various business purposes and sample multiple platforms before making a commitment.

Popular AI cloud offerings include the following:

- Amazon AI
- IBM Watson Assistant
- Microsoft Cognitive Services
- Google AI

8.7.1.2   AI in Cyber Security

A network has a nominal baseline that can be used to identify threats. AI cybersecurity addresses the need to automate the assessment of threats in complex environments. Specifically, here are two use cases for AI in AI cybersecurity:

- **Detecting anomalies**. AI will often detect anomalies in a network's daily operation. This helps you see when and where your users are accessing the network. Gateway devices also have AI integration for analytics. In case of unusual behavior, some solutions lock users out. Other solutions only send alerts.
- **Classifying data**. AI is effectively a classification utility. This speeds up the screening process for malware or bad actors. This is useful in organizations that have a lot of data.

Now you know the two main uses of AI in cybersecurity, let's take a look at its benefits and drawbacks!

- **AI Benefits and Drawbacks**: As mentioned, AI has a lot of benefits. It runs repetitive tasks to identify anomalies or to classify data in particular in your business. That said, a few large drawbacks may offset its benefits. Here, we'll look at the drawbacks.
- **AI Accuracy vs. Resource Demand**: The first drawback is the AI cybersecurity solution's accuracy. This accuracy also depends on many factors. This includes the neural net's size and the decisions defined for filtering. It also depends on the number of iterations used to reach the predefined error percentage.

  Imagine you have a decision tree with three layers. And each layer has several nodes for each decision route. Even though this is a fairly simple matrix, it needs a lot of calculations. Your system's finite resources will compromise your solution's intelligence.

  An AI cybersecurity solution provider may stunt its solution's intelligence/accuracy to meet the target demographic. But sometimes, the problem isn't intelligence. Instead, it's low latency and security vulnerabilities. When searching for an AI cybersecurity solution, consider how secure it is in your network.

8.7.1.3   Static and Continual Training

Once trained, an AI statistical weighted matrix is often not re-trained in service. You'll find this is due to the lack of processing resources available in hardware. Sometimes, the system learns something that makes it worse, reducing its effectiveness. Conversely, humans learn iteratively. This means they cause a lot of accidents. As a result, solution providers must ensure the software meets specification requirements during use.

Cybersecurity often requires updates to counter new exploits. To this end, it takes a lot of power to train your AI. Additionally, your AI cybersecurity vendor will need to update regularly to address cyber threats.

That said, the AI component of an AI cybersecurity solution is for classifying data and assessing anomalies in baseline data. As a result, it doesn't cause an issue for malware list updates. This means you can still use AI cybersecurity.

Now you know the benefits and drawbacks of AI cybersecurity, let's take a look at some uses for this technology!

AI cybersecurity acts like a security guard to your network.

8.7.1.4   Where You'll Find AI Cybersecurity

As mentioned, highly automated businesses have the weakest cybersecurity. Generally, automated environments will overlap information technology (IT), operational technology (OT), and the Internet of Things (IoT). This is to improve productivity, reduce the unit cost of a product, and undercut the competition.

But this also creates vulnerabilities. To this end, AI cybersecurity is great for finding potential exploits in these companies. Solutions either inform the administrator or automatically apply patches. However, this may not be enough. Cybercriminals are currently attacking large, highly integrated companies. To do that, they exploit OT, which has no security. This OT was meant for wired networks to send commands to hardware like plant equipment. This means it never posed a security weakness. But today, attackers use OT to access the rest of a network or take plant equipment offline.

8.8   OT RISK MANAGEMENT FOR MANUFACTURING AND AUTOMATED PLANTS

OT risk management tools are becoming popular for the reasons mentioned above. These systems effectively take a real-time clone of the production environment. Then, they run countless simulations to find exploits.

The AI part of the system generally finds exploits. In that case, an administrator provides a solution. OT risk management software continually runs as manufacturing plant arrangements change to meet orders, projects, or supply demands.

In this scenario, AI systems use known malware from antivirus lists to try and find an entry route into the system. The task requires automated repetitive functions of a complex system. And this makes it perfect for AI.

8.8.1   WHEN YOU SHOULD USE AI CYBERSECURITY

As discussed above, businesses that use manufacturing and plant equipment should use AI cybersecurity. In most cases, you'll also need to look for an OT risk management solution to reduce risks associated with OT.

You also can use AI cybersecurity if your business uses IoT and IT. This way, you can reduce the risk to the network from exploits. IoT devices generally undercut competitors, so you bypass the cost of adding adequate security measures.

Finally, you can use AI even if your company only uses IT. AI helps assess irregular traffic, so it protects your gateways. Additionally, you can leverage AI's data analytics. This way, you'll know if someone is using your hardware for malicious purposes.

Now you know all you need to get started with AI cybersecurity, let's wrap things up!

8.8.2   Benefits of Using AI for Cybersecurity

Artificial intelligence endeavors to simulate human intelligence. It has immense potential in cybersecurity. If harnessed correctly, Artificial Intelligence or AI systems can be trained to generate alerts for threats, identify new types of malware and protect sensitive data for organizations.

According to TechRepublic, a mid-sized company gets alerts for over 200,000 cyber events every day. A team of security experts in an average company cannot deal with this volume of threats. Some of these threats will, therefore, naturally go unnoticed and cause severe damage to networks.

AI is the ideal cybersecurity solution for businesses looking to thrive online today. Security professionals need strong support from intelligent machines and advanced technologies like AI to work successfully and protect their organizations from cyber attacks. Let's check them out.

8.8.2.1   AI Learns More Over Time

As the name suggests, AI technology is intelligent, and it uses its ability to improve network security over time. It uses machine learning and deep learning to learn a business network's behavior over time. It recognizes patterns on the network and clusters them. It then proceeds to detect any deviations or security incidents from the norm before responding to them.

The patterns that artificial neural networks learn over time can help to improve security in the future. Potential threats with similar traits to those recorded get blocked early enough. The fact that AI keeps learning makes it difficult for hackers to beat its intelligence.

8.8.2.2   Artificial Intelligence Identifies Unknown Threats

A human being may not be able to identify all the threats a company faces. Every year, hackers launch hundreds of millions of attacks with different motives. Unknown threats can cause massive damage to a network. Worse still is the impact they can have before you detect, identify, and prevent them.

As attackers try new tactics from sophisticated social engineering to malware attacks, it is necessary to use modern solutions to prevent them. AI has proven to be one of the best security technologies in mapping and stopping unknown threats from ravaging a company.

8.8.2.3   AI Can Handle a Lot of Data

A lot of activity happens on a company's network. An average mid-sized company itself has huge traffic. That means there's a lot of data transferred between customers and the business daily. This data need protection from malicious people and software. But then, cybersecurity personnel cannot check all the traffic for possible threats.

AI is the best solution that will help you detect any threats masked as normal activity. Its automated nature allows it to skim through massive chunks of data and traffic. Technology that uses AI, such as a residential proxy, can help you to transfer data. It can also detect and identify any threats hidden in the sea of chaotic traffic.

8.8.2.4 Better Vulnerability Management

Vulnerability management is key to securing a company's network. As mentioned earlier, an average company deals with many threats daily. It needs to detect, identify and prevent them to be safe. Analyzing and assessing the existing security measures through AI research can help in vulnerability management.

AI helps you assess systems quicker than cybersecurity personnel, thereby increasing your problem-solving ability manifold. It identifies weak points in computer systems and business networks and helps businesses focus on important security tasks, making it possible to manage vulnerability and secure business systems in time.

8.8.2.5 Better Overall Security

The threats that business networks face change from time to time. Hackers change their tactics every day. That makes it difficult to prioritize security tasks at a company. You may have to deal with a phishing attack along with a denial-of-service attack or ransomware at a go.

These attacks have similar potential but you must know what to deal with first. Bigger threats that can make security a challenge are human error and negligence. The solution here is to deploy AI on your network to detect all types of attacks and help you prioritize and prevent them.

8.8.2.6 Duplicative Processes Reduce

As mentioned earlier, attackers change their tactics often. But, the basic security best practices remain the same every day. If you hire someone to handle these tasks, they may get bored along the way. Or they could feel tired and complacent and miss an important security task and expose your network.

AI, while mimicking the best of human qualities and leaving out the shortcomings, takes care of duplicative cybersecurity processes that could bore your cybersecurity personnel. It helps check for basic security threats and prevent them on a regular basis. It also analyzes your network in depth to see if there are security holes that could be damaging to your network.

8.8.2.7 Accelerates Detection and Response Times

Threat detection is the beginning of protecting your company's network. It would be best if you detected things like untrusted data quickly. It will save you from irreversible damage to your network.

The best way to detect and respond to threats in time is by integrating AI with cybersecurity. AI scans your entire system and checks for any possible threats. Unlike humans, AI will identify threats extremely early and simplify your security tasks.

8.8.2.8 Securing Authentication

Most websites have a user account feature where one logs in to access services or buy products. Some have contact forms that visitors need to fill out with sensitive information. As a company, you need an extra security layer to run such a site because it involves personal data and sensitive information. The additional security layer will ensure that your visitors are safe while browsing your network.

AI secures authentication anytime a user wants to log into their account. AI uses various tools such as facial recognition, CAPTCHA, and fingerprint scanners among others for identification. The information collected by these features can help to detect if a log-in attempt is genuine or not.

Hackers use credential stuffing and brute force attacks to access company networks. Once an attacker enters a user account, your whole network could be at risk.

Today's largest and most successful enterprises have used AI to improve their operations and gain advantage over their competitors.

8.8.3   ADVANTAGES AND DISADVANTAGES OF AI

Artificial neural networks and deep learning artificial intelligence technologies are quickly evolving, primarily because AI processes large amounts of data much faster and makes predictions more accurately than humanly possible.

While the huge volume of data being created on a daily basis would bury a human researcher, AI applications that use machine learning can take that data and quickly turn it into actionable information. As of this writing, the primary disadvantage of using AI is that it is expensive to process the large amounts of data that AI programming requires.

Advantages
1. Good at detail-oriented jobs;
2. Reduced time for data-heavy tasks;
3. Delivers consistent results; and
4. AI-powered virtual agents are always available.

Disadvantages
1. Expensive;
2. Requires deep technical expertise;
3. Limited supply of qualified workers to build AI tools;
4. Only knows what it's been shown; and
5. Lack of ability to generalize from one task to another.

8.9   NETWORK MODEL

In the EIDR system, we assume that the network consists of randomly distributed high-density nodes and malicious nodes without movement. The sensors present in the network have the same transmission range and unique ID for user identification. The routing pattern is followed by the basic LEACH protocol with the help of our computed trust values. That is to say, the sensed information from each sensor are forwarded to the next node that is selected by trust value.

The routing implies that nodes only directly communicate with their highest trust neighbor nodes. Also, the information forwarded between neighbor nodes depend on the trust value, which cannot only transfer the packets from source nodes to destination nodes but also process the packets based on specific requirements. The assumed network model of the proposed EIDR system is shown in Figure 8.1 with example trust values and attacks.

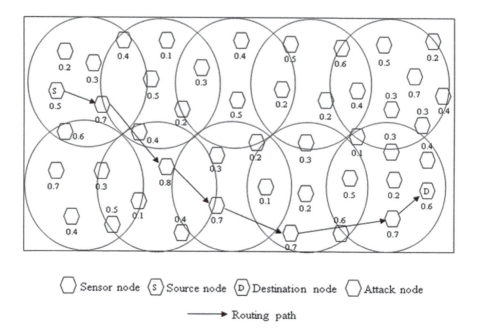

FIGURE 8.1   EIDR systems with example trust values and attacks.

8.10   ENHANCED INTRUSION DETECTION AND RESPONSE SYSTEM

The IDS is used to detect the attacks. Even if the system cannot prevent the attacks from getting into the network, noticing the intrusion will provide the security officer with valuable information. A detailed description of the proposed EIDR system is presented in the following section. EIDR consists of two algorithms namely clustering using CAO algorithm and Trust computation using the MODE algorithm.

8.10.1   CLUSTERING USING CHAOTIC ANT OPTIMIZATION (CAO) ALGORITHM

Deif and Gadallah (2017) proposed Ant colony optimization (ACO) is a metaheuristic figuring for combinatorial change issues. The key idea of ACO figuring is the mix of from earlier data about the structure of a promising plan with a posteriori data about the structure of formally got staggering systems. Metaheuristic estimation are checks which, with a specific common made obsession to escape from neighborhood optima, drive some enormous heuristic: either a central heuristic begins from an invalid method and then add ups the bits for validity, or uses a heuristic approach and iteratively changing some of its parts to accomplish a typical one. The metaheuristic part interfaces with the low-level heuristic to secure plans superior to anything it could have accomplished alone, paying little regard to whether it is iterated. The controlling piece is pro either by influencing or by randomizing the philosophy of close neighbor answers for considers in neighborhood look or by joining parts taken by various structures. The standard key thought, everything considered began by the lead of veritable ants, is that of a parallel range for after in excess of a not a lot of computational strings in a setting of neighborhood issue information and on a dynamic memory structure containing data on the probability of early got result. The aggregate direct moving out of the relationship of the specific demand strings has shown a standard in controlling combinatorial streamlining issues.

Here, the central ACO computation is invigorated in a chaotic manner, i.e., CAO count to make the best faultless squeezing. Exactly when ants see assistance, they attempt to keep up a proportionate edge with the light to fly in a straight line. Here, the game plan of ants is tended to in a structure. For each and every one of the ants, there is a get-together to secure the looking regards. The second part in the estimation is foods tended to in a structure F, and a social gathering for securing the looking regards. The CAO algorithm starts with the initialization process, which approximates the global optimal of the optimization problems and is defined as follows:

$$\text{MFO} = (P, S, T) \qquad (8.1)$$

where P represents the function of random population $P \rightarrow \{X, X_a\}$, S represents the moth's movement around search space $S \rightarrow X$, and T represents the termination criteria $T \rightarrow \{\text{True, False}\}$. After the instatement, the S function is iteratively kept running until the T point that the minute that the cutoff returns outstanding kept. For refinement in reflecting the direct of ants, the condition of every underground offensive irrelevant creature restored concerning sustenance as takes after:

$$X_i = s(X_i, F_i) \qquad (8.2)$$

where s represents the spiral function and i and j represents the ith moth, jth food, respectively. The spiral's initial point should begin from the underground bug and end at the last point ought to be the condition of the sustenance. The change of the level of winding pound the intrigue space. A logarithmic spiral is defined for the CAO algorithm as follows:

$$s(X_i, F_i) = |F_j - M_i| e^{bt} \cos(2\pi r) + F_j \qquad (8.3)$$

where $|F_j - M_i|$ indicates the distance of the ith ant for the jth food and b, r represents the shape of the logarithmic spiral, and random number, respectively. From this condition, the "running with position" of an underground bug is portrayed as one concerning a help. The parameter in the winding condition depicts how much the running with position of the moth is ought to be near sustenance. With a specific extraordinary obsession to collect the sensible approach of individuals against troublesome joining and enable the mixing speed, we enhance the CAO check using the Levy-flight. It has unmistakable properties to cover away the not dazzling get-together of masses, innovatively, which can make this appropriately ricochet out of the zone wrap up. The new position of ants is updated as follows:

$$X_i^2 = X_i^1 + u \, sign[r - 0.5] \oplus \text{Levy}(O) \qquad (8.4)$$

where t, u is a random parameter which conforms to a uniform distribution, *sign* $[r - 0.5]$ is taken as 1, 0, and −1. Levy-flights are a kind of random walk in which the steps are determined by the step lengths, and the jumps conform to a Levy distribution as follows.

$$\text{Levy}(O) \approx \frac{\left[\frac{\Gamma(1+O) \times \sin\left(\pi \times \frac{O}{2}\right)}{\Gamma\left(\left(\frac{(1+O)}{2}\right) \times O \times 2^{(O-1)/2}\right)} \right]^{\frac{1}{O}} \times \mu}{|v|^{\frac{1}{O}}} \qquad (8.5)$$

where μ, v represents the standard normal distributions, $O = 0.5$, Γ represents the standard Gamma function. To show up, global search cutoff of this figuring upheld utilizing remarkable stroll around Levy-flight, it is being gotten in neighborhood smallest is adjusted, and it to the degree anyone knows gives more triumphs especially to strike and multimodal benchmark limits. The planning improvement of the proposed CAO estimation is given in Algorithm 1.

ALGORITHM 1:   CLUSTER FORMATION USING CAO ALGORITHM

Input: *X← population size, F← number of design variables, termination criterion*
Output: *cluster formation*

1. *Initialize the position and distance of populations.*
2. *Compute initial solution using Equation (8.3), and identify best and worst solution in the population.*
3. *Modify the population solution using Equation (8.4).*
4. *Update the new solution if is better than old, otherwise maintain old one.*
5. *Stop the process if termination reached.*
6. ***Return:*** *Cluster formation*

8.10.2   TRUST COMPUTATION USING MULTI-OBJECTIVE DIFFERENTIAL EVOLUTION (MODE) ALGORITHM

The differential evolution (DE) algorithm [33] is a branch of transformative programs for reestablishing issues over pleasing spaces. The upsides of DE are its sensible structure, solace, speed, and power. DE striking harm from other fundamental effects suggests coordinating issues with the colossal encircled to respected domains. DE is a procedure contraption of gigantic utility that is in an inconsequential minute open for satisfying applications. DE has been utilized as a touch of two or three science and building applications to find influencing reactions for sensibly unmanageable issues without join as one with star information or complex strategy estimations. In the event that a structure is obliging to being continually analyzed, DE can give the best way to deal with oversee manage sort out expelling the best execution from it. DE utilizes change as a demand structure and choice to amass the power toward oversaw regions in the possible locale. Here, to vivify the consistent DE figuring by multi-objective DE (MODE) estimation utilizing the moving focuses, for example, criticalness utilize, got hail quality, administer lifetime, and stop up rate.

8.11   SIMULATION EXPERIMENTS

We use a simulation model based on NS2 in our evaluation (Kathirvel and Srinivasan, 2011a, 2011b). Our performance evaluations are based on the simulations of 200 wireless sensor nodes that form a wireless sensor network over a rectangular (1000 × 1000 m) flat space. The MAC layer protocol used in the simulations was the Distributed Coordination Function (DCF) of IEEE 802.11. The performance setting parameters are given in Table 8.2.

Before the simulation, we randomly selected 40% of the network population as generic malicious behavior nodes. Each flow did not change its source and destination for the lifetime of a simulation run. We kept the simulation time at 600s, so as to enable us to compare our results with that of ETUS.

Simulation studies have been done using NS2. We have carried out our focus attention on four parameters—packet delivery ratio, false negatives probability, false positives probability, and control overhead when node density and percentage of malicious nodes vary.

The performance evaluations for investigations are based on the simulations of 200 sensor nodes that form a WSN over a rectangular (1000 × 1000 m) flat space discussed in this section. Parameter settings are given in Table 8.1.

8.11.1   INVESTIGATIONS

Before the simulation, we randomly selected a certain fraction, ranging from 0% to 40% of the network population as malicious nodes. We considered only two attacks—modifying the hop count and dropping packets. Each flow did not change its source and destination for the lifetime of a simulation run.

TABLE 8.1
Parameter Settings

Property	Values
Simulation Time	600 seconds
Propagation Model	Two Rays Ground Reflection
Antenna	Omni Antenna
Initial Energy	14.3
Transmission Energy	0.395
Receiving Energy	0.660
Traffic Type	CBR (UDP)
Payload Size	512 bytes
Number of Flows	10 / 20 flows
Node Placement	Random
Transmission Range	200 meters
Radio Bandwidth	2 Mbps

TABLE 8.2
EIDR Throughput in Varying Node Density

Node Density	Percentage of Malicious Nodes				
	0%	10%	20%	30%	40%
50	99.48	99.59	99.58	99.48	90.54
75	99.16	99.48	97.41	96.45	83.44
100	98.38	98.60	95.91	96.15	78.42
150	97.19	97.77	93.95	93.24	72.64
200	97.40	95.96	93.44	91.33	65.57

TABLE 8.3
EIDR False Negatives in Varying Node Density

Node Density	Percentage of Malicious Nodes				
	0%	10%	20%	30%	40%
50	0	0.0934	0.1415	0.1425	0.1598
75	0	0.0933	0.1215	0.1239	0.1047
100	0	0.0531	0.0517	0.0622	0.0630
150	0	0.0639	0.0724	0.0729	0.0737
200	0	0.0731	0.0839	0.0799	0.0841

8.11.1.1 Throughput

In the world of MANET, the packet delivery ratio has been accepted as a standard measure of throughput. The packet delivery ratio is nothing but the ratio between the number of packets received by the destinations to the number of packets sent by the sources. We present in Table 8.2 the packet delivery ratios of EIDR with node density varying between 50 and 200.

From Tables 8.2 and 8.3, the following conclusions can be drawn:

i. In general, the packet delivery ratio decreases as the node density and the percentage of malicious nodes increase.
ii. We find that EIDR yields a much higher packet delivery ratio compared to generic ETUS, IDSEM, and ETUS in the presence of 40% malicious nodes. It is found that with EIDR, there is a higher packet delivery ratio ranging from 10.21% (ETUS, 50 node density) to 15.3% (ETUS, 200 node density).

8.11.1.2 Failure to Deduct (False Negatives) Probability

False Negatives Probability can be defined as

$$\text{False Negatives Probability} = \frac{\text{No. of malicious nodes left undetected}}{\text{Total number of malicious nodes}} = \frac{N_{LU}}{T_{MN}}$$

TABLE 8.4
EIDR False Positives in Varying Node Density

Node Density	Percentage of Malicious Nodes				
	0%	**10%**	**20%**	**30%**	**40%**
50	0	0	0	0	0
75	0	0.0021	0.0057	0.0064	0.0078
100	0	0.0067	0.0104	0.0113	0.0311
150	0	0.0087	0.0216	0.0245	0.0438
200	0	0.0079	0.0381	0.0318	0.0471

Table 8.3 presents the failure to deduct probability as a function of node density and percentage of malicious nodes.

The above definition requires some elaboration. We can think of two groups of malicious nodes that are left undetected. In the first group are those nodes, which never played a part in the network operation; they were probably traveling along the boundaries and never had a chance to participate in the network activity.

Tables 8.3 and 8.4 present the failure to detect probability as a function of node density and percentage of malicious nodes of generic ETUS, IDSEM, and ETUS, respectively. We have calculated the failure to detect probability by taking into consideration only those nodes that took part in the network activity. Other researchers have also adopted the same approach. A false negatives probability, which is the chance that umpires fail to convict and isolate a malicious node, can be defined as the ratio of the number of malicious nodes left undetected to the total number of malicious nodes. From Table 8.4, we can see that the false negatives probability has decreased in EIDR compared to ETUS.

8.11.1.3 False Accusation (False Positives) Probability

False accusation probability (refer to Table 8.4) is the chance that umpires incorrectly convict and isolate a legitimate node. In other words, this is the probability of wrongly booking innocent nodes. Table 8.5 presents false accusation probability as a function of node density and percentage of malicious nodes for EIDR and

TABLE 8.5
EIDR Communication Overhead in Varying Node Density

Node Density	Percentage of Malicious Nodes				
	0%	**10%**	**20%**	**30%**	**40%**
50	12151	15137	18764	20274	22174
75	12357	15934	18969	20386	22889
100	12554	17835	20061	21395	23898
150	12947	18042	21172	21563	24889
200	13534	18069	21789	22984	25541

ETUS, respectively. We find a similar decrease in the false accusation probability for all other combinations of malicious node percentages and node density values with ETUS. We find that false positives probability increases with the increasing percentage of malicious nodes and increased node density. We present a comparison of false positives probability values between generic ETUS, IDSEM, EIDR, and ETUS of 40% of malicious nodes. It is seen that with EIDR, false positives probabilities decrease slightly.

8.11.1.4 Communication Overhead

The communication overhead for EIDR is given in Table 8.5. Table 6 Communication overhead for GETUS, plain AODV, ETUS, IDSEM, and EIDR in the presence of 40% of malicious nodes.

i. In general, the communication overhead increases as the node density and the percentage of malicious nodes increase.
ii. We find that EIDR yields a much lower communication overhead compared to generic ETUS and ETUS in the presence of 40% malicious nodes, as shown in Table 6.6. It is found that with EIDR, there is a lower communication overhead ranging from 18% (ETUS 50 node density) to 38.75% (ETUS 200 node density).

8.12 CONCLUSION

The proposed model AI-based EIDR system using a combination of clustering and trust model was implemented. In EIDR, the CAO algorithm is utilized to form the optimal clustering with a balanced network, and the MODE algorithm is utilized to compute the trust value of each node. Then, the IRA system was perfomed using the computed trust values. The simulation result shows the effectiveness of the proposed EIDR system in terms of delay, loss ratio, energy consumption, network lifetime, throughput, detection rate, and false positive rate.

REFERENCES

Akbani, R., Akdemir, K. C., Aksoy, B. A., Albert, M., Ally, A., Amin, S. B., ... & Kwong, L. N. (2015). Genomic classification of cutaneous melanoma. *Cell*, *161*(7), 1681–1696.
Bleda, A. L., Fernández-Luque, F. J., Rosa, A., Zapata, J., & Maestre, R. (2017). Smart sensory furniture based on WSN for ambient assisted living. *IEEE Sensors Journal*, *17*(17), 5626–5636.
Carss, K. J., Arno, G., Erwood, M., Stephens, J., Sanchis-Juan, A., Hull, S., ... & Krishnakumar, D. (2017). Comprehensive rare variant analysis via whole-genome sequencing to determine the molecular pathology of inherited retinal disease. *The American Journal of Human Genetics*, *100*(1), 75–90.
Deif, D. and Gadallah, Y., An Ant Colony Optimization Approach for the Deployment of Reliable Wireless Sensor Networks. *IEEE Access*, 5, 10744–10756, 2017.
Erbacher, R. F., Walker, K. L., & Frincke, D. A. (2002). Intrusion and misuse detection in large-scale systems. *IEEE Computer Graphics and Applications*, *22*(1), 38–47.
Hoyle, B., Rau, M., Paech, K., Bonnett, C., Seitz, S. & Weller, J. (2015). Anomaly detection for machine learning redshifts applied to SDSS galaxies. *Monthly Notices of the Royal Astronomical Society*, *452*(4), 4183–4194.

Jokhio, F., Ashraf, A., Lafond, S., Porres, I., & Lilius, J. (2013, February). Prediction-based dynamic resource allocation for video transcoding in cloud computing. In *2013 21st Euromicro International Conference on Parallel, Distributed, and Network-Based Processing* (pp. 254–261). IEEE.

Kathirvel, A. and Srinivasan, R., ETUS: An Enhanced Triple Umpiring System for Security and Performance Improvement of Mobile Ad Hoc Networks. *International Journal of Network Management*, 21, 5, 341–359, September/October 2011a, John Wiley & Sons.

Kathirvel, A. and Srinivasan, R., ETUS: An Enhanced Triple Umpiring System for Security and Robustness of Mobile Ad Hoc Networks. *International Journal of Communication Networks and Distributed Systems, Inderscience*, 7, 1/2, 2011b, 153–187.

Mishra, S. K., Jain, M. K., & Singh, V. P. (2004). Evaluation of the SCS-CN-based model incorporating antecedent moisture. *Water Resources Management*, 18, 567–589.

Sun, L. Y., Aryee, S., & Law, K. S. (2007). High-performance human resource practices, citizenship behavior, and organizational performance: A relational perspective. *Academy of Management Journal, 50*(3), 558–577.

Valeur, F., Vigna, G., Kruegel, C., & Kemmerer, R. A. (2004). Comprehensive approach to intrusion detection alert correlation. *IEEE Transactions on Dependable and Secure Computing, 1*(3), 146–169.

Wu, J., Zhang, C., Xue, T., Freeman, B., & Tenenbaum, J. (2016). Learning a probabilistic latent space of object shapes via 3d generative-adversarial modeling. *Advances in Neural Information Processing Systems, 29.*

Yang, H., Luo, H., Ye, F., Lu, S., & Zhang, L. (2004). Security in mobile ad hoc networks: challenges and solutions. *IEEE Wireless Communications, 11*(1), 38–47.

Ye, W., Heidemann, J., & Estrin, D. (2004). Medium access control with coordinated adaptive sleeping for wireless sensor networks. *IEEE/ACM Transactions on Networking, 12*(3), 493–506.

9 Methodology for Programming of AI-Based IDS

Krishnamoorthy Parkavi and
Rajayan Christy Jeyavim Sherin

Vellore Institute of Technology, Chennai, India

CONTENTS

9.1   WHAT IS METHODOLOGY FOR PROGRAMMING?

A programming methodology is a method for explaining multiple actual issues, making software development plans, and trying to control application development.

DOI: 10.1201/9781003346340-9

179

The following are the Methodologies for Programming:

Sequential

- The issue is divided into techniques, or code frames, that each accomplishes a specific task.
- The programme is made of all procedures taken together.
- Only suitable for small programmes
- For instance, consider the calculator programme.

Object-Oriented

- The solution is centred on entities or objects that are a part of the problem.
- Employees, salary structure, leave rules, and so on are examples of entities in a payroll management system on which the solution should be developed.

9.2 MACHINE LEARNING ALGORITHMS FOR INTRUSION DETECTION

9.2.1 INTRODUCTION

An intrusion detection system (IDS) is a piece of software that detects network intrusions by utilising various ML algorithms. An IDS detects a network or system for fraudulent attacks and provides protection to a computer system from unauthorised access by users, including potential insiders [1]. The attack detector is required to learn the task by developing a predictive model (i.e., a classifier) that can tell the difference between "wrong interconnection" (detection and mitigation) and "great (standard) connections." There are four different types of attacks:

- DOS: denial-of-service
- R2L: unauthorised access from a remote machine, e.g., guessing password;
- U2R: unauthorised access to local super user (root) privileges, e.g., various "buffer overflow" attacks;
- Probing: surveillance and another probing, e.g., port scanning.

Dataset used: KDD Cup 1999 dataset.

9.2.2 FEATURES KDD CUP 1999

The KDD CUP99 dataset was used in DARPA's IDS evaluation programme. This dataset contains seven gigabytes of network traffic packets [1]. This method can hold approximately 5 million records. Each feature extraction is one of two types: attack vectors or normal feature vectors [2]. Table 9.1 presents the features of the KDD CUP99 Dataset.

9.2.3 RELATIONSHIP AMONG ARTIFICIAL INTELLIGENCE, MACHINE LEARNING, AND DEEP LEARNING

Nowadays, there are a lot of misconceptions about machine learning, deep learning, and artificial intelligence (AI). In general, the word AI is often associated with

TABLE 9.1
Features of KDD CUP99 Dataset [2]

w	Name	Description
1	Duration	Duration of connection in seconds
2	Protocol type	Connection protocol (tcp, udp, icmp)
3	Service	Dst port mapped to service (e.g., http, ftp, …)
4	Flag	Normal or error status flag of connection
5	Src bytes	Number of data bytes from src to dst
6	Dst bytes	Bytes from dst to src
7	Land	1 if the connection is from/to the same host/ port; else 0
8	Wrong fragment	Number of "wrong fragments" (values 0, 1, 3)
9	Urgent	Number of urgent packets
10	Hot	Number of "hot" indicators
11	Num failed logins	Number of failed login attempts
12	Logged in	1 if successfully logged in; else 0
13	Num compromised	Number of failed login attempts
14	Root shell	1 if root shell is obtained; else 0
15	Su attempted	1 if "Su root" command attempted; else 0
16	Num root	Number of "root" accesses
17	Num file creations	Number of file creation operations
18	Num shells	Number of shell prompts
19	Num access files	Number of operations on access control files
20	Num outbound cmds	Number of outbound commands in an ftp session
21	Is hot login	1 if login belongs to "hot" list (e.g., root, adm); else 0
22	Is guest login	1 if login is "guest" login (e.g., guest, anonymous); else 0
23	Count	Number of connections to the same host as the current connection in the past two seconds
24	Srv	Number of connections to the same service as the current connection in the past two seconds
25	Serror rate	% of connections that have "SYN" errors
26	Srv rate	% of connections that have "SYN" errors
27	Rerror rate	% of connections that have "REJ" errors
28	Srv rerror rate	% of connections that have "REJ" errors
29	Same srv rate	% of connections to the same service
30	Diff host rate	% of connections to different services
31	Srv diff host rate	% of connections to different hosts
32	Dst hot count	Count of connections having the same dst host
33	Dst host_srv_count	Count of connections having the same dst host and using the same service
34	Dst_host_same_srv_rate	% of connections having the same dst host and using same service
35	Dst host diff srv rate	% of different services of the current host
36	Dst host same src _post rate	% of connections to the current host having the same src port
37	Dst_host_srv_diff_host_rate	% of connections to the same service coming from diff. hosts
38	Dst host serror _rate	% of connections to the current host that have an S0 error
39	Dst_host_srv_serror_rate	% of connections to the current host and specified service that have an S0 error
40	Dst_host_rerror_rate	% of connections to the current host that have an RST error
41	Dst_host_srv_rerror_rate	% of connections to the current host and specified service that have an RST error

machine learning or vice versa [3]. There is a strong relation between them but they are not the same.

9.2.4 ARTIFICIAL INTELLIGENCE

AI is broadly the method of incorporating machines with human intelligence using policies or algorithms. The two words in AI are "artificial," which refers to human-made or unnatural, and "intelligence," which refers to the capability to comprehend or think appropriately. It also might be defined as follows: "AI is the study of training your machine (computers) to mimic a human brain and its thinking capabilities." To achieve maximum efficiency, AI focuses on three major factors (skill sets): studying, rationality, and self-correction. Different AI-based methods are used for IDSs and Intrusion Protection Systems (IPSs) [1, 4]. The implementation of Expert Systems is a current development trend. Expert IDSs are being developed in using Neural Network algorithms, Genetic Algorithm, Fuzzy Logic algorithms, and other algorithms for pattern recognition and learning [5]. An expert system is comprised of a knowledge base in which rules are stored and inferences are made for the purpose.

9.2.5 MACHINE LEARNING

Before looking deeper into machine learning, consider another concept known as data mining. Data mining is a method for examining a large database and extracting techniques similar to machine learning, in fact, and it is one of the data mining techniques [1]. "Machine Learning is a method of parsing data, learning from it, and then applying what they have learned to make an informed decision."

9.2.6 DEEP LEARNING

Deep learning is a subdivision of machine learning. It has different capabilities but machine learning technically works in the same way [6]. The main distinction between machine learning and deep learning is that models of machine learning improve over time, whereas require guidance in the deep learning models. If there is an incorrect prediction in the machine learning model, the programmer manually intervenes to fix it; however, in the same scenario, deep learning models do it on their own [7]. Differences between AI, ML, and DL is shown in Table 9.2.

9.3 USING AI FOR NETWORK-BASED INTRUSION DETECTION SYSTEM

1. **Machine Learning**
   With the increased quantity of confidential data flowing in and through numerous connections, intrusion is a growing problem that concerns today's world and intrusion detection is the key focus area for research [8]. The anomalies are detected using a variety of techniques in Machine Learning. Different learning techniques are highly useful compared to single techniques which are frequently used in anomaly detection. In recent years, hybrid or ensemble learning techniques have also been used. These techniques are

TABLE 9.2
Differences between AI, ML, and DL

Artificial Intelligence	Machine Learning	Deep Learning
Artificial Intelligence is to train machines to mimic human behaviour using a particular algorithm.	Machine Learning is the study of the statistical methods that allow machines which can improve with experience through learning.	Deep Learning is the study of neural networks to mimic human brain function.
It employs find trees and other complex mathematical functions.	It involves complex functionalities such as k-mean, Support Vector Machines (SVM).	DL aspect by breaking the complex functionalities into linear or lower-dimension features by adding more layers.
AI refers to a computer algorithm that demonstrates intelligence through decision-making.	ML is an artificial intelligence algorithm that allows a system to learn from data.	DL is a machine learning algorithm that analyses data and provides output using deep (multiple-layer) neural networks.
AI is a broader term that includes ML and DL as components.	Machine Learning is the subset of Artificial Intelligence.	Deep Learning is the subset of Machine Learning.
The efficiency of AI is essentially the efficiency provided by ML and DL.	It is less efficient than DL because it cannot work with longer dimensions or larger amounts of data.	It is more powerful than ML because it can work with larger datasets.
The goal is to increase the chances of success rather than accuracy.	The goal is to improve accuracy without regard to the success ratio.	When trained with a large amount of data, it achieves the highest accuracy ranking.

used in conjunction with a classifier. The classifier analyses the packets and determines bad or good connections. The machine learning pattern classification technique is primarily used for detecting anomalies, achieved using machine learning supervised and unsupervised learning methods [9]. Supervised learning is accomplished by training a function using training datasets, using the supervised learning to train dataset input, and the output vector is produced.

2. **Neural Networks**

Neural Networks creates a software behaviour profile that differentiates software behaviour between normal and malicious. The Neural Networks used in Intrusion Detection can distinguish between malicious and safe networks [10]. The network of artificial neural networks consists of connections that connect the processing units or also called nodes. The connection weight is useful to determine between two units the effect of one unit on the other. It implements a mapping from one set of values to another set of values using an activation function. The IDS can be created using the classical feed-forward multi-layer perceptron rule. Also, the backpropagation networks are successfully used in network intrusion detection as they are useful for the learning in the IDS that helps to learn and build profiles to detect any anomalous behaviour [11].

9.4   GENETIC ALGORITHM (GA)

Computational model algorithmic type that adopts the fundamentals of natural evolution and natural selection. In the genetic algorithm model, the problems are converted into a specific domain. The data structure in the algorithm is like a chromosome, that uses mutual operators, recombination, and selection as the chromosomes. Simple network access rules can be defined using a genetic algorithm [12]. These rules help to avoid the passage of known malicious attacks. The rules are stored as "if" and "then" statements with regular expressions.

9.5   FUZZY LOGIC (FL)

Fuzzy logic works best when dealing with complex problems. It consists of a set of fuzzy elements, which includes the range between 0 and 1 [13]. It lacks sharp values found in Boolean sets, such as 0 and 1. The elements' membership can be perfectly represented. In the first step, symbolic-valued attributes are converted to numeric-valued attributes (like tcp, udp, icmp, etc.). Features were then scaled linearly to each range. Then combining the testing data, and training datasets using fuzzy inference define rules. Techniques of Data Mining are applied to a TCP data packet that helps to extract non-explicitly mentioned parameters in the packet. These parameters used are very critical in distinguishing between normal and abnormal behaviour. In a nutshell, it is the creation of parameters that are critical for providing fuzzy inputs. The source and destination TCP control bits, IP addresses, port numbers, and other information are extracted [5, 14]. The source IP, destination IP, and port fields of the destination are combined to generate an aggregate key, then from the mined data, the key is used to generate counts and measure other statistics. After the completion of the extraction phase, fuzzy sets are generated based on the previous inputs and the applicable range is calculated. The calculations of these data feeds are based on three distinct variables: VARIANCE, UNIQUENESS, and COUNT. The data elements are also represented by five fuzzy sets: LOW, MEDIUM-LOW, MEDIUM, MEDIUMHIGH, and HIGH [15].

9.6   OTHER METHODS

i) **K-Nearest Neighbours (KNNs)**

K-nearest neighbour (KNN) is a new technique used to differentiate between normal behaviour and intrusive programme behaviour. The frequency of system calls is used by KNNs to detect malicious network activity [16]. Adopting KNNs technique with text categorisation feature categorises texts and convert them into vectors, then uses it to compare and differentiate two programme activities. Text categorisation is the process of grouping predefined categories of system-called documents. Text categorisation can also benefit from a variety of machine learning techniques. The vector space model is used to translate it into words first. The document's neighbours are then ranked using the classifier algorithm KNN. Classes are weighted based on how similar the vector is to each of its neighbours. As a result, they are analogous in terms of detection. The computation complexity is reduced because the generation of programme profiles is no longer required. Furthermore, when compared to other techniques, KNN false positives are very low. The following Python code shows the KNN model.

```
## Using KNN
#Remember that we are trying to come up with a model to predict whether someone
#will TARGET CLASS or not. We'll start with k=1.
from sklearn.neighbors import KNeighborsClassifier
knn = KNeighborsClassifier(n_neighbors=1)
knn.fit(X_train,y_train)
KNeighborsClassifier(algorithm='auto', leaf_size=30, metric='minkowski',
            metric_params=None, n_jobs=1, n_neighbors=1, p=2,
            weights='uniform')
            pred = knn.predict(X_test)
```

ii) **Naïve Bayes**

Naïve Bayes is grounded on the Bayes theorem for most classification problems. We know the relationship between system variables. The basis is that some predefined variables have the potential to influence these system variables [17]. Furthermore, expressing the relationship between these variables precisely may be difficult. The probabilistic graph model is created based on statistical, structural, and casual relationships that exist between the variables; it is also known as the Naïve Bayes network. This model predicts and answers questions related to the likelihood of reoccurrence of a certain type of attack, based on the recording of previous events. A conditional probability formula is used to provide an answer to the question. The structure of the Naïve Bayes Network is represented by the Direct Acyclic Graph (DAG). A node in the graph represents each system variables and the links that represent the relation between one node to another node. What we will find in the Naïve Bayes classifier is the probability that a given data point belongs to a specific class; we will have predictions for all of the classes in our target Equation (9.1).

$$P(x) = \frac{P(c)P(c)}{P(x)} \tag{9.1}$$

The following Python source code shows the Naïve Bayes binary classifier model.

```
##Naïve Bayes
import numpy as np
class NaiveBayesBinaryClassifier:
    def fit(self, X, y):
        self.y_classes, y_counts = np.unique(y, return_counts=True)
        self.phi_y = 1.0 * y_counts/y_counts.sum()
        self.phi_x = [1.0 * X[y==k].mean(axis=0) for k in self.y_classes]
        return self
    def predict(self, X):
        return np.apply_along_axis(lambda x: self.compute_probs(x), 1, X)
    def compute_probs(self, x):
    probs = [self.compute_prob(x, y) for y in range(len(self.y_classes))]
    return self.y_classes[np.argmax(probs)]
    def compute_prob(self, x, y):
    res = 1
    for j in range(len(x)):
        Pxy = self.phi_x[y][j] # p(xj=1|y)
        res *= (Pxy**x[j])*((1-Pxy)**(1-x[j])) # p(xj=0|y)
    return res * self.phi_y[y]
    def score(self, X, y):
    return (self.predict(X) == y).mean()
```

iii) **Decision Tree**

A supervised learning algorithm type that has a flow-graph-like structure with each of the internal nodes in the tree representing a test case. It organises the sample in a way that the current decision makes subsequent decisions that reach a conclusion [18]. A decision tree is used to represent such a series of decisions. The path from the root to the leaf is designed such that each leaf represents a different type of classification. Attributes are assigned to each node, and a decision is made after computing all of the attributes for that node. As a result, a path like this from the root to the leaf node represents classification rules. These classification rules are defined based on anomalies detected by the machine or encountered in the past. They are defined based on the behaviour and are classified based on the attributes such that when a sample is run through, the decision tree will progress through by making decisions and arriving at a conclusion, indicating whether the behaviour is malicious or not. A classification tree is a decision tree with a range of discrete (symbolic) class labels, whereas a regression tree has a range of continuous (numeric) values. According to their applications, any tree can be used for intrusion detection [19]. The following Python source code shows the Decision Tree classifier model.

```
## DecisionTreeClassifier
from sklearn.tree import DecisionTreeClassifier
# instantiate the DecisionTreeClassifier model with criterion gini index
clf_gini = DecisionTreeClassifier(criterion='gini', max_depth=3, random_state=0
# fit the model
clf_gini.fit(X_train, y_train)
DecisionTreeClassifier(class_weight=None, criterion='gini', max_depth=3,
            max_features=None, max_leaf_nodes=None,
            min_impurity_decrease=0.0, min_impurity_split=None,
            min_samples_leaf=1, min_samples_split=2,
            min_weight_fraction_leaf=0.0, presort=False, random_state=0,
            splitter='best')
```

iv) **Support Vector Machine (SVM)**

Support vector machines (SVM) are used to solve problems of binary classification. It is a supervised learning algorithm; the concept is built on decision planes which are defined by decision boundaries [5]. During the training of the IDS, SVM that is multiclass constructs k phases [20]. Hence, the IDS uses multiclass SVMs for classification. The greatest margin in hyperplane between classes is best for SVM and it is used for classification.

```
#Import svm model
from sklearn import svm

#Create a svm Classifier
clf = svm.SVC(kernel='linear') # Linear Kernel

#Train the model using the training sets
clf.fit(X_train, y_train)

#Predict the response for test dataset
y_pred = clf.predict(X_test)
```

v) **Swarm-Based Algorithm (SBA)**

Collective intelligence is also known as swarm intelligence (SI). Scientists were interested in the social insects' behaviour, for their unique ability that they adopt to solve complex problems, such as finding the shortest path between their nests and food sources [5]. Without individual education, they perform amazing achievements as a group by intercommunication with their surroundings. There are eight types of swarm intelligence algorithms in swarm-based optimisation – Ant colony optimiser, particle swarm optimiser, artificial bee colony algorithm, glow worm algorithm, firefly algorithm, cuckoo search strategy, bat algorithm, and hunting search algorithm are some of the tactics that were used.

SI aims to solve complex problems by using computational intelligence methods. The study of how individuals interact with each other at the local level is known as swarm intelligence. When it comes to biological systems, nature is a great source of inspiration. The agents follow rules because there is a lack of centralised control. The uneven iteration between agencies outcomes in the "smart" behaviour is exhibited by the individual agents.

vi) **Simulated Annealing**

Simulated Annealing is a global search optimisation algorithm that is stochastic. This means that it incorporates randomness into the search process. This makes the algorithm suitable for nonlinear objective functions, where other local search algorithms fail [21]. It modifies a single solution and searches the relatively local area of the search space until the local optima are found, similar to the stochastic hill-climbing local search algorithm. In contrast to the hill-climbing algorithm, it may accept less desirable solutions as the current working solution. The probability of accepting worse solutions increases at the start of the search and decreases as it progresses, allowing the algorithm to first locate the region for the global optima, avoiding local optima, and then hill-climbing to the maxima itself. The function optimisation algorithm is based on simulated annealing.

The simulated annealing algorithm using Python is as follows:

```python
##Simulated Annealing
def Sim_Ann(ini_x, fac, T, t_fac, n_fac):
    x1 = ini_x
    x2 = rand_point(x1, fac)
    delta = dist(x1, x2)
    del_f = del_fun(x1, x2)
    good_x = [x1]              ## LIST OF GOOD POINTS
    good_f = [f(x1)]           ## LIST OF FUNCTION VALUES OF GOOD POINTS
    while (delta > 0.0001):
        n = 0
        while n < n_fac:
            if del_f <= 0:
                good_x.append(x2)
                good_f.append(f(x2))
                x1 = x2
                x2 = rand_point(x1, fac)
            elif (del_f > 0) and (T != 0):
                p = boltz_prob(del_f, T)
                if random.choices([0, 1], weights = [1-p, p]) == [1]:
                    x1 = x2
                    x2 = rand_point(x1, fac)
                else:
                    x2 = good_x[good_f.index(min(good_f))]
            else:
                x2 = good_x[good_f.index(min(good_f))]
            del_f = del_fun(x1, x2)
            n += 1
        T = t_fac*T
        delta = dist(x1, x2)
    return x1, f(x1), good_x
```

```
## Objective function
def f(x):
    f_v = 100*((abs(x[1] - (0.01*(x[0]**2))))**0.5) + 0.01*(abs(x[0]+10)) + x[2]**2
    return f_v

ini_x = [-5, 0, 0] ## INITIAL SEARCH POINT
fac = 1          ## FACTOR OF SEARCH
T = Temp(ini_x, 1) ## INITIALIZING TEMPERATURE
t_fac = 0.5      ## TEMPERATURE FACTOR
n_fac = 10000    ## n FACTOR

(min_x, min_f, good_x) = Sim_Ann(ini_x, fac, T, t_fac, n_fac)
print(f'Minimum point: {min_x}')
print(f'Function value: {min_f}')
```

9.7 EVOLUTIONARY ALGORITHM (EA)

Evolutionary Algorithm (EA) is a meta-heuristic-based method which solves difficult problems easily. It contains processes such as initialisation, selection, genetic operators, and termination. EAs include genetic algorithm (GA), genetic programming (GP), evolutionary strategy (ES), differentiated evolution, and the recently developed Paddy Field Algorithm.

More features are shared by the EA family. All of them are survival-based population-based stochastic search methods. Each algorithm starts iteratively, first with a feasible solution population and it matures from generation to generation until the best-discovered solution is found. Within the population of solutions, fitness-based choosing occurs in consecutive iterations of the EA algorithm [6]. The learning is prioritised based on better solutions that are carried to the next generation. Figure 9.1 shows the processing steps of the EA algorithm.

9.8 DEEP LEARNING ARCHITECTURE

The main goal of deep learning in the development of intrusion systems is to extract features and perform classification tasks [22]. Auto-Encoder (AE), Recurrent Neural Networks (RNNs), Deep Belief Networks (DBNs), Convolutional Neural Networks (CNNs), and Hybrid Deep Learning are commonly used in deep learning techniques for intrusion detection [23]. Figure 9.2 illustrates the architecture of deep learning.

Unsupervised learning can benefit from deep learning approaches. This is a significant advantage because unlabelled data outnumbers labelled data.

9.9 AUTO-ENCODER (AE)

In literature, auto-encoder (AE) is the most commonly defined method, mainly useful for the task of dimension reduction and classification [24]. This method's function is to copy the input encoder to the output decoder. It's used in a variety of

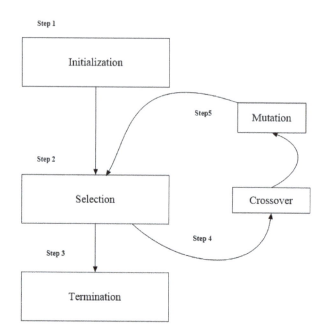

FIGURE 9.1   Processing steps of evolutionary algorithm (EA).

applications with compression and classification features. The extensions of AE are stacked, sparse, and denoising [25].

9.10   RECURRENT NEURAL NETWORKS (RNNs)

RNNs are a subset of artificial neural networks (ANNs) that is used for classification and regression [26]. RNNs are commonly used in two ways: the first is Long Short-Term Memory (LSTM) and the second is Gated Recurrent Units (GRU). This technique in deep learning helps to predict time series data. It requires access to previous data in current iterations. A variety of applications uses them, including robot control, especially in speech recognition and intrusion detection models. Numerous studies have been conducted to demonstrate that RNN adopted in IDS resulted in satisfactory results.

9.11   DEEP BELIEF NETWORKS (DBNs)

DBN is based on stacked Restricted Boltzmann Machine methods. A DBN from an original dataset learns the probability distribution and draws conclusions for unknown datasets. It can be applied to classification, dimensionality reduction, and regression [27]. The aim is to attain well-feature learning. During the training phase, a hidden layer is trained individually for input rebuilding, achieved by adjusting the weights and using rapid algorithms.

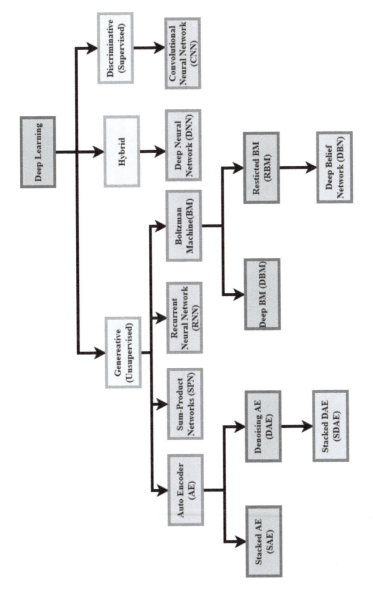

FIGURE 9.2 Deep learning architecture.

9.12 CONVOLUTIONAL NEURAL NETWORKS (CNNs)

The CNN is a neural network structure of deep learning, it is intended for complex data processes. It is a supervised learning model applied to various patterns classification [11]. It strengthens the DNN layers links. CNNs use nonlinear, fully connected networks to train multiple layers. CNNs' hidden layers consist of complex layers that combine with other layers in the network. CNN extracts complex features to perform the task with better accuracy. Applications like intrusion detection, face recognition engine, image feature extraction engine, and video analysis engine use CNNs [22].

CNNs clear the hurdles in traditional machine learning methods and is mainly used in IDSs. Several CNN-based approaches are used in IDS to address privacy concerns and security threats.

In CNN architectures, the convolutional operation across input feature maps and convolutional layers is represented by the following Equation (9.2).

$$h_j^{(n)} = \sum_{k=1}^{K} h_k^{(n-1)} \otimes w_{kj}^{(n)} + b_{kj}^{(n)} \tag{9.2}$$

where $\otimes$ denotes the output of the jth feature map in the nth hidden layer and represents a 2D convolution. Meanwhile, $h_j^{(n)}$, $h_k^{(n-1)}$ represents the kth hidden layer channel, $w_{kj}^{(n)}$ represents the kth channel weights in the nth layer's jth filter, and $b_{kj}^{(n)}$ represents the relevant bias term. A large number of feature maps is generated by collecting multiple convolutional layers, and then an additional layer is added to the convolutional layers to reduce the dimensionality of these properties [11]. This is

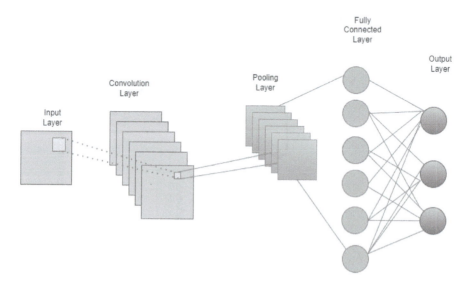

FIGURE 9.3 Architecture of CNN [28].

called a pooling layer and it helps reduce computational expense, which is essential to train networks while also reducing the likelihood of overfitting. Figure 9.3 shows the CNN architecture.

9.13 HYBRID DEEP LEARNING

Both generative and discriminative models are used in hybrid architectures. A Hybrid Model can effectively combine different methods of deep learning (e.g., LSTM with GRU, BiLSTM, and CNN with other techniques) [29]. The learning was performed in a progressive manner and it yielded the best results. Various techniques are used to extract features from various deep learning methods, combine these features, and classify them.

9.14 DEEP NEURAL NETWORKS (DNNs)

DNN is an ANN and has multiple hidden layers between input and output layers. A neural network's main purpose is to receive a set of inputs, perform increasingly complicated math on them, and output results to solve real-world problems such as classification [22, 24]. It limits us to forward-feeding neural networks. Deep neural networks offer a lot of value to statisticians, particularly, it will be increasing the accuracy of a machine learning model [29]. Figure 9.4 shows the DNN architecture.

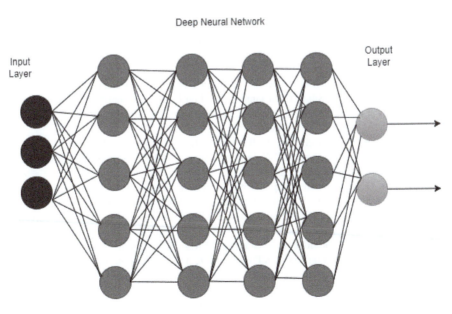

FIGURE 9.4 DNN architecture [28].

9.15   CONCLUSION

The deep learning IDS is exceptionally effective in detecting and classifying different types of malicious attacks. Deep learning methods outperform traditional machine learning algorithms in handling complex data which is one of the key challenges of IDS. The hybrid or combined deep learning method is highly effective in detecting threats with very high accuracy.

REFERENCES

[1] R. Malik, Y. Singh, Z. A. Sheikh, P. Anand, P. K. Singh, and T. C. Workneh, "An Improved Deep Belief Network IDS on IoT-Based Network for Traffic Systems," *J. Adv. Transp.*, vol. 2022, 2022, doi: 10.1155/2022/7892130.

[2] R. C. Jeyavim Sherin and K. Parkavi, "Investigations on Bio-Inspired Algorithm for Network Intrusion Detection – A Review," *Int. J. Comput. Networks Appl.*, vol. 9, no. 4, pp. 399–423, 2022, doi: 10.22247/ijcna/2022/214503.

[3] S. K. Shandilya, S. Upadhyay, A. Kumar, and A. K. Nagar, "AI-assisted Computer Network Operations testbed for Nature-Inspired Cyber Security based adaptive defense simulation and analysis," *Futur. Gener. Comput. Syst.*, vol. 127, pp. 297–308, Feb. 2022, doi: 10.1016/j.future.2021.09.018.

[4] C. Science and C. Centre, "PARKAVI. K, SWAMINATHAN. A, VIVEKANANDAN P Computer Science and Engineering, Anna University, Chennai, India. 3 Computer Centre, Anna University, Chennai, India.," vol. 23, pp. 487–498, 2015.

[5] G. Kocher and G. Kumar, "Machine learning and deep learning methods for intrusion detection systems: recent developments and challenges," *Soft Comput.*, vol. 25, no. 15, pp. 9731–9763, 2021. doi: 10.1007/s00500-021-05893-0.

[6] L. Ashiku and C. Dagli, "Network Intrusion Detection System using Deep Learning," *Procedia Computer Science*, 2021, vol. 185, pp. 239–247. doi: 10.1016/j.procs.2021.05.025.

[7] Y. K. Saheed and M. O. Arowolo, "Efficient Cyber Attack Detection on the Internet of Medical Things-Smart Environment Based on Deep Recurrent Neural Network and Machine Learning Algorithms," *IEEE Access*, vol. 9, pp. 161546–161554, 2021, doi: 10.1109/ACCESS.2021.3128837.

[8] E. Alhajjar, P. Maxwell, and N. Bastian, "Adversarial machine learning in Network Intrusion Detection Systems," *Expert Syst. Appl.*, vol. 186, no. May, p. 115782, 2021, doi: 10.1016/j.eswa.2021.115782.

[9] S. Idris, O. Oyefolahan Ishaq, and N. Ndunagu Juliana, "Intrusion Detection System Based on Support Vector Machine Optimised with Cat Swarm Optimization Algorithm," *2019 2nd Int. Conf. IEEE Niger. Comput. Chapter, Niger. 2019*, 2019, doi: 10.1109/NigeriaComputConf45974.2019.8949676.

[10] A. E. Ibor, O. B. Okunoye, F. A. Oladeji, and K. A. Abdulsalam, "Novel Hybrid Model for Intrusion Prediction on Cyber Physical Systems' Communication Networks based on Bio-inspired Deep Neural Network Structure," *J. Inf. Secur. Appl.*, vol. 65, no. January, p. 103107, 2022, doi: 10.1016/j.jisa.2021.103107.

[11] T. Saba, A. Rehman, T. Sadad, H. Kolivand, and S. A. Bahaj, "Anomaly-based intrusion detection system for IoT networks through deep learning model," *Comput. Electr. Eng.*, vol. 99, no. February, p. 107810, 2022, doi: 10.1016/j.compeleceng.2022.107810.

[12] M. Sazzadul Hoque, "An Implementation of Intrusion Detection System Using Genetic Algorithm," *Int. J. Netw. Secur. Its Appl.*, vol. 4, no. 2, pp. 109–120, 2012, doi: 10.5121/ijnsa.2012.4208.

[13] G. Wang, "Research on Network Security Risk Assessment Method Based on Improved Analytic Hierarchy Process," *Int. J. Netw. Secur.*, vol. 23, no. 3, pp. 515–521, 2021, doi: 10.6633/IJNS.202105.

[14] K. Parkavi and P. Vivekanandan, "A novel cluster based energy efficient protocol for wireless networks," *IEEE-International Conf. Adv. Eng. Sci. Manag. ICAESM-2012*, pp. 645–650, 2012.

[15] P. Kanchan, "Rainfall Analysis and Forecasting Using Deep Learning Technique," *J. Informatics Electr. Electron. Eng.*, vol. 2, no. 2, pp. 1–11, 2021, doi: 10.54060/jieee/002.02.015.

[16] T. S. Naseri and F. S. Gharehchopogh, "A Feature Selection Based on the Farmland Fertility Algorithm for Improved Intrusion Detection Systems," *J. Netw. Syst. Manag.*, vol. 30, no. 3, 2022, doi: 10.1007/s10922-022-09653-9.

[17] S. Mukherjee and N. Sharma, "Intrusion Detection using Naive Bayes Classifier with Feature Reduction," *Procedia Technol.*, vol. 4, pp. 119–128, 2012, doi: 10.1016/j.protcy. 2012.05.017.

[18] K. Peng, V. C. M. Leung, L. Zheng, S. Wang, C. Huang, and T. Lin, "Intrusion Detection System Based on Decision Tree Over Big Data in Fog Environment," *Wirel. Commun. Mob. Comput.*, vol. 2018, 2018, doi: 10.1155/2018/4680867.

[19] S. Shilpashree, S. C. Lingareddy, N. G. Bhat, and G. Sunil Kumar, "Decision tree: A machine learning for intrusion detection," *Int. J. Innov. Technol. Explor. Eng.*, vol. 8, no. 6 Special Issue 4, pp. 1126–1130, 2019, doi: 10.35940/ijitee.F1234.0486S419.

[20] M. N. Mohammed and N. Sulaiman, "Intrusion Detection System Based on SVM for WLAN," *Procedia Technol.*, vol. 1, pp. 313–317, 2012, doi: 10.1016/j.protcy.2012.02.066.

[21] A. A. Obeidat, "Novel Approach for Intrusion Detection Using Simulated Annealing Algorithm Combined with Hopfield Neural Network," *Int. J. Commun. Networks Inf. Secur.*, vol. 12, no. 3, pp. 289–294, 2020.

[22] D. Akgun, S. Hizal, and U. Cavusoglu, "A new DDoS Attacks Intrusion Detection Model Based On Deep Learning for Cybersecurity," *Comput. Secur.*, vol. 118, p. 102748, 2022, doi: 10.1016/j.cose.2022.102748.

[23] D. Selvapandian and R. Santhosh, "Deep Learning Approach for Intrusion Detection in IoT-multi Cloud Environment," *Autom. Softw. Eng.*, vol. 28, no. 2, pp. 1–17, 2021, doi: 10.1007/s10515-021-00298-7.

[24] Y. N. Kunang, S. Nurmaini, D. Stiawan, and B. Y. Suprapto, "Attack Classification of an Intrusion Detection System Using Deep Learning and Hyperparameter Optimization," *J. Inf. Secur. Appl.*, vol. 58, no. March, p. 102804, 2021, doi: 10.1016/j.jisa.2021.102804.

[25] Eul H. Qazi, M. Imran, N. Haider, M. Shoaib, and I. Razzak, "An Intelligent and Efficient Network Intrusion Detection System Using Deep Learning," *Comput. Electr. Eng.*, vol. 99, no. February 2021, p. 107764, 2022, doi: 10.1016/j.compeleceng.2022.107764.

[26] N. Gupta, V. Jindal, and P. Bedi, "CSE-IDS: Using Cost-sensitive Deep Learning and Ensemble Algorithms to Handle Class Imbalance in Network-based Intrusion Detection Systems," *Comput. Secur.*, vol. 112, p. 102499, 2022, doi: 10.1016/j.cose.2021.102499.

[27] O. Belarbi, A. Khan, P. Carnelli, and T. Spyridopoulos, "An Intrusion Detection System Based on Deep Belief Networks," pp. 377–392, 2022, doi: 10.1007/978-3-031-17551-0_25.

[28] H. Gu, Y. Wang, S. Hong, and G. Gui, "Blind Channel Identification Aided Generalized Automatic Modulation Recognition Based On Deep Learning," *IEEE Access*, vol. 7, pp. 110722–110729, 2019, doi: 10.1109/ACCESS.2019.2934354.

[29] R. Vinayakumar, M. Alazab, K. P. Soman, P. Poornachandran, A. Al-Nemrat, and S. Venkatraman, "Deep Learning Approach for Intelligent Intrusion Detection System," *IEEE Access*, vol. 7, pp. 41525–41550, 2019, doi: 10.1109/ACCESS.2019.2895334.

Index

Pages in *italics* refer to figures and pages in **bold** refer to tables.